Two we
loan

...on or before the last
date stamped below.
Charges are made for late return.

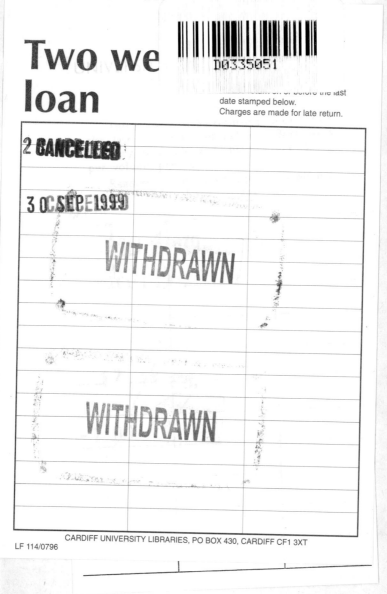

THE TRADE UNION MOVEMENT
IN AFRICA

THE
TRADE UNION MOVEMENT
IN AFRICA

Promise and Performance

BY

WOGU ANANABA

WITH A FOREWORD BY
OMER BECU

LONDON
C. HURST & COMPANY

First published in the United Kingdom by
C. Hurst & Co. (Publishers) Ltd.,
1–2 Henrietta Street, London WC2E 8PS

© Wogu Ananaba, 1979

ISBN 0–905838–13–0

Printed in Great Britain by
Billing & Sons Limited,
Guildford, London and Worcester

To my Mother

CONTENTS

                    page

Foreword   xi

Introduction   1

Part 1:   The General Trade Union Situation

1. WEST AFRICA

(i) English-speaking areas   9
    Ghana   9
    Nigeria   13
    Sierra Leone   16
    The Gambia   17

(ii) French-speaking areas   21
    Before UGTAN   21
    Emergence of UGTAN   22
    'Nationalisation' of UGTAN Branches   25
    After UGTAN   28
    Benin   28
    Cameroun   29
    Central African Empire   30
    Chad   30
    Mauritania   30
    Senegal   30
    Togo   31
    Upper Volta   31

(iii) Guinea-Bissau   32

2. EASTERN AFRICA

    Tanzania   34
    Kenya   38
    Uganda   40
    Ethiopia   45
    The Seychelles   47
    Burundi   49

Rwanda	49
Somalia	50

3. CENTRAL AFRICA

Malawi	51
Rhodesia	52
Zambia	57
Congo	59
Gabon	60
Zaire	61

4. SOUTHERN AFRICA

Angola	63
Botswana	64
Swaziland	65
Mauritius	67
South Africa	70
Madagascar	73
Mozambique	73

5. NORTH AFRICA

Algeria	74
Egypt	77
Libya	78
Morocco	82
Sudan	83
Tunisia	84

6. CASE STUDIES

Lesotho	89
Liberia	101

7. CONTINENTAL TRADE UNION ORGANISATIONS

AFRO	120
AATU	124
ATUC	131
OATUU	135

Part 2: Promise and Performance

8. AFRICAN TRADE UNIONS AT WORK

Organising	141
Education	144
Finance	149
Administration	154
Grievance Handling	160

Publicity 163
Collective Bargaining 164
Elections 171
Defence of Human and Trade Union Rights 175
Non-bargaining Activities 177

9. FACTORS AFFECTING AND INFLUENCING UNION ACTIVITIES

The Legal Framework 180
International Relations and Aids 188
Government Policies and Tactics 193
Employers' Attitude 198
Quality of Union Leadership 201
Effects 204

10. PROSPECTS AND PROBLEMS 207

Notes 227

Guide to Abbreviations and Terminology 232

Index 239

FOREWORD

It is with pleasure that I respond favourably to the request of the author to write a Foreword to his book. I spontaneously accepted it since I have known him for several years as a faithful and most reliable trade unionist. I am all the more pleased, after reading the manuscript of his book, that he has proved in no uncertain terms that I was right in my judgment about his straightforward and unbending character.

Every reader of his book who has been in a position to follow to some extent the development of African affairs since the acquisition of independence of the major part of that large and important continent, will no doubt subscribe to my judgment.

The analysis and description of the political and social situation as it has developed in the countries of Africa that he takes under review are, without doubt, most objective, accurate and factual. As a black African he needed courage and a great sense of impartiality to write what he did. It may well be that some of his fellow workers and even some of his friends will feel to some extent offended, for the truth is not always readily accepted.

I felt that I had to bear this out in the first place, so that there can be no doubt that I subscribe fully to the narrative of the facts.

For more than three decades I myself have been keenly interested and absorbed by the political, social and economic developments in Africa, and even more so since so many countries have acquired independence from a nasty inhuman colonial rule. My first visit to Africa was as a seaman and dates back to 1926 at a time when no law protected the indigenous people—to the extent that the white settlers or colonialists, as one may call them, could, in many African countries, decide upon the life or death of a black African without any fear of prosecution. In other words there was no law protecting the black African.

I was a witness at several ceremonies in different countries of their independence day, which were events never to be forgotten, particularly as we of the ICFTU had, since its foundation, made every possible contribution to such achievement. But we had at the

xi

same time to point out that independence was not an end in itself, but that the workers of these countries would also have to face exploitation from their own greedy national employers and would have to fight for their human rights. The text of this book is, from the beginning to the end, an illustration of that statement.

There are, however, so many factors which have contributed to the present regrettable situation in Africa that they could constitute sufficient material for the text of another book. It is not my intention nor certainly the writer's wish to dwell upon them.

Although this book deals primarily with trade union development since the attainment of independence, I note with some measure of satisfaction that the author has tried, in his Introduction, to cover some of the earlier developments. Some of the difficulties of the trade union movement in Africa today owe their origin to the colonial rulers and the wicked policies they pursued. I can only guess that the writer does not refer to the crimes committed under the colonial regimes because he is too much imbued by the responsibilities of the present leaders and rulers in Africa.

I for one would like to point out that the former colonial powers should be most strongly blamed for having kept the indigenous population to the greatest possible extent ignorant, uneducated and inexperienced. Should one be surprised, that, for instance, a sergeant, who becomes a general overnight at independence, and later President of his country, acts contrary to the general interest?

Whilst it is true that the policies of the former colonial powers varied considerably, it is also true that their behaviour was all meant to subdue and exploit the black African.

Where the writer, with good reason, can hardly accept that African trade unionism has not been able to develop into pressure groups and responsible social partners in their national structure, one can also plead for patience and the application of a long-term policy based upon the principle for progress achieved by trial and error.

Many of us have probably felt frustrated that, notwithstanding good advice and assistance in many forms, we have not as yet reaped the so much expected fruits. African trade unions have been repeatedly told not to make the same mistakes as we have made in the industrialised and more advanced countries, or at least to learn a few lessons from them. We were no doubt too optimistic and did not think deep enough, as for instance a father has to come to terms with the fact that his own son does not need his advice and must learn to stand on his own feet. One can surely not expect that the Africans and other peoples in developing countries will achieve in a decade or two what took us in the developed world almost a century.

Having made these points I want to emphasise that in my candid opinion the social, economic and political development of any country depends largely upon the existence—and indeed the degree of strength and political independence—of the trade union movement. Where the trade union movement is non-existent, weak or subjugated to any power whether from within or without, either economic or political, there will be poverty, hunger, slavery and total lack of human rights and freedom.

It requires a continuous struggle and a long-term process to achieve some kind of humanitarian life, lasting peace and human dignity. It should be the common objective of all people to eradicate the exploitation of men by men, if we are ever to reach that goal. In any case let us not despair, and fight for it with all our might.

Finally I want to congratulate the author for having always fought, with all the means at his disposal, for the crucial necessity of creating stable unions able to stand up against so many odds and in the face of the calamities under which the African workers are labouring.

Let us beware of one-party states which have fallen, or are bound to fall, into despotism.

OMER BECU
Ex-General Secretary of the ITF and the ICFTU

INTRODUCTION

The development of trade unions in Africa may be classified under three main periods. The first is the period before the end of the Second World War; the second is from 1945 to 1960, and the third covers what has been happening since 1961. Although this book is primarily concerned with the last, a brief consideration of some of the major developments during the first two periods is necessary for an understanding and appreciation of some of the problems of the third. Before 1939 trade unions of African employees existed in only a handful of countries. Such unions were few in each country, and were craft- or plant-based. There were hardly any national trade union centres. Organisation on a broader basis and the creation of national trade union centres were a later development. Most of the few unions which existed were unions either of European or Asian workers. The reasons for this state of affairs are not far to seek: there can be no unions without workers, and there can be no workers without some measure of industrial activity. Before 1939 the level of industrial activity in most African countries then under colonial rule was very low. A devastating world war from 1914 to 1918 was followed, after a decade of slow recovery, by the Great Depression of 1929–35, which left millions of people unemployed in Europe and North America. Its consequences were felt in other parts of the world including Africa.

The colonial policy of racial segregation and discrimination also played its part. Colonial authorities and white settlers looked at every attempt by Africans to organise with suspicion and did whatever they could to discourage it. In 1930 Lord Passfield, then Britain's Secretary of State for the Colonies, addressed his famous circular letter to colonial governments urging them to take the necessary steps to enact a law authorising the organisation of trade unions. That circular was not necessarily inspired by a desire to improve the lot of colonial workers, but by an anxiety that the bitter conflicts which had occurred in the West Indies should not spread to other areas. In the late 1920s West Indian workers took the law into their own hands in revolt against the denial of trade union

1

rights. Widespread rioting ensued, leading to thousands of pounds worth of damage and loss of property. Official sources interpreted the events as the handiwork of extraneous elements outside the trade union movement who wanted to use the workers to achieve certain political objectives. It was to ensure that disaffected persons did not manipulate workers to attain their personal ambitions that prompted Lord Passfield to act. The 1930 directive was followed by similar dispatches in 1935, 1937, 1938 and 1939.

Some colonial administrators and white settlers set about sabotaging the directives. Three developments however forced them to change their attitude. In 1938 the Colonial Office appointed its first permanent labour adviser and thus gave indication that it was prepared to insist on the introduction of labour legislation, the creation of labour departments, the appointment of labour inspectors and the establishment of a machinery for the settlement of industrial disputes. The outbreak of the Second World War in 1939 caused thousands of Africans to join the army ostensibly to fight for the survival of democracy. War production programmes created employment facilities hitherto unknown. As large numbers of people entered the labour market—and quite often in unfamiliar surroundings, as workers were required to work long hours and under difficult conditions—the problems of social adjustment and some of the conflicts which generally arise between employers and workers developed. In 1940, the British Parliament passed the Colonial Development and Welfare Act which provided for economic aid to the colonies, but the Act stipulated that 'no territory might receive aid under its provisions unless it had in force legislation protecting the rights of trade unions, and unless the works for which the aid was to be used were carried out under a contract which embodied a fair wages clause, and which forbade the employment of children under the age of fourteen'. Trade Unions Ordinances were passed in various countries after the coming into operation of that Act, Kenya, Nigeria and Sierra Leone being the few colonial territories where such legislations had been enacted a few years earlier.

The organisation of trade unions began in earnest when the laws regulating them came into operation. The first trade union in Nigeria was registered in 1940. By the end of that year there were five registered unions with a membership of 3,500. At the end of 1942 sixty-two unions claiming a membership of 21,000 had been registered. The tremendous increase in the cost of living during the war inspired the agitation for a cost of living allowance. In 1942 the Nigerian unions won a 100 per cent increase in the minimum wage following the granting of a cost of living allowance. The failure of the colonial government to honour its promise of reviewing the cost of living allowance if there were further increases in the cost of living provoked the General Strike of 1945 which lasted for forty-four days in Lagos and fifty-two in the Provinces. In Ghana, railway workers organised a successful strike in 1940 in furtherance of a pay claim. A general strike was organised in 1950 in support of the meteorological employees' claim for a wage increase. Kwame Nkrumah exploited the general discontent among the workers to unite them with his Convention People's Party in the struggles for independence. A 'Positive Action' programme was launched which included, among other things, 'the constitutional application of strikes, boycotts, and non-co-operation based on the principle of absolute non-violence'. In Uganda a general strike was organised in January 1945 in furtherance of a pay claim. A commission of inquiry into the riots which followed found that the motives behind the riots were political rather than economic.

Before 1945, labour departments had been set up in a number of countries. After the war trade union sections were created to help and advise the nascent unions on various aspects of their work, the aim being, as far as possible, to create the same model of industrial relations practice as was then existing in the United Kingdom. The labour departments were staffed with people with various backgrounds. Some were local administrative officers, some were seconded from the Ministry of Labour in Britain, while others were recruited from the ranks of the British trade unions on the recommendations of the Trades Union Congress. But it was in the day-to-day operation of the departments, and particularly in their dealing with trade unions, that a world of difference existed between official posturing in favour of strong trade unions and the practical demonstration of helping African workers to achieve that objective. Two instances may be cited. J. S. Brandie, a trade union adviser in Uganda, was dismissed from his job because he acted against official policy by advising African trade unions on negotiating techniques. In Kenya, James Patrick, another trade union adviser, was told on his arrival by white settlers and the Commissioner of Labour himself that the time had not arrived for the establishment of trade unions in the country, and that he should come back in twenty years' time. It was only in Sierra Leone that a former British trade unionist seemed to have achieved some success in introducing a system of industrial relations similar to the British pattern.

What was the official policy against which Brandie acted and which cost him his job? Lord Passfield outlined them in his directive of 1930 when he suggested that the legislation to be enacted should provide for the compulsory registration of trade unions, which should be carefully guided and supervised. The British TUC added insult to injury when they insisted—and their insistence was accepted—that trade unions in the colonies should be 'non-political', a standard which the British trade unions themselves cannot maintain in view of their history and relationship with the Labour Party. These things became the justification for the colonial authorities to employ various devices to control the trade unions. During the struggles for independence the colonial authorities tried to discourage trade unions from participating in politics and saw many industrial disputes as political agitation. The shooting of twenty-one mine workers in 1949 in Nigeria is a case in point. A commission of inquiry which investigated the matter found the Lieutenant Governor wrong in considering a pure industrial dispute as a political agitation. African trade unions considered the struggle for independence as a national issue deserving the support of every organised group, and periodically tried to help by organising strikes which, though purely economic, nevertheless gave a fillip to the political issues of the day. Nkrumah soon supplied an answer to the ban on political activity by trade unions when he coined the slogan 'Seek ye first the political kingdom and every other thing would be added unto you thereafter.' This slogan was echoed by workers in many countries. In Kenya, where Africans were forbidden to engage in politics during the emergency, the trade union movement provided the only platform for Africans to speak out on basic issues involving human rights. The Kenya Federation of Labour took advantage of the opportunity to express the yearnings of the African population for freedom.

Discussing the role of labour departments in British colonial Africa and what followed the registration of trade unions, Ioan Davies reports (*African Trade Unions*, p. 42) that the unions were:

closely supervised by the labour departments, accounts were scrutinised, political affiliation was discouraged, union offices were closed, and, in practice, the right to strike was severely circumscribed by the emergency actions of Governors or by the introduction of long lists of 'essential services' in which strikes were illegal. ... The effect of this was to give labour departments a real or potential power rare in Britain's industrial experience. At independence this power was used by most of the new governments to establish a structure of industrial relations that was very different to that advocated by Britain. The policy of close administrative control prepared the way for the integration of party, bureaucracy and trade unions that is a marked feature of several African countries today.

In the French colonies a slightly different approach was adopted to achieve the same objective, though changing circumstances sometimes led to different results. The right to organise was granted in North Africa in 1932 and in West Africa in 1937, but trade union membership was restricted to those who were literate in French and possessed elementary school certificate. In 1944 the literacy qualification was abolished, and this provided an opportunity for organising the majority of the wage earners. In Morocco, although the right to organise had been granted to non-Moroccans—who were mainly French citizens—in 1936, indigenous Moroccans had the legal right to organise in 1950 when the Lamine-Gueye Law came into operation. This law prescribed the working conditions in the civil service, and the Overseas Territories Labour Code of 1952 established the machinery for collective bargaining, works inspection and provided for equal pay for equal work, regardless of race or origin. As in the British colonies, employers in the private sector as well as administrators in the colonial service were not particularly keen to negotiate with African trade unions, but the policy of assimilation pursued in the French colonies gave the unions there a lever over their counterparts in the British colonies. Moreover, Africans were directly represented in the French Parliament and this provided a useful opportunity to press the claims for improved working conditions. The Lamine-Gueye Law itself derived its name from the prominent Senegalese Deputy who played a leading part in drafting it. After its introduction the Deputies and the African trade unions worked in close co-operation for its implementation.

There was a great difference between the process of law implementation in the French colonies and the British. 'If in the British colonies the effectiveness of labour policy depended more on the enthusiasm of the local administration and the co-operation of the employers, in the French it relied on the power of the popular movements to urge the implementation of the extensive labour laws' (Davies, p. 43). The French had three national centres none of which had any close relationship with the government of the day. Instead of collaborating with the Government as the British unions did over labour and colonial policies, they formulated theirs which included provisions for the colonies because the colonies were considered to be 'Overseas France'.

In the Belgian territories of Congo and Rwanda-Urundi labour policy was regulated by four laws governing employment in the public service and in the private sector of industry. There were different laws for senior government officials who were Europeans, junior government officials who were Africans, senior European officials in the private sector and also Africans in the private sector. Africans were not allowed to organise trade unions until 1946. Even then, those who were eligible for union membership were Africans who had been continuously employed in their jobs for at least three years. The unions were craft- and plant-based, and were not allowed to federate even on a provincial basis. Local authority officials had the power to inspect union records, files and accounts, to attend union meetings and to insist that the unions exclude certain persons from their meetings. None of the laws made any provision covering collective bargaining. It was not until 1957 that the unions were allowed to form federations. The Belgian unions assumed the responsibility of representing African unions in the Belgian colonies at international bodies. Until 1959 no Africans represented their organisations in meetings of such organisations like the ILO, ICFTU and IFCTU (the former name of the World Confederation of Labour).

Since independence the trade union movement in Africa has had a rough existence. So turbulent has been its history that it is sometimes very difficult to recount the developments with accuracy and precision. Certain common features, however, may be noted. Laws and policies which violate international labour standards abound in most African states. Bona fide trade union organisations have ceased to exist in many countries, and have been replaced by outfits created or sponsored by governments, politicians or military leaders. Trade unionists have been arrested and jailed without trial; some have been detained for months or years, and some have been shot in cold blood. There are probably more African trade unionists in jail or in detention, killed or driven into exile by independent African countries than was the case during the whole period of colonial rule. In certain countries, so-called union leaders have been imposed on trade unions without any reference to them or the workers they are supposed to represent, while in others elected officials have been removed from office by persons or organisations which did not elect them.

The movement in most countries has not overcome its basic weaknesses and contradictions. Fragmentation, maladministration, indiscipline, abuse of office and undemocratic procedures are still the order of the day. Although many unions now operate check-off, and in some countries the check-off has been made mandatory by law, several unions still do not pay dues to their national trade union centres and international trade secretariats; and those unions which do pay dues invariably pay less than they ought to.

To what extent then, if at all, may political developments, government policies, Pan-Africanism, aids from international trade union organisations and international development agencies, and the quality of union leadership and membership be blamed for the current trade union situation in Africa? In the following pages an attempt is made to examine these and other questions.

Almost every trade union in the world has as its primary objective the protection and improvement of the economic and social interests of its members. This book has been written in order to provide a bird's-eye view of what African trade unions have been doing in this respect since independence. If it can bestir the unions in taking a critical look at themselves, their promises and per-formances, or help labour policy makers, labour administrators, teachers of industrial relations, industrial relations practitioners and international trade union organisations in understanding and appreciating the problems of African trade unions, then it would have served its purpose.

The book is purely the product of a personal initiative, and the views expressed therein are personal and in no way reflect the official views of the ICFTU on the matters discussed. It is divided into two parts. The first is a survey of the general trade union situation. The survey has been done on a regional basis. A chapter has been devoted to case studies of two countries (Lesotho and Liberia) and another has been devoted to an examination of continental trade union organisations like AFRO, AATUF, ATUC and OATUU. The second part deals with what the unions have been doing in the various fields of trade union work, factors affecting and influencing union activities and prospects and problems of the movement.

Several individuals and organisations have assisted me in one way or the other in producing it, and I sincerely thank them. My gratitude goes to the unions and international trade secretariats which were kind enough to answer the questionnaires I sent out in 1975, to some of the national centres which granted me interviews and supplied very useful materials, and to participants in trade union courses and seminars in several parts of Africa and neigh-bouring islands who brought interesting documents relating to their unions and national centres, and made worthwhile contributions during discussions on trade union problems in Africa. Special thanks go to my colleagues in the ICFTU secretariat, to Charles Ford, General Secretary of the International Textile, Garment and Leather Workers' Federation, and to my friend and former colleague, Paul Kanyago, Africa Representative of the Inter-national Metalworkers' Federation, for their encouragement, com-ments and advice. I am deeply indebted to Omer Becu, former General Secretary of the ICFTU, who read the manuscript. Finally, I am grateful to my wife, Edith, without whose assistance and encouragement it would have been impossible for me to complete the work at the time I did.

11 January 1978   *WOGU ANANABA*

PART 1
The General Trade Union Situation

1. WEST AFRICA

(i) *English-speaking areas*

Ghana

Trade union development in post-independence Africa has, in many respects, followed patterns which were developed in Ghana and Guinea in 1956. During that year, two significant developments took place in both countries. In Ghana at its thirteenth annual conference held in Takoradi, the Trades Union Congress decided to restructure the trade union movement by replacing the existing craft and house unions, numbering more than a hundred, with national industrial unions 'with a sense of direction and purpose'.[1] In Guinea, Sekou Toure and his colleagues founded the Union Générale des Travailleurs d'Afrique Noire (UGTAN) which was to have no organic link with any international trade union organisation or with any of the three national centres in France. Shortly after the Takoradi conference, the TUC General Secretary, John Kofi Tettegah, visited Israel and the Federal Republic of Germany to study the trade union structure of both countries, and the relationship existing between the trade unions and political parties. He seemed highly impressed by what he saw, and at the TUC's fourteenth annual conference held in Cape Coast in January 1958 he stressed the need for adopting 'whatever structure and whatever measures we deem peculiar and necessary for Ghana'.[2] He proposed that the sixty-four unions then affiliated to the TUC be amalgamated into sixteen national industrial unions and that each union, while enjoying complete autonomy in collective bargaining, should operate 'subject to an overall policy decided by the TUC'.[3] He went on: 'We do not want to be bothered with Cambridge essays on imaginary ILO standards with undue emphasis on voluntary association.'[4]

The proposal was enthusiastically accepted. Another proposal which was equally accepted was that the TUC should enter into an alliance with the ruling Convention People's Party (CPP) because the party's programmes were in consonance with those of the TUC.

9

The CPP was duly informed of these decisions. In time, action was taken to integrate the trade union movement with the party. In consequence of that relationship the Ghana Government gave the TUC a grant of £25,000 for organisational work, and the Ghana Parliament passed the controversial Industrial Relations Act 1958 which repealed the Trades Union Ordinance 1941, and created a 'Trades Union Congress which shall act as the representative of the trade union movement in Ghana and perform the functions conferred on it by this Act'.[5] Twenty-four national unions were to constitute the new TUC, which had as one of its primary objectives 'to uphold the aims and aspirations of the Convention People's Party through financial and organisational support in its struggle to create a socialist state in Ghana'.[6]

At that time the TUC was an affiliate of the International Confederation of Free Trade Unions (ICFTU), and its General Secretary, John Tettegah, was a member of ICFTU Executive Board. The ICFTU noted a number of weaknesses in the Industrial Relations Bill, and tried without avail to persuade the TUC and the Ghana Government to see the wisdom of removing them. In identical letters to Tettegah and Prime Minister Kwame Nkrumah, the ICFTU pointed out that 'a bill which "establishes" a trade union centre; decides which unions are to be represented in it and how they shall be represented; gives the Government the power to add to and delete from the list of affiliates of the trade union centre; subjects the rules of procedure of the trade union centre to Government approval; and gives the Government the power to freeze the funds of the trade union centre if any of its actions is "not conducive to the public good" violates the most elementary principles of trade union freedom. We are further of the opinion that a bill which deprives all public servants and teachers of the right to strike, outlaws any strike called before a union is certified as a collective bargaining agency, as well as any strike over the interpretation of agreements and strikes which follow a compulsory award, violates the workers' right to strike'.[7]

There were, of course, a few welcome sections in the Act namely those covering check-off,[8] the payment of its proceeds on an agreed basis to the TUC and the national unions and others relating to unfair labour practice.

Some unions, notably the UAC (United Africa Company) Workers and Railway Workers, were vehemently opposed to the new structure and the relationship between the TUC and the CPP. Both unions remained outside the TUC until 1960 when the Industrial Relations Act was amended slightly, and the number of unions was reduced from twenty-four to sixteen and fair and foul means were employed to bring dissident unions in line.

Alongside these developments was another which had far-reaching consequences on trade union development in several African countries. An All-African People's Conference (a gathering of representatives of political parties irrespective of their ideological orientation) was held in Accra in December 1958. The conference adopted a resolution urging African workers to 'realise their unity in the interest of the struggle for independence and the affirmation of the African personality'. There was no disagreement among African trade union leaders as to the desirability of setting up such an organisation. Indeed, the First African Regional Trade Union Conference held in Accra from 14 to 19 January 1957, under the chairmanship of John Tettegah, had voted unanimously in favour of such a body. The difference, however, was that the organisation envisaged at the First African Trade Union Conference was to have been an African Regional Organisation of the ICFTU and not one whose constituent members were to have no organic links with international trade union organisations like the ICFTU, the World Federation of Trade Unions (WFTU) and the World Confederation of Labour (WCL). In 1957 very few, if any, African trade union leaders thought that Africa was a world unto itself, completely different and separate from the rest of the world, or that workers' problems in Africa were basically different from those of their opposite numbers in other parts of the world. That school of thought emerged after 1958, when the heat generated by Pan-Africanism spread all over the continent like wild fire.

There were several issues involved in the proposal to set up a Pan-African trade union organisation, the most important being how to finance the organisation and whether its constituent members should or should not maintain their affiliations with international trade union organisations. The advocates of a Pan-African trade union organisation seemed to have paid very little attention to the problem of financing apparently because the Ghana Government was willing to foot the bill. What created much concern was international affiliation: the Ghana Government and its ally, the GTUC, felt that national centres should not affiliate. From 1959 onwards they spent a good deal of time, effort and money to ensure that other African trade union centres, political parties and governments followed their thinking.

Between 1958 and February 1966, when the Nkrumah Government was overthrown by military coup, the TUC existed under the tight control of the CPP and the Ghana Government. But for a shilling a day gesture which the Government made in 1960 to avert trouble, there was no general wage increase for public employees during the period. Constant reports of violation of trade union rights in Ghana forced the ICFTU to file a complaint with the ILO in June 1962 against the Ghana Government. This complaint was investigated by the special committee on Freedom of Association which upheld most of the points raised by the ICFTU. Consequently, the Ghana Government, hitherto unmoved by public opinion, amended some sections of the Industrial Relations Act 1958. Another reason for amending the Act was the Government's anxiety to ensure that the Ghana TUC was free from criticism, and that the TUC developed an organisational model which would be followed by other trade unions in Africa. The Minister of Labour, K. Amoa-Awaah, expressed the Government's feelings when he said: 'It is a well-considered view that the success of the organisation of the All-African Trade Union Federation (AATUF) is dependent largely on the prestige of the Ghana TUC. This means that the TUC has to do everything possible to attract as much following and support throughout Africa, and its organisational machinery built up as a model to be followed by the other trade union movements in Africa. The Ghana TUC must therefore be free from criticism internationally and the new law is aimed at achieving this.'[9]

After the fourteenth annual conference of the TUC, there were no free union elections in Ghana until the overthrow of the Nkrumah Government. The workers' right to elect their leaders in freedom and to order the administration of their unions to suit their interests was restored when Benjamin A. Bentum, a former General Secretary of the Agricultural Workers' Union and Minister of Forestry in Nkrumah's Government, was appointed acting General Secretary of the TUC by the National Liberation Council. He was eventually elected to the post by an extraordinary congress held at Legon from 4 to 5 June 1966.[10]

The extraordinary congress adopted a 'Programme for Progress' which said, among other things, that 'the first task which the trade union movement in Ghana shall tackle is to transform itself into an organisation which has a meaning to the workers, and responsibly advances their interests in the social and economic spheres. The only form of organisation that can do this with any measure of success is one which draws its authority and its power from the workers themselves and is responsive to their aims and aspirations.'[11] It was probably in an attempt to live up to that expectation that the TUC had one of its greatest confrontations with the Ghana Government in 1971. Busia's Progress Party Government had introduced a National Development Levy to which the workers

were obliged to contribute 5 per cent of their wages and salaries
every month. The Cedi was devalued the same year by about 48 per
cent which meant that the workers' purchasing power had been
seriously eroded. To ameliorate the situation, the TUC demanded a
minimum wage of NC 1.50 per day: the Government offered NC
1.00 per day. There being no agreement between the Government
and the TUC on the minimum wage issue, a smouldering discontent
among workers developed into a conflagration of labour unrests.
The Progress Party Government reacted by introducing an
Industrial Relations (Amendment) Bill, which was passed by
Parliament under a certificate of urgency. The law dissolved the
TUC and dismantled the basis of operating the check-off. The
Government tried to justify its action by arguing that it was wrong
in the first place to constitute the TUC by an Act of Parliament,
and quoted a section of the Ghana Constitution in support, but it
was quite obvious that the intention was to weaken the trade union
movement.

After dissolving the TUC, the Progress Party and its Government tried to create divisions among the national unions and to use
some of the union secretaries in starting an alternative national
centre. Thanks to the determination of the majority of the union
secretaries to maintain solidarity, these efforts failed. Under the
Industrial Relations (Amendment) Act 1971 union dues were no
longer to be deducted from workers' pay packets whether or not
they were members of trade unions. Deductions were to be made
strictly on the basis of written authorisations freely signed by trade
union members. Leaders of the various unions tried to get their
members to comply. Although the unions did not earn as much
income as before, nevertheless they earned enough to run their
administration and thus prove that they could pay their way
without the aid of the law.

In January 1972 the Progress Party Government was overthrown
by another military coup. The new regime of Colonel Ignatius
Achampong took immediate steps to repeal the Industrial Relations
(Amendment) Act, 1971. This had the effect of reviving the TUC,
but it did not restore the old system of check-off which was
mandatory on all workers. In January 1976 the TUC was made up
of seventeen national industrial unions representing a paid-up
membership of 350,000. Most unions collect their dues by voluntary
check-off, and the proceeds are shared among the TUC, the
national unions and their branches.

Nigeria
The year 1956 is a momentous one in Nigerian labour history. At

the founding conference of the third national trade union centre in 1953 (there had been two before then) Nigerian trade union leaders decided not to affiliate the All-Nigeria Trade Union Federation (ANTUF) to any international trade union organisation. That decision was changed in 1956 when there was a general interest in international affiliation. A motion in favour of the principle of international affiliation was unanimously adopted by the third annual conference of the ANTUF. But another motion in favour of affiliation to the ICFTU was defeated by one vote. At the first General Council meeting following the conference, ANTUF General Secretary, Gogo Chu Nzeribe, a member of one of the Marxist Groups in the country, interpreted the result of the motion on affiliation to the ICFTU as a decision in favour of affiliation to the WFTU.[12] The stage was thus set for another split which occurred in 1957. Although unity was achieved again in 1959, it proved to be short-lived because another Marxist, Samuel U. Bassey, lost the election to the post of General Secretary of the Trades Union Congress of Nigeria (TUCN) (the second congress bearing that name) founded that year.

A split also occurred in 1960, a few months before Nigeria attained independence. That split was masterminded by external influences, but the dissidents in the Nigerian trade union movement claimed that the main cause of the split was the decision to affiliate the TUCN to the ICFTU. The truth, however, is that before the merger conference of 1959 both the ANTUF and the National Council of Trade Unions of Nigeria signed an agreement in which both sides agreed, among other things, to accept the existing international affiliation of either parties. At the time of signing that agreement the only international affiliation known to be existing was the affiliation of the NCTUN to the ICFTU. By ratifying that agreement, the merger conference was giving unqualified approval to affiliation to the ICFTU.

The split of 1960 was healed in 1962 but not until after a protracted negotiation in which the special committee of the All-Nigeria People's Conference played a leading role. Before the unity conference in May, the Trades Union Congress of Nigeria (TUCN) and the die-hard ANTUF group which called itself Nigerian Trade Union Congress (NTUC) signed another agreement which provided, among other things, 'that both the TUCN and the NTUC are quite prepared to accept the verdict of the Nigerian workers on the issue of international affiliation. Towards this end both the TUCN and the NTUC agree that there should be a joint unity conference of the two organisations at a place easily accessible to the Nigerian trade union delegates to take a decision on the question of international affiliation. The conference should be presided over, for the purpose, by an independent chairman acceptable to both the TUCN and the NTUC.'[13] The Ibadan conference eventually became a conference of all registered trade unions willing to participate, and that modification of the merger agreement was made on NTUC insistence. Yet when the conference voted by 659 to 407 in favour of affiliation to the ICFTU and the African Trade Union Confederation (ATUC), NTUC leaders and their supporters felt they were not bound by the undertaking to respect the verdict of Nigerian workers. Rather than return to the conference after lunch break, they retired to another venue in Ibadan where they founded what they called the Independent United Labour Congress (IULC).

Within one year the IULC split into two, and by the following year the splinter groups had increased to three. At this stage the IULC changed its name back to the NTUC. By the end of 1964 there were four national centres in the country: the United Labour Congress (ULC), the Nigerian Trade Union Congress, the Nigerian Workers Council and the Labour Unity Front (an amorphous grouping of individual union leaders who believed that they could promote labour unity by their unions remaining unaffiliated to any of the other national centres). The unity promoters eventually became a national centre and were recognised as such by the Federal Ministry of Labour.

Bickering and rivalry continued among the centres until 1974 when the Apena Cemetery Declaration issued at the burial of J. A. Oduleye, former Treasurer of the ULC, formed the basis of achieving yet another unity. Unfortunately the Nigerian Government refused to register the Nigerian Labour Congress or accord it recognition, arguing that it was undemocratically set up and workers' representatives were not given the opportunity to elect its leaders. In a swift move the Government banned international affiliation by Nigerian trade unions, prohibited international trade union organisations from operating in Nigeria, except the Organisation of African Trade Union Unity and the ILO—which is not strictly a trade union organisation—and set up a commission of inquiry into the activities of Nigerian trade unions. It later appointed an Administrator to reorganise the trade union movement and set up a properly constituted national centre.

By January 1976 Nigeria had a total of 983 registered trade unions representing a membership of about 800,000.[14] The number of registered unions was arrived at apparently after the registrar of trade unions had taken action in keeping with the provisions of the Trade Unions Decree No. 31 of 1973 to ensure that his register was a record of bona fide trade unions. The former trade union law authorised the registration of all sorts of groupings in so far as they satisfied the definition of a trade union as specified in the law. The definition was loose and broad-based, and covered organisations of wage earners, self-employed craftsmen, employers' organisations and even petty traders. At the end of 1972 there were 1,032 registered 'trade unions' in the country of which 783[15] representing 665,615 members could be said to be genuine trade unions. Majority of them, however, were ineffectual plant unions whose membership was limited to the employees of a particular company, government ministry or public corporation. The reason for this is partly historical and partly the failure of union leaders to evolve an organising pattern which would achieve strength.

In spite of the perennial divisions which had seriously sapped the energy of the Nigerian trade union movement, the unions occasionally displayed some strength and unity. An example is the Joint Action Committee (JAC) set up in 1963 to prosecute the claims for wage increase. The JAC organised the general strike of June 1964 which paralysed the economy for thirteen days. In 1971 the four national centres formed the United Committee of Central Labour Organisations (UCCLO) which pressed the pay claim leading to general wage increases for workers following the recommendations of a commission of inquiry headed by Chief Adebo, a former Nigerian representative at the United Nations. A new national centre, the Nigeria Labour Congress, was inaugurated at Ibadan on 28 February 1978. Hassan Sunmonu was elected President, and Aliya Musa Dangiwa was appointed General Secretary.

Sierra Leone

In Sierra Leone the trade union movement had taken a decision from the outset that it would not be involved in politics. Even when two of its leading officers went into partisan politics in 1957 and 1961 the Sierra Leone Council of Labour (SLCL) refused to be drawn. In 1962 a split occurred when three unions pulled out of the Council of Labour and set up the Trades Union Congress. The new organisation accused the Council of Labour of misusing financial assistance from ICFTU and of poaching its members. (The Sierra Leone trade union movement was one of the few founding members of the ICFTU. Its international relations date back to the early days of the WFTU. When the split occurred in the international trade union movement in 1949 and national centres from Western Europe and North America walked out of WFTU, the Sierra Leone Trades Union Congress also followed.) Unity was restored in 1963 through ICFTU assistance, but antagonism did not cease. Outwardly it seemed that disagreements were over policy matters, but in fact they were differences between the old and new generation of trade unionists. In spite of these difficulties the movement as a whole made steady progress.

In 1964 it was reported that the SLCL had an estimated book membership of 12,000 of which 4,000 were paying regular dues.[16] Dues-collection was often by check-off, and six unions (Railways, Transport and General Workers, Dockworkers, United Mineworkers, Clerical and Mercantile and Construction Workers) were operating it. But it was only SLCL full-time staff who toured various parts of the country, organising meetings, recruiting workers into their unions and urging the unorganised to sign up.

In February 1965 a new split occurred over the election of SLCL General Secretary. The splinter group, called the Sierra Leone Federation of Trade Unions, was led by George E. E. Palmer. Hitherto H. N. Georgestone who, with Marcus Grant, had dominated the trade union scene for many years, had been the General Secretary of SLCL. The younger elements wanted a young man to take over the leadership of the SLCL, but to do so the candidate had to win through the ballot box. In 1965 Palmer and his supporters were not yet ready. Undaunted efforts were made to restore unity, and in May 1966 these efforts were rewarded when a representative meeting of both organisations presided over by the Minister of Labour agreed to set up a new national centre called the Sierra Leone Labour Congress. E. T. Kamara, General Secretary of the United Mine Workers' Union was elected General Secretary of the new organisation. Kamara resigned in 1968 and was succeeded by George Palmer, who held the post until 1976.

The Gambia

Until January 1977 the Gambia had four general workers' unions: the Gambia Workers' Union (membership 10,500) affiliated to the ICFTU; the Gambia Labour Union (membership 100) affiliated to the WCL; the Drivers and Mechanics' Union and the National Farmers' and General Workers' Union (membership of both unions unknown) were unaffiliated. The Gambia Workers' Union (GWU) embraces technical and manual workers in the public service, parastatal organisations and the private sector of industry, and has been responsible for securing improvements in the wages and working conditions of workers in the low income groups.

In 1970 it organised a general strike in furtherance of a pay claim for a minimum wage of 8s. 3d. per day. A government-appointed commission had recommended a daily minimum wage of

7s. 2d. and £40 per month car allowance for Ministers. While accepting the recommendation in respect of car allowance, the Government rejected the one on minimum wage. The strike began on 27 January, and almost paralysed the whole country. Sir Dawda Jawara, then Prime Minister, broadcast to the country appealing to the workers to return to work or face dismissal. The strike was called off after two days not as a result of the Prime Minister's appeal and threat, but because the union leaders had learnt from 'reliable sources' that the Government was planning to take advantage of the strike to achieve a political objective it was uncertain to win through the ballot box.

The Jawara Government had been toying with the idea of turning the Gambia into a republic with an executive president. The GWU was opposed to the idea. The first referendum on the subject which was held in 1965 failed to secure the necessary two-thirds majority largely as a result of the combined opposition of the trade unions spearheaded by the GWU and other organised groups. In December 1969 the Gambian Parliament adopted a Republican Constitution which was to be put to the electorate for approval in April 1970. Although the Jawara Government was becoming increasingly popular, it was by no means certain that the new constitution would be approved by the electorate. The fact that M. E. Jallow, General Secretary of the GWU, and other union leaders were political rivals of the Prime Minister increased the uncertainty. During the strike information was received that the Government was planning to arrest union leaders, declare a state of emergency and promulgate a republic without testing the will of the electorate through the ballot box. States of emergency had been used in and out of season by many African governments to introduce unpopular measures, harass and persecute their political opponents, and it was feared that the same thing might happen in the Gambia. The GWU leaders felt that, if an emergency was declared and they were arrested and detained, such a development would not only adversely affect the union but the workers' claims for improvement in wages and working conditions would continue to be ignored as they seemed to have been ignored for quite some time. The April referendum was held and the country voted in favour. Sir Dawda Jawara became the country's first President.

As far back as 1967 the GWU put up proposals to the Government for the introduction of wage differentials reflecting the various skills. These proposals were rejected on the ground that they were premature. Another claim for a general review of the wages in view of the rising cost of living was also rejected. In 1970, two civil servants staff associations which, by law, could not be members of the GWU, supported the claim for a general review of the wages and salaries. It was not until 1972, and probably in anticipation of the effect which the action would have on the general elections of that year, that the Government agreed to appoint a commission of inquiry commonly known as the Waller Commission. Although the employers were represented, there was no workers' representation on the commission. During the first eight months of the commission's work, no invitation was sent to any of the unions to give evidence: people knew of the existence of the commission only through radio annoucements. After six months' work, the Waller Commission felt that there was a case for an interim award and made recommendations graduated according to income. These gave wage increases varying from 5 per cent for those in the higher income brackets to 35 per cent for workers in the lowest categories. The recommendations were immediately implemented in the public service, but problems arose with regard to their implementation in the parastatal corporations and the private sector.

The Government convened the Joint Industrial Council (JIC) which determines minimum wages, and the Council was asked to endorse the interim awards. The GWU took the stand that the Council should not endorse them because there had been no trade union involvement in determining them. The GWU's stand was supported by all other trade unions in the country. In consequence, the Waller Commission held a meeting with the JIC. Jallow acted as a spokesman of the unions, and made a great impression on members of the commission. From then henceforth there were regular consultations between the unions and the commission aimed at reducing the wage gap. The Waller Commission submitted its report in April 1975, and its recommendations were accepted by the Government and Parliament. As usual the recommendations in respect of workers in the higher income brackets were implemented. As far as those relating to the workers in the lower income groups were concerned they could not be implemented because 'there was a feeling among some top government officials that the Commission had been unduly influenced by the views of the Gambia Workers' Union'.[17]

In August 1975 a general strike was organised in protest of the failure to implement the Waller Commission recommendations. The strike was called off after five days following an undertaking from the Government that they would be implemented. But while steps were taken to pay certain workers many others were not paid until there had been wild-cat strikes in many parts of the country. In March 1976, the first differentials for skilled artisans were paid retrospective from April 1975, but not all categories benefited, and this caused a great resentment among the workers. In the Gambia Utilities Corporation and the Ports Authority only those in the higher income brackets benefited from the Waller awards. In consequence the junior employees of the Electricity Corporation went on a one-day protest strike. The GWU persuaded them to return to work after obtaining a firm promise from the management to pay. Management's failure to honour its pledge forced the GWU to threaten another general strike. That threat led to the appointment of another commission known as the Agege Commission, which was charged with the responsibility of ensuring that the Waller awards were paid by the Utilities Corporation.

The Agege Commission reported to the Minister of Labour in September. Six weeks after the submission of the report there was still no implementation of the Waller awards. In the meantime the Government had rushed through Parliament a bill obliging trade unions to give at least twenty-one days' notice before their members could go on strike. Hitherto unions were required to give twenty-one days' notice in respect of strikes in 'essential services' and fourteen days in respect of others. GWU leaders interpreted the new law as 'a calculated attempt to suppress a fundamental right of workers—the right to strike'.[18] In view of the continued failure to implement the Waller awards, the employees of the Utilities Corporation threatened strike action, but were persuaded by the GWU to wait until there had been another round of talks between Jallow, the Bargaining Committee of the Utilities Corporation employees and the appropriate Ministries on 15 November 1976. The meeting was held and lasted a whole day. Government again promised to pay and to do so the same week. Two days after the meeting, however, members of the Bargaining Committee were sacked because of so-called 'recent events' which were not specified. This was the last straw that broke the camel's back.

The Gambia Utilities Corporation employees went on strike on 18 November. That same day the GWU decided to call a general strike in sympathy with effect from 19 November. The strike took place and was a huge success. The Minister of Labour broadcast to the nation alleging that the strike was illegal and subversive, and that Jallow was planning to organise a political party to overthrow the Government. Workers were called upon to return to work or face dismissal. In spite of the dismissal threat, the strike continued. Government then called the police who raided workers' homes and arrested those who refused to go back to work. On the second day, two officials of the GWU, A. Bah, Deputy General Secretary, and M. A. Cessay, Organiser, were arrested. Surprisingly the General

Secretary, M. E. Jallow, was not arrested, apparently because such a development would have unleashed an incontrollable workers' revolt. During the trial which followed Bah and one other employee of the Utilities Corporation were acquitted and discharged, and six others were fined between 300 Dalasies (£75) and 400 Dalasies (£100). The ICFTU sent a protest telegram to the Government and provided legal assistance for those prosecuted. In January 1977 the GWU was deregistered for failing to submit its annual financial returns and its funds were frozen.

(ii) *French-speaking Areas*

(a) *Before UGTAN*

Three important periods may be identified in the development of African trade unions in French-speaking West Africa. The first is the period before 1957, which may be called the pre-UGTAN era; the second covers developments between 1957 and 1961, which may be called the UGTAN era; and the third covers what has been happening since 1961. Until 1957 most African unions in French-speaking West Africa were mere extensions of the three national centres in France: the communist dominated Confédération Générale du Travail (CGT); the Catholic outfit known as the Confédération Française des Travailleurs Chrétiens (CFTC); and the socialist oriented Confédération Générale du Travail–Force Ouvrière (CGT–FO). There were also independent unions, for example those of the railway workers, teachers, doctors, veterinarians, pharmacists and midwives. Most of the organised workers, however, belonged to the CGT, and a minority was shared by the CFTC and CGT–FO.

Several factors explain the great support which the CGT enjoyed among African workers. The first is that it supported the inter-territorial nationalist movement, the Rassemblement Démocratique Africain (RDA), founded in Bamako in 1954. This organisation was affiliated to the French Communist Party, and most of its leaders were also leaders of the trade union movement in the various territories. The RDA also played a popular role in the religious antagonism of French colonial Africa. The colonial authorities were predominantly catholic: the majority of the population in all the territories under French colonial rule were Moslem. The Moslem population had always accused the administering authorities of not giving their religion its rightful place in the scheme of things, and tended to see every action taken against CGT and RDA leaders as persecution because of their religious belief. Added to this allegation was the fact that between 1948 and

1950 a systematic attempt was made to suppress communist organisations in French-speaking West Africa, and the CGT and its ally, the RDA, were the principal targets. Common suffering tends to strengthen solidarity, and this was what happened to the CGT in French-speacking West Africa.

The emergence of African trade unions created opportunities for African workers to protest against low wages, poor working conditions and the enormous disparities in pay and fringe benefits between African and European workers with the same qualifications and doing the same type of work. There was no uniform labour code regulating the terms of employment of Europeans and Africans, so pressure began to build up for the introduction of such a code which could be applied in all French colonial territories. Between 1947 and 1950 a series of strikes was organised in furtherance of this claim. The climax came in November 1952, when a general strike was organised throughout French West Africa. In an effort to palliate the workers the French National Assembly enacted the Overseas Labour Code on 15 December 1952.

During the long struggle for the introduction of the uniform labour code, union membership declined from 25 to 20 per cent. In the RDA/CGT—dominated areas (Guinea, Ivory Coast, Mali and Senegal) the decline in membership was even heavier—between 35 and 40 per cent. The CGT was particularly hard hit, its part of total union membership dropping from 65 per cent in 1948 to 45 per cent in 1952.[19] It is one thing to win an industrial victory, but quite another thing to reap the fruits of that victory. Mere enactment of the Overseas Labour Code did not necessarily mean that it was being applied everywhere. Between 1952 and 1958 the unions turned their attention to achieving equal application of the provisions of the Code in all the territories and building strong and effective trade unions to achieve that objective and to protect and promote African workers' economic and social interests. In Guinea, for example, Sekou Toure, head of the CGT in that country, led a seventy-two-day strike (23 September–25 November) in 1953 to achieve equal application of the provisions of the Labour Code. That victory added a considerable stature to his name.

(b) Emergence of UGTAN

By 1954 the unions had developed strong local leadership and a passionate desire to direct their own affairs. These trends created stresses and strains with their mentors in France, and a feeling of frustration and disengagement began to develop. Mamoudou Sy, General Secretary of the Guinean Trade Union Federation CNTG puts it this way: 'Our central labour bodies could not continue to be branches of the French labour bodies, receiving orders from the metropolitan centres, waiting for their instructions before acting and sharing in their internal fights which led to divisons, particularly when there was an important action to be taken.'[20]

At the end of 1954, Sekou Toure took the first bold step to create autonomous organisations in French West Africa. He persuaded his organisation to sever connections with the CGT in France and disaffiliate from the WFTU. The local CGT and other unaffiliated unions then disbanded and reformed as the Confédération Générale des Travailleurs Africains (CGTA) which, though unaffiliated to either the CGT or the WFTU nevertheless maintained friendly relations with both. At about the same time the local branch of the CFTC also broke relations with France and set up the Confédération Africain des Travailleurs Croyants (CATC) changing the word 'Chrétien' to 'Croyant' (believing) apparently to differentiate it from the uniquely christian French organisation.

Things moved fast after these dramatic developments. There were, of course, dissidents to Sekou Toure's initiative. For example, Diallo Abdoulaye, a die-hard Marxist and head of the CGT in Mali, objected and openly declared his intention to remain loyal to the CGT in Paris. But this could not last for long. Sekou Toure's initiative seemed to have answered the cravings of thousands of African workers who wanted an organisation in which they could have a feeling of belonging. To them the connection with the French organisations was useful at the outset, but as time went on the relevance of that connection to their problems and aspirations became increasingly questionable. No matter what the French organisations did, and were prepared to do, to protect and promote their interests, African workers tended to feel that they were nothing more than black men in white men's organisations. This explains why thousands of them flocked to the CGTA soon after it was formed. Abdoulaye could not resist the temptation to join.

Five months after the founding of the CGTA, he resigned his position of Vice-President of WFTU and joined Sekou Toure and others in arranging a unity congress which inauguarated the Union Générale des Travailleurs d'Afrique Noire (UGTAN) in Cotonou in January 1957. Former CGT, CATC and unaffiliated unions attended the congress. CGT–FO did not attend, and the CATC as an organisation refused to join because of political differences. In due course UGTAN represented about 80 per cent of organised labour in French West Africa. Its structural organisation was as follows: (a) local unions composed of workers in the same type of activity constituted the base; (b) unions in the same town or region were grouped together to form local or regional union; (c) the local or regional unions within the framework of a state constituted the national union or the national branch of UGTAN; and (d) all the national unions constituted UGTAN.

The Contonou congress outlined the aims of UGTAN as being 'to unite and organise the workers of black Africa; to co-ordinate their trade union activities in the struggle against colonial regimes and all other forms of exploitation; to defend their moral and material interests and to affirm the personality of African trade unionism'. UGTAN was not to be affiliated to any international trade union organisation. At its second congress held in Conakry in January 1959, Sekou Toure defended the decision against international affiliation. He said that the extension of metropolitan trade unionism to Africa had broken African trade union unity, weakened the workers' power and made some trade unionists forget their sense of mission. Instead of fighting for concrete objectives, instead of combining workers' struggles with those of the people against colonialism, African trade union leaders had been carried away by ideological differences which had paralysed their actions. After discovering these weaknesses, and considering UGTAN's primary objective of emancipating the common people, promoters of African trade unionism since Cotonou had come to the conclusion that trade union ideology must be considered in the context of the immediate surroundings and conditions around which it was to develop. UGTAN had rejected any form of assimilation and any form of integration with national trade union federations in metropolitan countries, although it recognised proletarian internationalism as an effective factor in its development and in the implementation of its programmes. The congress appealed to African workers' unions still connected with French national centres to sever connections not later than May 1958. Mamoudou Sy, General Secretary of the CNTG, reports that most of them responded to the appeal.[21] The congress decided to establish a bi-monthly newspaper with correspondents in certain areas, who would meet periodically to discuss matters of common interest. It was also agreed that a trade union school be set up. Sekou Toure was elected President; six other persons were elected vice president; and four others were elected general secretary. UGTAN did not believe in the concept of one general secretary. Each general secretary was to be responsible for a certain activity like external relations, press and propaganda, economic and social affairs, and orientation. One of the vice-presidents was John K. Tettegah, Secretary General of the Ghana TUC and a member of the ICFTU delegation which attended the congress as an observer.

The significance of the congress may be judged from many angles. Under de Gaulle's referendum French colonies were required to indicate their preference for membership of the French community or outright independence. Any colony which voted 'non', i.e. a simple majority against, was automatically granted its independence. Sekou Toure's Guinea has the distinction of being the only country which voted 'non' during de Gaulle's referendum of 1958, and the outcome of that exercise won Guinea her independence. France's decision to cut off aid immediately from Guinea created speculations that the country would collapse within a short time. The fact that this did not happen, although there were great economic difficulties, tilted the scale in Sekou Toure's favour, and his popularity increased inside and outside Guinea. On the other hand it created strains for political leaders in other countries whose people had to wait for another twenty-four months before independence because they voted 'oui'. An observer at the Conakry congress reported that 'although Sekou Toure still represents a political minority in the fight against other African leaders like Senghor and Houphouet-Boigny in the French areas, I have the impression that he is the wave of the future while his opponents resemble more and more of the past. The freak of Guinean independence achieved by the mere vote of a "non" has begun to spread like wild fire throughout the French areas. The "oui" leaders are fast trimming their sails in order to show their independence and eventually anti-French orientation.'[22]

(c) 'Nationalisation' of UGTAN Branches
On attainment of independence Sekou Toure became President of Guinea. Combining that office with the office of President of UGTAN soon created the fear, rightly or wrongly, that he might use UGTAN's great influence to subvert other countries whose political leaders he had often denounced as imperialist stooges. That fear caused the governments and political leaders of those countries to 'nationalise' UGTAN national branches, a process which accelerated with independence as the inter-territorial links, which existed among the various countries during the colonial period disappeared. Different methods were employed to achieve the same objective. In some countries governments and political parties encouraged dissident groups to break away from UGTAN national branches and set up new organisations which were accorded recognition immediately irrespective of the unrepresentative character of such organisations. In others, governments took undue advantage of any mistakes which UGTAN national branches made to declare them illegal. A few examples may be cited.

In Senegal, the ruling Union Progressiste Sénégalaise, helped to create what was known as UGTAN-Autonome under the leadership of Abbas Gueye, a former member of the CGT and the Parti Sénégalais Démocratique (PSD), and a member of Parliament. In 1959 Alioune Cisse, former General Secretary of UGTAN, broke away from Conakry and established UGTAN-Unitaire. UGTAN-Autonome and UGTAN-Unitaire later formed the Union Générale des Travailleurs Sénégalais (UGTS), which merged with CATC-Sénégal in 1962 to form Union Nationale des Travailleurs du Sénégal (UNTS). In Ivory Coast where union–party relationship was closer than in any other country in French-speaking West Africa, differences had arisen in the trade union movement over the 'oui' or 'non' question during the French Community referendum with a majority of individual unions led by the civil servants supporting UGTAN's stand that the people should vote 'non'. The ruling Parti Démocratique de la Côte d'Ivoire objected sharply to UGTAN's stand as it was contrary to its recommendation to the electorate, and threatened the unions with reprisals. The party's general secretary, Philippe Yace, declared at the 1959 congress that it was 'dangerous for Ivory Coast unions to take directives from abroad because the central federation might not take account of the country's own social and economic problems.'[23]

UGTAN's supporters stayed away from the congress and later developed working relations with CATC which paved the way for the creation of Intersyndicat des Travailleurs de la Fonction Publique led by Blaise Yao Ngo. On 28 August 1959 France published the *Statut de la Fonction Publique* which provided elaborate labour relations policies applicable in the four West African Community States whose people had voted 'oui' during the 1958 referendum. Under the *Statut* the right to strike in the public service was severely curtailed, vacation period was reduced from three months every two years to one month every year and family allowances were reduced. Joint councils of workers were given more restricted functions than hitherto and most decisions were to be left to the Government. The *Statut* created a lot of embarrassment for union leaders who believed in working with the ruling party and the Government and reinforced Intersyndicat's militancy. Workers, apparently acting under the inspiration of Intersyndicat, took to the streets of Abidjan shouting slogans and denouncing Houphouet-Boigny's Government as 'worse than any form of colonialism'.[24] The Government warned Intersyndicat that any union which maintained relations with a 'hostile country' would be outlawed. The warning had no effect on Intersyndicat's militancy and its opposition to the hated *Statut*. On 7 October the Ivory Coast Government deported

Yao Ngo to Guinea. Intersyndicat reacted by organising a strike the following day, which lasted for three days and created chaos in Abidjan. The police broke up a protest demonstration with baton charges and tear gas. On 11 October twelve union leaders were arrested, 200 government employees were sacked and over 300 others were suspended. In 1961, plans were made to create a single national centre which would have close ties with the Government. That centre, the Union Générale des Travailleurs de la Côte d'Ivoire, was created in 1962. In September 1963 seven ministers were dismissed from the Cabinet and imprisoned following the discovery of an alleged plot to overthrow the Government. At their trial in January 1965, four of them and two local politicians were sentenced to death. Among them was Camille Gris, a former UGTAN leader, who became Minister of Labour. Since that time the trade unions in Ivory Coast have been thoroughly subdued.

In Niger, the union of postal, telegraph and telecommunications workers broke relations with Conakry, and within a few months and (in co-operation with other unions) set up a new federation. Government decree 18 of March 1960 forbade all meetings of UGTAN, and the national branch had to be dissolved in August because it was considered 'a potential danger to public order'. In Dahomey (now Republic of Benin) a dissident group within UGTAN formed the Union Générale des Travailleurs du Dahomey (UGTD) in February 1961, and immediately declared its support for government policy restricting the right to strike. It was quickly accorded recognition by Government. Sekou Toure himself did not help to improve UGTAN's image if judged from certain events in Guinea. Economic difficulties encountered within the first three years of independence had evaporated the euphoria of the 'non' vote. By 1961 the country's national centre, the Confédération Nationale des Travailleurs de Guinée (CNTG), looked like an uneasy alliance of rival interest groups, some groups believing that their first duty was to help the Government survive, the others arguing that their primary responsibility was to protect and promote the economic and social interests of the workers. In spite of earlier indications of being a nation-wide movement embracing wage earners and peasants it had become what Ioan Davies has described as 'a pressure group of the urban elite'.[25]

The teachers' union began a campaign for a review of salaries, and circulated a memorandum to this effect among party leaders, UGTAN and the AATUF offices. The CNTG congress of 1961 devoted a good deal of time discussing the teachers complaints. Delegates thought that a government headed by their former colleague would try to listen to the teachers' complaints and explore the possibilities of rectifying them. It was a forlorn hope. In November 1961 the teachers' union executive was suspended by government order: its leaders were arrested, prosecuted and sentenced to various terms of imprisonment ranging from three to ten years for 'conducting subversive activities'. The ruling Parti Démocratique de Guinée (PDG) threatened to convert the union's headquarters into a youth centre and the Government severely restricted CNTG's international activities as well as those of the individual unions. Plans to introduce check-off were abandoned. In 1962 the Government nationalised UGTAN's educational centre set up two years previously with the aid of East German trade unions. Since then the trade union movement in Guinea has been under strict government control.

(d) After UGTAN

Perhaps the most important aspect of the UGTAN congress of 1959 is its impact on the international relations of African trade unions, the ambivalence of their national centres to international trade union organisations, the creation of continental trade union organisations in Africa, and the notion that international affiliation is necessarily incompatible with the concept of African trade union unity. Since 1966, several governments in French-speaking Africa, like their counterparts in the English-speaking areas, have changed hands, some peacefully, others violently. A new brand of unionism has been emerging, and African workers have been witnessing an interesting, though sometimes bewildering, relationship between trade unions and government. The following developments may be noted:

Benin. Before 1973 there were six national centres and fifteen independent unions in this country. On 1 January 1973 President Kerekou asked the unions to prepare for unity, which was eventually achieved in November 1974, when a single national centre, the Union Nationale des Syndicats des Travailleurs de Dahomey (UNSTD) was formed. In April 1975 UNSTD organised an extraordinary congress to determine the principles of a new orientation for the unions. The new orientation meant a total rejection of Article 17 of UNSTD constitution which forbade national union officials from taking active part in politics. The congress decided that henceforth the new orientation should include (a) support of 'the new policy of national independence' (the Republic of Benin has been independent since 1960); (b) true belief in Marxist–Leninist ideology for the construction of a socialist society; and (c) effective participation in all the political activities of the country.[26]

Two months after the congress, Captain Michael Aikpe, Minister of Interior and Security, was shot dead by Presidential guards having, it was alleged, been caught in adulterous relations with the President's wife. Captain Aikpe was one of the principal architects of the 1972 coup which brought Colonel Kerekou to power, and was known to be one of the young Marxist officers whose support had continued to keep President Kerekou in power. According to *West Africa* (30 June 1975), the Dakar newspaper *Le Soleil* commented that 'these bedroom tales appear rather to be a cover for a far more serious crisis brewing in Dahomey'. The public were deeply shaken by the incident: some trade unionists took exception arguing that the 'punishment' was too severe. They organised a strike on 24 June in an attempt to force the President to resign. The strike was supported by public demonstration. According to a complaint filed with the ILO by the World Confederation of Organisations in the Teaching Profession (WCOTP), 'the President of the Republic ordered troops to open fire on the demonstrators and several trade unionists were among those killed and wounded.[27] The organisers of the strike were arrested and taken to a military camp where, according to press reports, they were maltreated. Workers who went on strike from 24 to 27 June had their wages and salaries reduced for the number of days they were on strike; those who were not on their jobs on 30 June lost them; those who signed the strike resolution were suspended from their jobs and sent to an agricultural centre where they underwent a six-month 're-education'.[28] UNSTD leaders issued a statement denouncing 'a group of activist trade unionists using the UNSTD's name to incite the workers to go on strike'. Later they met President Kerekou and reaffirmed the workers' determination to contribute actively to the success of the revolution.[29]

Cameroun. After the UN plebiscite in 1961 which resulted in the former British Cameroon joining the Cameroun Republic, President Ahidjo issued an appeal for trade union unity. This led to the grouping of four national centres, the Union des Syndicats Libres du Cameroun (USLC), Confédération Générale des Travailleurs Camerounais (CGTC), Union Générale des Travailleurs Camerounais (UGTC), and Union des Syndicats Autonomes du Cameroun (USAC) into the Fédération Syndicale du Cameroun (FSC). Two Christian groups, the Union Camerounaise des Travailleurs Croyants (UCTC) and Confédération Camerounaise des Syndicats Croyants (CCSC), merged in 1962 to create the

Union des Syndicats Croyants du Cameroun (USCC), but the new organisation refused to join the FSC. Trade unions in the English-speaking area of West Cameroon were united in the West Cameroon Trades Union Congress. In March 1969 the ruling Union Nationale Camerounaise (UNC) called for trade union unity. The call was heeded in February 1972, when the FSC, USCC and the West Cameroon Trades Union Congress (WCTUC) agreed to dissolve themselves and create the Union Nationale des Travailleurs du Cameroun (UNTC) which maintains close ties with UNC. In 1975 all the members of UNTC Executive were removed on the orders of the party and the government and new Executive members were appointed.

Central African Empire. Between 1964 and 1970 the Union Nationale des Travailleurs Centrafricains (UGTC) had a series of difficulties with the Government and there was widespread dis-content among workers with trade union leaders. Two congresses held in 1970 and 1974 adopted programmes aimed at revitalising UGTC. An ICFTU mission which visited the country in 1976 reported encouraging progress.

Chad. In 1963 four rival trade unions agreed to unite and form a new national centre called the Union Nationale des Travailleurs du Tchad (UNATRAT). Nahaur Oudalbaye Gorralah was elected General Secretary. Following the military coup which toppled Tombalbaye's Government, Gorralah was arrested and imprisoned and was replaced by his assistant Gabriel Dombal.

Mauritania. In April 1974 the trade union movement was integrated with the ruling party. Cheikh Melainine, Secretary General of the Mauritanian trade union federation (UMT) has described the integration as 'a political choice' reflecting the belief of both the workers and the party. He added that the integration had existed before, particularly since the 'institutionalisation of the party in 1965', but conflict arose in 1969 and 1972 over political and ideological differences.[30]

Senegal. Against trends towards a rigid control of the trade union movement through the device of integration with the ruling political party or military junta, Senegal's ruling political party, the Union Progressiste Sénégalaise (UPS) appears to have set an example in modifying its relations with the country's trade unions. A meeting of the party's National Council held in Dakar in January 1976 examined in depth the question of trade unions and political pluralism. During the meeting President Senghor was reported to have pointed out that the constitution of 20 February 1970, allowed the creation of political parties and groups in accordance with the prevailing political orientation of the electorate. He suggested that three political parties could exist, each reflecting one of the current orientations which he identified as liberal and democratic, socialist and democratic and Marxist–Leninist. Several trade unions, he added, could exist within the framework of a multi-party system.

After the meeting, it was announced that Senegalese workers would be allowed to set up more than one national centre if they so desired; that it would no longer be obligatory for a member of the country's national centre, Confédération Nationale des Travailleurs du Sénégal (CNTS), to become a member of the UPS; and CNTS would no longer be 'integrated' with the UPS, but would be 'affiliated' to it.[31]

Togo. Until 1971, two trade union groupings existed in Togo—the Union Nationale des Travailleurs du Togo (UNTT ex-UGTAN) and the Confédération Syndicale des Travailleurs du Togo (CSTT ex-CATC). In November 1971 the ruling Rassemblement du Peuple Togolais (RPT) congress urged Togolese trade unions to unite. In December 1972 the party appointed a committee to prepare for a unity congress. In January 1973 the UNTT and CSTT dissolved themselves and created the Confédération Nationale des Travailleurs du Togo (CNTT) which is more or less an industrial wing of the RPT.

Upper Volta. Upper Volta has the distinction of being the only country in French-speaking West Africa which has more than one national centre. There are five national centres: the Confédération Nationale des Travailleurs Voltaïques (CNTV), the Union Syndicale des Travailleurs Voltaïques (USTV), Organisation Voltaïque des Syndicats Libres (OVSL), Confédération Syndicale Voltaïque (CSV), and Union des Forces Ouvrières Voltaïques (UFOV). Relations between the government and the unions have often been strained because of disagreements over policy matters. A case in point is a law passed on 25 April 1964, prohibiting trade unions from having affiliation at international level and giving trade union centres already affiliated to international trade union organisations three weeks to disaffiliate. At the time when this law was passed Upper Volta had ratified ILO Convention 87 which guarantees freedom of association and the right to organise.

The ICFTU affiliate, OVSL, quickly complied with the provisions of the law, and ICFTU lodged a complaint with the ILO against the Republic of Upper Volta. It came to light later that the other national centres, notably the CATC, did not severe their international ties, despite the legislation in force. At the end of December 1965, the Government tried to induce the National Assembly to pass a law reducing wages by between 10 and 20 per cent. The unions unanimously opposed the measure, and a general strike was called. After three days of hostile demonstrations against the Head of State, President Yameogo, the army intervened and Lt. Col. Sangoula Lamizana took over the Government. He has been the President since then.

In December 1975 the unions organised another general strike which paralysed the economy for two days. In a letter to the General Secretaries of the national centres, the President announced that consultative meetings would be held with the trade unions in order to improve relations. He said that he had given orders to the appropriate authorities to study the grievances of the unions, particularly the revision of the minimum wage.

On 10 February 1976, the President announced the composition of his new cabinet which was largely civilian. The former cabinet had been suspended on January 29 after two months of crises between the Government and the unions. Before the cabinet changes, the President had conceded some of the demands of the unions, for example wage increases, the setting up of price controls and a promise to return to constitutional rule. In another attempt to satisfy the unions he announced that Zoumana Traore, General Secretary of USTV, an affiliate of WFTU, had been appointed Minister of Labour.

(iii) Guinea-Bissau

Before independence, there was a General Workers' Union of Guinea-Bissau (UGTGB) which operated in exile in Senegal. UGTGB was affiliated to the ICFTU and worked closely with FLING, one of the nationalist movements which fought the Portuguese army for more than a decade. UGTGB had three regional sections (branches): in the Gambia, Guinea and Senegal, each composed of Guinea-Bissau nationals working in these countries.

Guinea-Bissau was proclaimed an independent state on 24 September 1973 by PAIGC—the more representative and more successful nationalist movement—and was recognised by 90 member states of the United Nations. On 26 August 1974 Portugal finally accepted the 'fait accompli' when the Portuguese Foreign Minister, Dr. Mario Soares, signed an agreement to that effect with Major Pedro Pires of the PAIGC.

As PAIGC had no trade union wing, it was thought advisable that UGTGB should reconcile with PAIGC so as to pave the way for organising workers in the country. Such efforts at reconciliation were tried, but all to no good avail. In the meantime reports reaching the ICFTU secretariat in Brussels allege that a number of UGTGB and FLING members who returned to their country had disappeared.

2. EASTERN AFRICA

Tanzania

Tanzania seems to have borrowed a leaf from the Nkrumah Government in dealing with its trade union movement, though with some differences. In 1964, following an army mutiny over a pay claim, the Tanganyika National Assembly passed a law which dissolved the Tanganyika Federation of Labour (TFL) and created in its place a monolithic organisation called the National Union of Tanganyika Workers (NUTA). Under the new law NUTA was to have an organic link with the Tanganyika African National Union (TANU). It was obliged to promote TANU and government policies and encourage union members to join TANU. NUTA was granted union shop facility (an arrangement which compels every worker in a given bargaining unit to belong to the union) in cases where more than 50 per cent of the workers concerned were already members. The principal officers of the new organisation, i.e. the General Secretary and his Deputy, were to be appointed by the country's President, and they were to hold office at his pleasure. Other NUTA officials were to be appointed by the General Secretary.

The union was to have industrial sectors corresponding roughly to the nine industrial unions which constituted the former TFL. Its governing bodies were to review policies, not to make them. In exercise of the powers vested in him by the National Union of Tanganyika Workers (Establishment) Act 1964, President Nyerere appointed Michael Kamaliza, the Minister of Labour, General Secretary of NUTA. The Tanganyika developments must be considered against the following background:

(a) Tanganyika had a longer history of union–party relations than any other country in English-speaking Africa, excepting perhaps Kenya. But that relationship must be understood in its proper context. There was no formal organic link between the TFL and TANU right from the outset. Individual union leaders merely co-operated with TANU leaders in their political activities. Organic

34

link between the TFL and TANU took place only in 1961 following a compromise in a conflict between the unions and TANU over a major industrial dispute.

(*b*) TFL–TANU relationship had been deteriorating since the TANU Government assumed office, and Ministers could not always see eye to eye with the unions on certain industrial and policy issues. (Alan Rake, writing in *African Development* (July 1974), reports that some of the policies advocated by TFL at that time were then being implemented).

(*c*) In 1963, shortly after becoming Minister of Labour, Michael Kamaliza, a former President of the TFL, proposed to his former trade union colleagues that the TFL and the unions be incorporated into the Ministry of Labour. The proposal was formally put to the TFL Executive Council in October of that year, and was rejected by an overwhelming majority, the union leaders suspecting, in view of Kamaliza's well-known pro-TANU posture, that the move was the first step in a TANU bid to take over control of the trade union movement.

(*d*) The rejection of the Kamaliza proposal was a personal defeat for the Minister and a humiliating defeat for the TANU Government which they did not take kindly. When the army revolted over a pay claim in January 1964, and it appeared that certain trade unionists supported the claim, the Minister and the Government found a convenient opportunity to fight back. About 200 trade unionists were arrested in various parts of the country and sent to jail without trial, although there was no evidence of complicity between the trade union movement and the mutineers. While the trade unionists were still in jail the National Assembly passed the National Union of Tanganyika Workers (Establishment) Act.

Some of the arrested unionists spent more than two years in jail. When they were released, not only were they deprived of their union positions but a good deal were put on the black list. No government department, public corporation, local authority, and no employer in the private sector dared offer them employment.

NUTA had an uneasy existence for about two years. In May 1966, President Nyerere appointed a commission of inquiry into its affairs with particular reference to its constitution, organisation and practical activities since its inception, and in the light of the purpose for which it was established. The commission reported after five months, and listed thirty-five categories of complaints against NUTA. A Government White Paper on the commission's report said that some of the complaints were not entirely attributable to

NUTA and the commission should have recorded that fact. It agreed, however, with the commission's conclusion that there was need to provide more effective contacts, at all levels, between union officials and members. The commission made a number of useful recommendations which were accepted by the Government. Among them were the need to remove criticisms levelled against NUTA's accounting system and pattern of expenditure, the need to reduce administrative expenditure to the 50 per cent limit provided in NUTA's constitution, and the need for the organisation to develop a comprehensive workers' education programme.

The White Paper explained the embarrassing problem of organisation and structure, particularly the appointment by the country's President of the General Secretary and his Deputy and the related appointment of the Minister of Labour as General Secretary of NUTA. The commission had recommended, after carefully examining the matter and considering the views of a vast majority of members, that 'the General Secretary should henceforth be a full-time paid official of the union and shall not be permitted to hold any other office.'[1] That recommendation was rejected on the ground that 'union members who criticised the dual appointment had failed to realise the very substantial benefit which it has helped to win for them in recent years ... To assume that improvements in wages and terms of employment would have been greater had the General Secretary of NUTA been an elected full-time union official is to ignore the benefits conferred by legislation sponsored by the Minister of Labour.'[2]

These arguments ignore the fact that wage increases and improved terms of employment are no alternatives to the exercise of the fundamental human rights of the workers to choose their leaders freely and to remove them from office when they forfeit their confidence. Secondly, wage increases and improved terms of employment secured not through the process of collective bargaining but through legislations sponsored by a Minister expose the fallacy of having a union which is supposed to cater for the interest of workers but which in fact does not discharge that responsibility. Thirdly, it ignores a peculiarity in workers' thinking in many parts of the world: namely, that concessions granted by employers in order to dissuade workers from exercising their human and trade union rights are always suspect and contrary to international labour standards.

The Government's argument, that the dual appointment helped ensure that wage earners' problems were known to the Government and were taken into account in decision-making, does not impress. If there was a genuine desire to know workers' problems and to take them into consideration in the decision-making process, that objective could have been better accomplished by receiving representations from leaders who derived their authority to function from the workers themselves.

It is not always easy for governments to admit their faults. This is particularly true of governments in the so-called 'Third World' countries which tend to justify almost every one of their mistakes with arguments of 'national security' or 'development'. The Tanzania Government continued its experiment of having the Minister of Labour as General Secretary of NUTA. But that experiment could not be continued for long. In 1967 the Minister of Labour was relieved of the post of General Secretary of NUTA and was succeeded by Alfred Tandau, until then Deputy General Secretary.

Another White Paper, this time on wages, incomes, rural development and price policy was issued in October 1967, following the publication of the controversial ILO-sponsored Turner Report, which claimed that wage earners were exploiting the peasant population in the rural areas. The White Paper limited wage increases to 5 per cent per annum and only when there was evidence of increased productivity. A permanent labour tribunal was set up to act as an arbitrator between NUTA and employers, and ensure compliance by both workers and employers with the wage policy. Later the tribunal was given the additional responsibility of deciding whether bonuses were justified in public enterprises claiming increased productivity.

In 1970 a Presidential Circular called for the launching of workers' committees and councils in factories which, along with TANU branches there, were to be responsible for influencing events in the factories. The following year, TANU issued 'Mwnogozo', a set of thirty-five guidelines mostly on the need for workers to have a greater say in their place of work. It called, among other things, for an end to 'colonial working habits and leadership methods' whereby one man gave the orders and the rest just obeyed. Alan Rake reports in the article quoted earlier that 'following this important information workers have been alert and have been quoting clause 15 [containing the above reference] as they "destool" their "bosses" through strikes, go slows, locking them out or taking over the firm.' He goes on: 'As NUTA enters its eleventh year, there is much need for its strengthening if it is to get the genuine support and respect of its members some of whom have been disillusioned about its effectiveness on many occasions: some strikers have decided to march to TANU headquarters or to State House rather than NUTA offices.'

Kenya

In Kenya, trade union development followed a different pattern from the experiences in Ghana and Tanzania. Although there was a long history of union–party relationship as in Tanzania and Ghana, the Kenya Government did not move as quickly as these countries to take over control of the trade union movement. Kenya achieved independence in December 1963. In January 1964 the Government concluded an agreement with employers and trade unions on measures to achieve unemployment relief. Under the agreement, the Government and private employers undertook to increase employment: the Kenya Federation of Labour (KFL) pledged, on behalf of the unions, that there would be no strikes for one year. An industrial court was to be set up, and the Government further undertook not to recognise any trade union splinter groups. The value of that agreement may be measured by the fact that during its existence some 32,000[3] unemployed persons were offered employment.

A few months after the tripartite agreement had come into operation, three officers of KFL (Walter Ottenyo, Deputy General Secretary; Dennis Akumu, Assistant General Secretary; and Ochola Mak'Anyengo, Director of Organisation) teamed up and demanded a meeting of the KFL General Council in order to discuss what the three officials described as four important subjects. These, they said, were certain aspects of the tripartite agreement, KFL disaffiliation from the ICFTU, KFL's proposals on economic planning since, they claimed, the Kenya Government lacked dynamism in the matter, and intensification of the Government's Africanisation policy. Walter Ottenyo had earlier issued a statement that his union, the Railway African Union, did not recognise the tripartite agreement, a statement which provoked a quick response from the Government, which promised to take swift action if the parties to the tripartite agreement did not respect its provisions. A few months earlier Mak'Anyengo, as Director of Organisation, had written to ICFTU for a substantial financial grant for an organisation campaign and thanked the Confederation warmly for previous financial support.

The KFL Executive met, and after considering the activities of its dissident officers and the image they were creating for the organisation, decided to suspend them from office. A subsequent meeting of the General Council not only approved the decision of the Executive, but went further and decided to dismiss the three officials summarily.

The dismissed officials organised what they called the Kenya Federation of Progressive Trade Unions (KFPTU), which was refused registration by the Registrar of Trade Unions. It was evident from the outset that the KFPTU had the backing of certain political forces inside and outside the country, including certain elements in the ruling Kenya African National Union. Financial support was also coming from Ghana and certain 'socialist' embassies in Nairobi. In due course, the new organisation attracted sympathy and tried to maintain it by arguing that the KFL was acting contrary to the Government's declared policy of non-alignment by remaining an affiliate of the ICFTU.

The KFPTU appealed against the decision to refuse it registration, and lost. Thereupon it was informed by the Minister of Constitutional Affairs, Tom Mboya, that consequent to the rejection of its appeal, the KFPTU had become an 'unlawful society in Kenya'. The KFPTU ignored that warning and publicly stated that they would continue their activities. They added that they would never return to KFL as long as that organisation was affiliated to the ICFTU. Strangely enough, and in spite of this apparent affront to its authority, the Kenya Government did nothing to contain the activities of this 'unlawful society in Kenya'. Rather, certain statements by government spokesmen would appear to indicate that the Government had accepted the argument that international affiliation was a sensitive issue in Africa and incompatible with the policy of non-alignment, and the removal of that issue from Kenya would lead to harmonious industrial relations. J. Odero-Jowi, Parliament Secretary to the Ministry of Labour, and a former Principal of the ICFTU African Labour College in Kampala, described ICFTU as belonging to the 'western bloc' when contributing to a debate in Parliament.[4] Speaking about the same time in Melbourne, Australia, Tom Mboya, Minister of Constitutional Affairs and a former member of the ICFTU Executive Board, urged the ICFTU 'to face some of the realities of Africa.'[5] Such statements by former ardent supporters of the ICFTU coupled with the wave of Pan-Africanism then sweeping across the continent became power ammunitions in the hands of the KFPTU leaders and their promoters, and they showed no scruples in exploiting them. It was against this background that a Presidential Committee comprising nine Cabinet Ministers was appointed to review the trade union situation and make recommendations.

Early in 1965 the KFPTU changed its name to the Kenya African Workers' Congress, and succeeded in obtaining registration. The change of name made no difference to its character or following. It increasingly attacked the KFL, which fought back like a wounded lion. Walter Ottenyo backed out early in the game when his union refused to support him. In August 1965 a nasty incident took place in Mombasa during the elections of the Distributive Workers' Union. An armed gang, believed to be the hirelings of the KFPTU, forced its way into the meeting. In the ensuing hand-to-hand fighting three persons were killed and about a hundred others wounded. The shock and dismay which the incident caused hastened the publication of the Presidential Committee Report. The Committee recommended the immediate deregistration of the Kenya Federation of Labour and the Kenya African Workers Congress. A new national centre was to be formed in their place known as the Central Organisation of Trade Unions (Kenya) (COTU). All trade unions were to terminate their affiliation with external bodies forthwith, and external affiliations applied not only to bodies outside Africa but also outside Kenya. No affiliations to external bodies could be made without government approval. The President of Kenya, in consultation with the Minister of Labour, was to appoint the General Secretary, Deputy General Secretary and Assistant General Secretary of COTU from a list of names submitted to him by COTU's Governing Council. There was to be a compulsory check-off for all unions, the proceeds being remitted to COTU, the national unions and an investment fund approved by the Government.

COTU was formally launched after the publication of the report and has been in existence ever since.

Uganda

Of all the countries in East and Central Africa, Uganda appears to be the only country where politics played an insignificant role in trade union development until after the attainment of independence. This is probably due to two factors. The first is the comparative absence of the white settler problem in that country. Before and after independence, the vast majority of land was always held by Africans. Roger Scott discussing 'The Uganda Setting' in his book *The Development of Trade Unions in Uganda* reports that 'only 1·5 per cent of the total area is held in freehold, half of which was given as gifts to early European pioneers.' This is a sharp contrast to the experience in neighbouring Kenya where African opposition to land grabbed by Europeans and white South Africans led to the Mau Mau movement and its tragic consequences.

The second factor is the special position of the Kingdom of Buganda, a position due partly to physical and partly to historical reasons. The Baganda are the largest ethnic group in Uganda, occupying about one-third of the land space, and they account for about one-third of the total population. The seat of government and the headquarters of churches are situated in Buganda. Until 1966 it was reported that Buganda had proportionally the most educated people in the country and accounted for more than 55 per cent of the total GNP. When the British were trying to impose their suzerainty on Uganda, other kingdoms opposed them, but the Kabaka of Buganda wholeheartedly co-operated with the British. Indeed the kingdom of Buganda was the staging post from which the British undertook their military expeditions which subdued the dissident kingdoms. In return for that co-operation, the British excised a considerable portion of Bunyoro land (commonly known as 'the last counties') and gave it to the Kabaka. The lost counties later became an important political issue, and was to some extent responsible for the late emergence of nation-wide political parties. The issue was eventually settled after independence when the vast majority of the population living in those areas voted in a referendum in favour of being merged with the Kingdom of Bunyoro.

Various attempts had been made before and after the second world war to organise trade unions in Uganda, but these failed. Some measure of success was achieved in 1952 when the first union was registered. In the six years which followed, thirteen trade unions representing 7,370 workers were organised. By 1961, the number of registered unions had increased to thirty-four representing a total membership of 39,862.[6] In 1955 the unions founded the Uganda Trades Union Congress (UTUC) which existed in relative peace and unity until 1960, although there were periodical schisms over leadership.

The incident which led to the final split was a simple matter of procedure. An invitation had been received from the Preparatory Committee of the All-African Trade Union Federation asking the UTUC to send two delegates to its meeting in Accra. The invitation had been received by the General Secretary, Angelino Banyanga. Banyanga did not consult his President or put the matter before the UTUC General Council for consideration. Instead, he consulted John Reich, General Secretary of the Amalgamated Transport and General Workers' Union, and both men nominated themselves as UTUC representatives and advised Accra accordingly.

UTUC General Council met while the AATUF meeting was still in session and decided to suspend Banyanga and Reich from office pending their appearance before a committee of inquiry. Banyanga and Reich refused to appear before the committee, arguing that they had been suspended unconstitutionally. Subsequent efforts to resolve the matter were of no avail, so Reich and his supporter set up a rival organisation called the Uganda Federation of Labour

(UFL). Reich was elected President and H. Kasolo, of the Tobacco Workers' Union, Secretary. Banyanga had earlier dissociated himself from any attempt to split the trade union movement. UFL existed for a while but folded up for lack of support, and Reich took up an appointment with AATUF.

Another split occurred in 1964. By this time a great deal of differences had arisen between the ruling Uganda People's Congress (UPC) and the UTUC leadership over union–party relationship. There were elements in the top echelon of the party and the Government who wanted to see in Uganda the same type of relationship that existed between TANU and NUTA. They took exception to the idea that the trade unions should be independent workers' organisations. One of them, the former Minister of Labour, George Magezi, once asked, 'Free from what?' when discussing the concept of 'free and democratic unions' with some union leaders. The anti-free trade union elements in the party encouraged the UPC Youth Wing to harass union leaders known to be supporters of free trade union principles. In the trade union movement itself, they found a few allies like Eriabu Kibuka, General Secretary of the Uganda Public Employees Union, and I. M. Sheja, General Secretary of the Oil and Chemical Workers' Union, whom they wanted to use to replace what they generally regarded as the uncompromising leadership of the UTUC.

But to lead the workers of Uganda at that time Kibuka and his associates had to win their votes. Kibuka made an attempt at the UTUC congress in 1963 and failed, though he was elected Vice-President. During the twelve months when he functioned in that capacity he showed no scruples in his efforts to impress the Government and the UPC of his willingness to co-operate. In 1964 he resigned his office of Vice-President and set up the Federation of Uganda Trade Unions (FUTU) which 'will co-operate with government and employers but will maintain the workers' independence'. His sincerity was tested that same year. During the passage of a controversial Bill which seriously limited the trade union rights of public employees, he showed such attitude of unconcern that baffled both his friends and opponents. Roger Scott, Kibuka's great admirer, was so shaken that he was compelled to remark, 'A union genuinely devoted to western principles of free collective bargaining might have stirred itself in effective protests. But the only people in UPEU (Uganda Public Employee's Union) devoted to such principles were the expatriate advisers, and they had gone home.'[7]

FUTU had only six affiliates as against twenty-six affiliated to the UTUC. Yet 'Kibuka appeared on political platforms introduced as the leader of Uganda's workers in the company of cabinet ministers, and a FUTU delegation was sent as the official workers' representatives to the 1964 ILO conference in Addis Ababa.'[8] It existed side by side with UTUC until 1966 when a seminar on 'Labour Problems in Uganda' organised by the Milton Obote Foundation, an outfit financed by the Fredrich Ebert Foundation of West Germany, recommended the dissolution of the two organisations and the setting-up a new national centre. The seminar appointed an interim committee to draw up the constitution of the proposed new centre. What followed is both interesting and revealing. A few days after the seminar, the Permanent Secretary to the Ministry of Labour, who was also the Registrar of Trade Unions, addressed a letter to UTUC General Secretary advising him that the Government had 'accepted the decision of the Delegates' Conference ... to dissolve the hitherto existing two national centres' and that 'you will now cease to style yourself as the General Secretary of a non-existent organisation'.[9]

The Uganda Labour Congress (ULC) was formally inaugurated in November 1966. Kibuka contested the offices of President and General Secretary and lost, but he was eventually elected Organising Secretary. He held that position until March 1968, when he resigned. On 22 April he announced at a press conference in the Uganda Club that a 'Revolutionary Council' had taken over control of ULC, dismissed its officers, dissolved the Executive and abrogated the constitution. Earlier, he and Sheja had led their supporters to the ULC offices but were ordered out by the police, who threatened to charge them with trespass.

The attempted trade union coup was a sign of things to come, and appeared to have been planned with the active support of influential quarters in the party and government. There had been allegations of mismanagement of ULC affairs, of union leaders receiving money from external sources without reporting it to the governing bodies of the unions concerned, and of failing to 'mobilise the workers and co-operate with the government in development efforts'. The ULC scheduled an extraordinary conference for 29 April to consider these and other matters. But that conference could not be held because of new dramatic developments. In a three-pronged attack on 27 April, the Government announced that it had closed with immediate effect all ULC offices in Uganda, taken custody of their assets and ordered the closure of the ICFTU African Labour College. No reasons were given. Another announcement by the Minister of Labour, Lameck Lubowa, said that the Minister had appointed a commission of inquiry into the dispute affecting the Executive Board of the Uganda Labour Congress, and the sole commissioner was Godfrey Binaisa, a former Attorney General of Uganda.

The Binaisa Commission reported after some months and found, among other things, 'that although the waters of the TUC and FUTU met in one stream on 13 November 1966, to form the Uganda Labour Congress they still continued to flow in different currents without ever mixing; that the reasons that prompted Kibuka and his friends in 1964 to form a splinter national trade union centre in the name of FUTU were the same pattern as the reasons given in 1968 when Kibuka led the revolutionary council and purported to take over the ULC and to dismiss its duly elected officers ... the same characters who took part in the drama way back in 1964 when FUTU was formed were the same. What they changed in 1968 were the tactics which they employed to achieve their objects ... the evidence recorded showed beyond doubt that FUTU was founded in hatred of the Uganda TUC and nourished in opportunism, hoping against hope that by posing as a pro-Government trade union movement it would get the blessing of Government and thus prosper much faster than the Uganda Trades Union Congress. These hopes were, however, dashed through inefficiency, bad organisation and lack of principles.'[10] About Kibuka himself the Commissioner remarked that the manner in which he gave evidence and his demeanour in the witness box 'gave me a picture of a disappointed man with unfulfilled ambition, who would stop at nothing until he realised his life-long ambition of being at the top of the Uganda trade union movement.'[11] Having failed in all his manoeuvres, Kibuka eventually dropped out of the trade union movement.

In 1970 the Uganda Parliament passed a new Trade Unions Act which repealed the Act of 1965. The new law dissolved all existing trade unions registered under the 1965 Act and created a national trade union on the NUTA pattern called the Uganda Labour Congress. All existing registered unions under the 1965 Act were deemed to belong to the new ULC automatically. The new organisation was to have fourteen branches covering all categories of work in Uganda. Branch and sub-branch elections were to be held in January 1971, and ten delegates from each branch were to attend a conference in February at which the new ULC was to be formally launched. Unfortunately that conference could not be held because of the military coup which toppled President Obote's Government and brought Idi Amin to power. It was not until 1974 that a new national trade union centre, the National Organisation of Trade Unions (Uganda), was formed. NOTU has sixteen affiliates and its principal officers are Humphrey Luande,

President, and J. K. Kalangari, General Secretary. Very little is known of its powers and activities.

Ethiopia

Although the oldest independent country in Africa, Ethiopia has one of the youngest trade union movements in the continent. The first union was formed in 1961 at a mass meeting held in Addis Ababa and attended by about 200 workers from various factories. In October 1962 the Labour Relations and Public Employment Administration Order was handed down by the Emperor, Haile Selassie II. It is doubtful whether this decree could have been promulgated at the time were it not for certain developments in the political arena. In 1962 the Ethiopian Emperor was making strenuous efforts to unite the various political groupings which had arisen following the All-African People's Conference of 1958. A meeting of African Heads of State had been scheduled to take place in Addis Ababa in May 1963, and there were indications that the meeting would agree to dissolve the Casablanca and Monrovia Groups of African States, set up one organisation in their place and make Addis Ababa the headquarters of that organisation. Policy makers in Addis Ababa thought that it would be most embarrassing if it were known, particularly by the more militant African leaders, that Ethiopia was the only independent African country which had no trade union movement; and that although it had been a member of the ILO since 1923 it had the 'distinction' of being the only country in the world to have participated in the activities of that organisation for thirty years with only a government rather than a tripartite delegation.

The decree served two main purposes. First, it provided for the legalisation and registration of trade unions and employers' organisations. Secondly, it tried to reduce the incidence of labour unrests (then taking a turn for the worse) by establishing machineries for settlement of labour disputes. It permitted the employees of a plant to form a union if there were fifty or more persons employed therein or to join any union if fifty or more persons were already members. The decree did not cover persons in managerial positions, public servants in non-profit-making government enterprises, domestic servants and agricultural workers in small farms. It did not introduce the concept of "exclusive bargaining agency".

Soon after the promulgation of the decree, the Ministry of National Community Development received a flood of applications for registration of trade unions. Within six months forty-two unions representing a paid-up membership of 10,000 had been registered. In April 1963 the registered unions set up the Confederation of

Ethiopian Labour Unions (CELU), and in June, Ethiopia was, for the first time in her history, represented at the ILO conference by a tripartite delegation. An employers' organisation was formed in 1964. By 1966 CELU's affiliates had increased to seventy-two representing 31,766 members. All the affiliates were plant unions, excepting the construction workers' union which tried to organise construction workers in various parts of the country. The Government was not well disposed towards national unions, fearing that a strike in one plant might spread to other plants if unions were organised on national or industrial basis.

Employers would not bargain with the unions. An ICFTU representative reported in 1966 that 'most employers still believed in "master–servant" relationship and will not really accept the unions.'[12] The experience of the Printing Workers' Union is a case in point. The union tried for more than two years to negotiate with the employers and failed. The matter was reported to CELU which took up the case with the Government. When the appropriate Ministry invited the employers for a discussion they failed to show up.[13] In July 1966 the Ethiopian Government lifted the ban on trade unions in Eritrea, which was imposéd in 1952 when Eritrea became an integral part of Ethiopia. Since unions had existed there under British administration it was not difficult to revive them. By the end of that year, nineteen unions representing 7,000 workers had been organised. During the period 1966–73, CELU's membership grew and it made encouraging progress in its administration. Increased financial and technical assistance from the ICFTU and the African American Labour Centre helped to bring this about.

In 1974, CELU's progress suffered a severe set back. Ethiopia came under military rule that year. A general strike which paralysed the country's economy for three days was called off when CELU received an assurance from the Government that its seventeen-point demand, which included free education for poor children, freedom of the press, land reforms, the setting up of price control boards, improved labour relations including the right to strike, would be met. Relations with the military administration began to cool with the reinstitution of press censorship, the ban of strikes and demonstrations, and efforts to keep the unions under tight control. 'Moreover, the officers who at first seemed content to wield power through a simple "Armed Forces Co-ordinating Committee" proclaimed the creation of a Provisional Military Government and failed to name a date on which they intended to hand over power to a civilian government.'[14]

Matters came to a head on 16 September when CELU's General Assembly adopted a resolution commending the Military administration for its pronouncements on social and economic recon-struction but criticising it for the creation of a military admin-istration without the participation of civilians. Other organised groups shared the same opinion. The following day, the Govern-ment reacted by appealing in a radio and television broadcast to workers to get rid of their leaders, whom they accused of being 'corrupt and wealthy collaborators of the old regime'. Two days after, representatives of the Military Council visited CELU office and asked the officials present to withdraw the resolution. They were told that the officials had no authority to withdraw a decision taken by the General Assembly. On 23 September the Military authorities summoned the President, Beyene Solomon, the Vice-President, Gidey Gebre, and Fisseha Tsion Tekie, General Secretary of CELU, to the Barracks of the Fourth Division. They asked them again to withdraw the resolution. Upon being told that they had no authority to do so, the three men were detained. They remained in detention until June 1976. In February 1975, CELU disaffiliated from the ICFTU and three months after it was dissolved by the Military administration.

The Seychelles

In the Seychelles, the trade union movement is sharply divided between the two main political parties: the Democratic Party (SDP) led by James Mancham, and the Seychelles People's United Party (SPUP) led by F. A. René. So sharp was the division that the Labour Department Report for 1967–8 noted that 'the rank and file members of the large unions usually referred to themselves as being members of the "SPUP Union" or the "SDP Union" rather than as members of the actual union to which each belonged'. The 1969–70 report also noted that 'politics once again played a considerable part in the trade union field and retarded development amongst the more mature and active unions'.

In 1973 there were fifteen registered unions representing a total membership of 3,309. The strength of the individual unions varied from thirteen to 1,049. Of the fifteen the SPUP had four represen-ting 1,946 members; the SDP had also four representing 675 members; the Christian Union had only fifty-three members; the rest were unaffiliated. The massive trade union support for the SPUP is due to a number of factors, some historical, some political and some cultural and industrial. The Seychelles is a group of ninety islands of which only thirty are inhabited. The estimated population of the islands in 1973 was 54,000 of which 16,500 were in paid employment. About 80 per cent of the population are of African origin. It was a British colony until June 1976.

About a decade before independence, the key political issue was whether the islands should remain a Province of the United Kingdom or whether it should become an independent country closely associated with East Africa. SDP supported mainly by whites and the so-called coloureds (persons of mixed blood) advocated local autonomy within the framework of the British political system, while SPUP advocated complete independence from Britain. Because of their desire to be associated with East Africa, the SPUP was supported by the OAU and its Liberation Committee allocated funds for the party's political campaigns.

The growing popularity of the SPUP at the national and international levels and the ruling party's anxiety not to be outdone, led the Mancham Government into a series of blunders. For example, bombs exploded in the Reef Hotel in Victoria in February 1972, and in three other places. The authorities tried to frame the leaders of the Opposition, but failed. The same tactic was used against trade unionists pursuing normal trade union activity during the Government Workers' Union strike of April that year. The union had submitted a pay claim of 40 per cent increase to the existing wages and salaries. Although the Government realised that the workers had a good case, it would not concede partly because the claim had been made by a union that was affiliated to the Opposition Party and partly because such a concession would weaken the position of the unions affiliated to the Democratic Party. The aggrieved unions reacted by calling out their members on strike. The Government denounced the strike as political, and this created greater solidarity among the workers. On 17 April other workers came out in sympathy, and the economy was almost brought to a standstill. The police moved in with tear gas, and pickets and sympathisers were arrested. Among those accused of supporting the strike were three Swiss priests who attended the demonstration of 12 April. The priests denied any involvement in politics, but admitted supporting the strike because they considered the demands to be justified.

The strike led to the appointment of an arbitration tribunal headed by the island's Chief Justice. The tribunal awarded three categories of wage increases ranging from 25 to 35 per cent.

In 1973 an attempt was made to achieve inter-union co-operation through the creation of a Workers' Education Committee under the chairmanship of the Labour Commissioner. All the unions were represented at the first meeting. Two subsequent meetings were held later. In one, the committee nominated two persons to attend a conference on Labour and Family Health organised by the African–American Labour Centre in Nairobi. In the other meeting four of the constituent unions withdrew for reasons which were not stated. Efforts to summon other meetings failed and the committee ceased to exist.

Two trade union courses organised by the ICFTU in 1974 made it possible for all the unions to share a common platform again. During the course the idea of reviving the Workers' Education Committee was canvassed and received a general support. A Seychelles Workers' Education Committee was later formed in 1974.

The Seychelles achieved independence in 1976. James Mancham became Executive President and Albert René became Prime Minister following a coalition government formed before independence. In June 1977, while in London attending the Commonwealth Prime Minister's Conference, Mancham, the 'Playboy President' was overthrown in a bloodless coup, and René took his place. The change of Presidency meant that René took into his government most of the ablest trade union leaders who, with him, had led the SPUP. The extent to which the drain of able trade union leadership has affected the movement as a whole is unknown, though it can be imagined.

Burundi

At independence four unions emerged from the former branches of the Belgian national centres. They were the Syndicat Libre des Travailleurs du Burundi (SLTB); Syndicat des Agents de l'Administration du Burundi (SAAB), a union of civil servants; Fédération des Travailleurs du Burundi (FTB) formed in 1963 but banned in 1965, and Syndicat Chrétien du Burandi (SCB).

Burundi came under military rule in November 1966, and Col. Micombero created a party called APRONA, the only legal political party in the country. In 1969 the unions created a national centre, the Union des Travailleurs du Burundi (UTB), which has very close ties with APRONA.

Rwanda

Trade unions in Rwanda have made little or no progress since independence owing to lack of encouragement from the Government. In 1973 a new military administration took over charge of the country under the leadership of Major General Juvenal Habyalimana. In his May Day address to workers in 1974, the General asked them to 'take all initiatives which will help you to improve your working conditions and your living standards'.[15]

Somalia

Until 1965, two national centres existed in Somalia: the Confederazione Somala dei Lavoratori (CSL) which had its headquarters in Mogadishu and the Northern Federation of Labour (NFL) based in Hargesia. Discussions for a merger began that year, but very little is known of further developments. The CSL was closely associated with the ruling Somali Youth League, but it maintained its independence as a union.

The October 1969 military coup which brought General Mohammed Siad Barre to power changed the trade union situation. After the coup, the trade union centres were dissolved and their leading officials were arrested and jailed. When they were released they were reassigned to other jobs.

3. CENTRAL AFRICA

Malawi

Trade union development in Malawi has always been affected by the low level of industrial development, the excessive migration of the labour force and the general political situation. The economy is predominantly agricultural, the main cash-crops being tea, tobacco, cotton, tung and groundnuts. Minerals have recently been discovered, but it will take some time yet before their impact on the economy is felt. During the period 1965–7 the average level of wage employment was estimated at between 140,000 and 160,000 out of a total population of 4,038,904.[1] In view of the limited number of employment opportunities, neighbouring countries with more developed economies (Rhodesia, South Africa and Zambia) had always attracted Malawian labour. Between 1963 and 1967 an average number of 56,000 people emigrated yearly to seek employment in these countries.

The first trade union, the Transport and Allied Workers' Union, was formed in 1949. During the decade 1950–9 only three additional unions were registered. In 1956 the four unions set up the Nyasaland (the former name of Malawi) Trades Union Congress, which became the Trades Union Congress of Malawi after independence. Between 1960 and 1963 fifteen other unions were registered bringing the total number of registered trade unions to nineteen with a paid up membership of 4,763.[2]

Malawi trade union leaders supported their nationalist movement, the Nyasaland African Congress (later the Malawi Congress Party) in its opposition to the Central African Federation of Rhodesia and Nyasaland. In the process some of them came in conflict with the law and were punished. Malawi achieved independence in July 1964. A few months later, differences arose between the Prime Minister, Dr. Hastings Kamuzu Banda, and some of his cabinet colleagues, notably Henry Chipembere and Kanyama Chiume, over policy matters. So serious did the differences become that the two men resigned their positions in the Government and fled the country with some of their supporters. There were allegations of conspiracy to topple the Government by force, and indications of armed insurrection were reported in certain parts of the country. The Government reacted by ordering a ruthless crackdown of Chipembere and his supporters. In the exercise some people were killed and others went into exile. Among them were trade union leaders known or suspected to have been Chipembere's supporters. The incident contributed immensely to weakening the trade union movement.

In 1965 a convention of the Congress party decided that trade unions could affiliate to the party. At the time of making that decision it was generally thought, at least by trade unionists, that the decision to affiliate or not would be left to the unions, and that 'affiliation would confer on the movement formal and overt recognition and thereby remove from the minds of the workers any suspicion as to its bona fides'.[3] The amendments made in the party's constitution to give effect to that decision went beyond that expectation. Not only were the unions required to affiliate, but also the TUC. Affiliation meant that the party had the power to approve the election of trade union officials. In other words, should an elected official, for one reason or the other, be unacceptable to the party, such an official could be forced out of office and fresh elections would then be held to ensure that a candidate of proven Malawi Congress party political soundness was elected.

The unions, and particularly the TUC, objected to this provision, and tried to convince the party to delete or modify it, but failed. The union leaders who objected were squeezed out of office and the trade union movement. Since then the trade unions have been under the tight control of the Party and the Government. Malawi trade unionists cannot get out of their country or participate in any international trade union activity without Government approval.

Rhodesia (now Zimbabwe)

Until 1960 African trade unions could not legally exist in Rhodesia. The only exception was the Railway African Workers' Union whose right to exist was guaranteed by the Rhodesia Railways Act 1949. The exception was due mainly to the fact that the railway was jointly owned by Southern Rhodesia and Zambia then known as Northern Rhodesia. When the railway broke up after Zambian independence the Rhodesian authorities brought African railway workers under the Industrial Conciliation Act, 1959, which, while not permitting racial discrimination *per se*, nevertheless provided a number of legal loopholes to perpetrate discrimination and weaken African trade unions. Knight Maripe, a former General Secretary of the Railway African Workers' Union (RAWU), has described the effect of the change on African workers as follows:

The government plan means that if RAWU is forced to belong to one industrial council with the two other white unions, it will, like all other African unions, come under the effective control of white workers and its membership will be outnumbered by at least three to one. Vote valuation, its manipulation and other devices under the terms of the 1959 labour legislation will take care of that.[4]

What is 'vote valuation' and how does it work? To understand this intriguing problem, it is necessary to look at some of the provisions of the Industrial Conciliation Act 1959. Section 7 (1) provides for 'the equitable representation on the governing body' of trade unions and employers organisations, and in particular, the 'adequate representation of skilled and minority interests'. Section 47 (2) provides not only for the voting rights of members, the system of voting, the method of counting votes, but also 'the value of votes'. The Act divides workers under three main categories: skilled, semi-skilled and unskilled. To be classified under the first and second categories, a worker must have undergone a course of apprenticeship or attended a technical college. These opportunities were not available to Africans on an equal basis. The job reservation policy of the Government added insult to injury. African workers generally qualified for grouping under the third category.

Under Section 46 (4), the Registrar of Trade Unions may require a trade union to amend its constitution if he considers that existing provisions regarding the protection of skilled and minority interests or the voting rights of members are inadequate. In practice what all these things mean is that at union meetings skilled workers have a full vote, semi-skilled half vote and unskilled a quarter vote. In other words, no matter the numerical strength of Africans in the so-called non-racial unions the voting power of white workers would always hold sway. Against this background the desire of African workers to set up their own unions must be considered.

Although African trade unions could not legally exist before 1960 there were nevertheless many such unions before then, but they could not engage in collective bargaining with employers. Pay claims and demands for improvement in terms of employment were usually submitted to labour boards specially created for the purpose by the Southern Rhodesia Government. Though the unions were statutorily denied collective bargaining right, the Government recognised them as respresentatives of African workers' opinion and periodically consulted them on important matters of labour policy.

In 1957, the African trade unions founded the Southern

Rhodesia Trades Union Congress (SRTUC) led initially by Knight Maripe and later by Reuben Jamela. From the early stages of the Congress, the leaders were divided over trade union relationship with the nationalist movement. The problem was particularly embarrassing when considered against the background of developments in the neighbouring countries of Malawi and Zambia, and the fact that some of the leading nationalists like Joshua Nkomo, Michael Mawema, J. S. Moyo, Benjamin Burombo and Charles Mzingeli were themselves former trade unionists. A decision not to support them and their struggles could be misunderstood or misinterpreted. But the matter had to be considered, bearing in mind the realities of the local situation. It was this overriding consideration that decided the formal stance of most union leaders not to be involved in politics.

There were probably two reasons for the decision. Southern Rhodesia, unlike Malawi and Zambia, was a self-governing colony, and the white population was more sensitive to African nationalist aspirations than the colonial authorities responsible to the British Government. Active involvement in politics could entail detention or restriction of the leaders and/or the banning of their unions. This would have been an expensive gamble at a time when the unions were just trying to get on their feet. Secondly, many Southern Rhodesian trade union leaders belonged to Lawrence Katilungu's school of thought about union–party relationship. But that school of thought could not survive for long the rising tide of nationalism, Pan-Africanism and anti-colonialism which followed the All-African People's Conference of 1958.

In 1962 a group of union leaders under the leadership of Josiah Maluleke broke away from the SRTUC and set up the Southern Rhodesia African Trades Union Congress (SRATUC) which tried to forge Pan-African links. The split was compounded by the split in the nationalist movement in 1963. SRTUC was split further in 1964 when some leaders joined the SRATUC and others formed the Zimbabwe African Congress of Trade Unions (ZACU), which immediately affiliated itself to Joshua Nkomo's Zimbabwe African People's Union (ZAPU). ZACU was banned in 1964 and was succeeded by the National African Federation of Unions (NAFU). By this time the SRATUC had identified itself with the rival nationalist movement, the Zimbabwe African National Union (ZANU) led by the Rev. Ndabaningi Sithole.

The Rhodesian authorities had often taken repressive measures against African trade union leaders. These measures were intensified as nationalism gained momentum; but union leaders showed an increasing tendency of fighting themselves instead of the common enemy. Several trade unionists were arrested and imprisoned without trial under the notorious Law and Order Maintenance Act. These developments forced the ICFTU and the International Trade Secretariats associated with it to work out an international solidarity programme for the trade union movement in Southern Rhodesia. In 1963 they sent William G. Lawrence, a British trade unionist from the Inland Revenue Staff Federation and the Public Services International, as a special representative in Rhodesia. His responsibilities included helping the trade union leaders to achieve a united movement, administering ICFTU International Solidarity Fund grants for the families of detained and restricted trade unionists, organising trade union courses and correspondence courses for detained and restricted trade unionists and generally offering advisory services on organising techniques, trade union administration and collective bargaining. Lawrence did a good job during his twelve year's stay in the country, but unity was not easy to achieve owing largely to the division in the nationalist movement.

For ten years, the African trade union movement was split between the SRATUC (or ATUC for short) and NAFU. In 1971, following the emergence of the African National Council and the apparent unity of African public opinion against the Pearce Commission Report, several unions affiliated to both the ATUC and NAFU appealed to both organisations to settle their differences, dissolve themselves and set up a new national centre. These appeals fell on deaf ears. It took three years of patient prodding by Lawrence to make the leaders appreciate the need for unity. In March 1974 a meeting organised by Lawrence and attended by representatives of thirty unions affiliated to both the ATUC and NAFU renewed the appeal, and went a step further by setting up a National Interim Committee (NIC) to act as a representative and spokesman of the African trade union movement, pending the founding of a properly constituted national centre. NAFU responded to the appeal and dissolved itself in August. The ATUC, according to its President, Phenias F. Sithole, refused to dissolve even though its General Secretary, Financial Secretary, and Treasurer were members of the NIC and leading officials of the ATUC's strongest affiliate and historically Rhodesia's most developed African union—the RAWU. For co-operating with the NIC, ATUC's General Council decided at its meeting in October to remove its General Secretary, Financial Secretary and Treasurer from office and membership of the General Council. But the trends towards unity continued to gather momentum. The following month, a conference attended by representatives of the unions which attended the March conference felt that enough was enough. It decided to set up the National African Trades Union Congress (NATUC), and elected John T. Dube of the RAWU President, and D. T. G. Chimusoro, General Secretary of the Engineering and Metal Workers' Union, General Secretary. Anderson J. Mhungu, General Secretary of the RAWU, later succeeded Chimusoro as General Secretary of the NATUC.

In 1976, NATUC split into three factions following the split in the nationalist movement which preceded the abortive Geneva conference of that year. Each faction claimed to be the 'true NATUC'. Faction 1 led by E. Tsvaringa, General Secretary of the Hotel and Catering Workers' Union, had Anderson Mhungu as its General Secretary, and supported the United African National Congress led by Bishop Abel Muzorewa. Faction 2 led by T. Chikura, President of the Bulawayo Municipal Workers' Union had B. Ngwerume, General Secretary of the Gemstone Workers' Union, as its General Secretary and supported the Zimbabwe African National Union led by Robert Mugabe. Faction 3 led by J. J. Dube, President of the recently formed National Associated Railway Workers' Union which caters for the interests of senior African railway employees, had as its General Secretary W. V. Masuku, Branch Secretary of the Railway Associated Workers' Union, and supported the Zimbabwe African People's Union led by Joshua Nkomo. Faction 3 had such powerful trade union figures as M. G. Khumalo, President of the Rhodesian Tailors and Garment Workers' Union; M. M. Gwetu, Treasurer of the same union and A. N. Nadabambi, Vice-President of the Railway Associated Workers' Union. Dube, Ndabambi, Mrs. L. Sihwa and M. G. Khumalo were later arrested and detained, but they were eventually released on 1 February 1978.

In 1977 several attempts were made to restore unity, but all to no avail. One of the principal characters behind the unity move was Reuben Jamela, a former President of the then united Southern Rhodesia African Trades Union Congress (SRATUC), who left the trade union movement in the early 'sixties to become an executive officer of the Salisbury Municipality. During his leadership of the SRATUC Jamela received tremendous support from the Americans, particularly from Irving Brown and Maida Springer of the AFL–CIO. A meeting called by Jamela in June was attended by several trade unionists, and it was agreed to set up a working committee which would pave the way for a merger conference. After the meeting, however, some trade unionists expressed some misgivings that Jamela was being used by the Americans, and therefore failed to co-operate. Early in November, Faction 1 of the

NATUC dissolved itself and one week later Jamela and others willing to co-operate with him formed the Zimbabwe Federation of Labour. E. Tsvaringa was elected President; Reuben Jamela, General Secretary; and Maodzwa Treasurer. The new federation is reported to be financed by the AALC.

Zambia

From the outset, trade union development in Zambia was bedevilled by politics. That country's labour history is, more or less, a history of the nationalist movement. Surprisingly, though there was always this twin relationship between unionism and politics, there were hardly any 'political strikes'. The strikes which took place were 'industrial' and were expressions of African workers' resentment against starvation wages, racial discrimination and deplorable conditions of work. But each successful strike added a new dimension to nationalist struggles for a say in the administration of their country. African trade unions and the nationalist movement started about the same time, and almost every union member was also a member of the nationalist movement, the African National Congress (ANC). But the leadership of the trade union movement and that of the ANC were kept apart scrupulously. The leaders of practically all the unions were committed to the nationalist cause, excepting that of the 32,000 strong Northern Rhodesia Mineworkers' Union. Lawrence Katilungu, President of this union, had a philosophy which his admirers and detractors expressed in one sentence—'politics and trade unionism don't mix'. A critical observer has described what eventually happened to him and his philosophy. 'When in the late 'fifties he abandoned this philosophy and joined the ANC his opponents used the same philosophy in deposing him. "Either Katilungu remains a trade unionist or he becomes a politician. He can't be both."'[5] To understand what happened and why it happened it is necessary to bear in mind the following facts:

(a) White settlers in Central Africa had been pressing for a federation of the two Rhodesias and Nyasaland ostensibly in the interests of 'all inhabitants'. In fact the real reason for the agitation was to enable them to extend to the three countries the land laws, racial segregation and other repressive legislations existing in South Africa from which they drew their inspiration.

(b) Africans in Northern Rhodesia and Nyasaland were vehemently opposed to any suggestion of incorporating them in any political arrangement with Southern Rhodesia. As far back as 1938, a commission of inquiry appointed by the British Government had established this fact.

(c) In the late 'fifties, the Federation of African Societies had decided to change its name and character, the new name being the African National Congress led by Harry Nkumbula. The change of name and character was necessitated by the fact that the Provincial Advisory Councils, later known as African Representative Councils, set up by the colonial regime 'to speak for and on behalf of the Africans in rural and urban areas' did not represent the true opinion of the Africans.

(d) In 1958 the Northern Rhodesia Trades Union Congress (NRTUC) led by Lawrence Katilungu underwent some reorganisation and new officers were elected. Most of the newly elected officers were staunch supporters of the ANC. A meeting of NRTUC General Council had decided in unequivocal terms that the TUC was opposed to the proposed Federation of Rhodesia and Nyasaland and would not participate either by way of representation on, or by submitting a memorandum to, any commission to be set up on the matter. The meeting further decided that any trade unionist who defied the decision would be disciplined.

(e) To the embarrassment of the African population, and particularly his colleagues in the trade union movement, Lawrence Katilungu defied the decision and accepted an invitation to serve on the Monckton Commission appointed by the British Government. A vote of no confidence was passed in his leadership, and subsequently the majority of the unions affiliated to the NRTUC withdrew and formed the 'Reformed Trades Union Congress'. Only the mineworkers' union remained with the NRTUC.

Hitherto, there had been no formal organic link between the trade unions and the ANC. As in most other countries, union–party relationship was merely an indication of the extent to which individual union members and/or their leaders were actively involved in politics. The formation of the Reformed TUC changed the picture. A meeting of the RTUC held at Ndola in May 1960, decided to support 'a progressive political party'. That progressive party was the United National Independence Party (UNIP), which had been formed by dissidents who broke away from the ANC. When in 1961 the NRTUC and the RTUC merged and became the United Trades Union Congress (UTUC) the new organisation decided to continue the relationship which existed between the RTUC and UNIP. The UTUC existed until 1965 when it was dissolved by an Act of Parliament which created in its place the Zambia Congress of Trade Unions (ZCTU).

The ZCTU has seventeen affiliated unions representing a total of 205,000 workers. This represented in January 1976, about 38 per cent of all wage earners and salaried employees in the country, and placed Zambia on the map as a country with one of the highest rates of organised labour in Africa.[6] Since independence the number of organised workers has nearly doubled, and the number of unions has fallen from twenty-seven to seventeen.

Yet with this splendid record, the ZCTU and the Zambian Government appear to be dissatisfied with the trade union structure. The ZCTU has said, for example, that 'the structure of the labour movement is so cumbersome that it is not suitable for Zambia'.[7] But how cumbersome really is the Zambian trade union structure? What features make it unsuitable for Zambia? The ZCTU itself has given some indications which may be summarised as follows: strength in real terms belongs to the unions and not to the Congress; affiliated unions are autonomous organisations with their own rules; the ZCTU has no authority over individual members of its affiliates except through the authority of those affiliates; and the Congress cannot instruct unions nor can it control strikes without the co-operation of the unions concerned. For these reasons a new thinking is developing in Zambia about trade union structure. The ZCTU gave a hint of the line of thought when it said, 'It has been found that in developing countries a centralised structure of trade union organisation is more effective for mobilisation and discipline; it works in Tanzania, Algeria, the UAR and other countries. The Ministry of Labour and Social Services is considering some changes in the structure of the trade union movement in Zambia.'[8]

Congo

In the early 1960s President Fulbert Youlou had a number of problems with the trade unions over a number of policy issues. The President wanted to set up a single political party involving also the creation of a single national trade union centre. At that time there were three national centres in the country: the CCSL affiliated to the ICFTU, the CGAT affiliated to the WFTU and CATC. A Trade Union Merger Committee had been created, and the unions suggested that the Committee be recognised as an industrial wing of the proposed party. Youlou rejected the suggestion and the unions began a general strike in mid August 1963. The strike lasted three days and led to the fall of the Youlou Government.

Under the provisional government of Massemba Debat the plan

of the previous regime was carried out, and all the former political parties were dissolved, leaving only one authorised party, the National Revolutionary Movement (MRN). At the elections which followed, Massemba Debat was elected President of the Republic and the union leaders from the CGAT and CATC who played a leading role in the Trade Union Merger Committee were given important political appointments. In March 1964, a provisional unified centre known as the Confédération Syndicale Congolaise (CSC) was formed on the understanding that pending the formal inaugural congress, the former national centres would retain their respective international affiliations. The inaugural congress did take place in September 1964, and confirmed the agreement on international affiliation.

A surprising development took place just before the inaugural congress. The CATC which had been in the vanguard in the efforts to create trade union unity and whose President had presided over the first meeting of the merger committee, withdrew its participation in the executive of unified provisional centre. Consequently it was not represented on the CSC Executive elected by the founding congress. The Executive comprised three representatives from the CGAT, three from CCSL, one from the civil servants' association and one from the postal workers' federation who was elected General Secretary of CSC. Eight months after the formation of the CSC, the Congolese National Assembly declared it the only legal trade union organisation in the country. The CATC President was arrested and jailed and its General Secretary, Gilbert Pongault, went into exile. The CSC is closely associated with the Congolese ruling party, the PCT.

Gabon
Relations between the Government and trade unions were not particularly good in the early 1960s. This was due in the main to the reluctance of the Government to be faced with the prospect of a powerful trade union movement. Unlike the neighbouring country of Congo where the combined strength of the trade union movement had led to the fall of an elected government, trade unions in Gabon were not implicated in the abortive coup of February 1964, which was crushed by French paratroopers. Although one union leader, Essone Ndong, General Secretary of the ICFTU-affiliated national centre CNTG, was arrested after that event, this was not in connection with the coup. President Mba told the ICFTU in a letter dated 9 April 1964, that the union leader was arrested and detained because of his 'having been implicated in the distribution of an anonymous tract, and as the investigation carried

out in this connection had not resulted in any specific charge being brought against him, he had been released immediately'.[9]

In April 1969, leaders of the three national centres—the CATC, CGTC and CNTG—held a meeting with President Bongo to discuss trade union unity. Six months later the three organisations merged and created the Fédération Syndicale Gabonaise (FESYGA) which has very close ties with the ruling party.

Zaire

African trade union development in the former Belgian colonies of Congo (now Zaire), Burundi and Rwanda followed more or less the same pattern as in the former French territories. Until 1946, African workers were not allowed to form or join trade unions. The unions which they managed to form during and after that year were affiliated to the two national trade union centres in Belgium: the socialist Fédération Générale du Travail de Belgique (FGTB) and the Christian Confédération des Syndicats Chrétiens de Belgique (CSCB). The FGTB helped to organise African and European workers, ignoring some of the restrictions imposed by the labour law of 1946. In August 1951 the unions thus organised became FGTB-Congo Belge, Rwanda-Urundi.

Before independence there were five national centres in Zaire, Burundi and Rwanda. These were the Confédération des Syndicats Chrétiens du Congo et Rwanda-Urundi (CSCC) which became the Union des Travailleurs Congolaise (UTC) when Zaire became independent in April 1960; the Fédération Générale du Travail de Belgique-Congo Belge, Rwanda-Urundi (FGTB–CBRU) which, also in April 1960, became the Fédération Générale des Travilleurs Kongolais (FGTK); Association des Fonctionnaires et Agents de la Colonie (AFAC), an organisation of European civil servants which ceased to exist after independence; Association Indigène de la Colonie, an organisation of indigenous civil servants which merged with the Confédération des Syndicats Libres Congolaise (CSLC) in 1961 and the Confédération Générale des Syndicats Libre de Belgique (CGSLB). The principal organisations were the UTC, CSLC and FGTK which represented about 90 per cent of all organised labour.

During the period 1960–5, characterised by unstable governments and civil wars, prices of essential commodities rose by about 400 per cent, but wages failed to keep pace. This led to strikes, demonstrations and the frequent arrest of union leaders. In November 1965, a military coup brought General Mobutu Sesse Seku to power, and an opportunity was created to bring some measure of stability to the country. In May 1967, Mobutu created a political party, the Mouvement Populaire de la Révolution (MPR), and dissolved all other political groupings. The following month representatives of the UTC, CSLC, FGTK and the teachers' union, SYNECO, met in Kinshasa to discuss trade union unity. They agreed to dissolve their organisations and create one national trade union centre called the Union Nationale des Travailleurs du Congo (UNTC) which became the UNTZa in 1971 when the country was renamed Zaire. André Bo-Boliko, former General Secretary of the UTC, was elected its first General Secretary. In 1970, Bo-Boliko, Raphael Bintou, Thomas Booka and Victor Beleke, the founding fathers of the UNTZa, were appointed to important political posts and left the trade union movement. In January 1971, an extraordinary congress elected Kikongi di Mwinsa as the new General Secretary. The UNTZa is closely tied to the MPR.

4. SOUTHERN AFRICA

Angola

Before the Portuguese coup of April 1974, there were fourteen trade unions in Angola which served mainly the interests of whites. The largest unions were those of commercial, banking, railway and metal workers. Africans joined these unions merely to benefit from social security which could not otherwise be obtained. After the coup, a number of Africans imprisoned in Angola for political reasons were released. Among them was Mauricio Luvualo who had been a trade union activist in exile prior to his arrest. He considered the existing trade unions inappropriate for the needs and aspirations of the African workers, and therefore began organising activities. In due course he succeeded in establishing the National Confederation of Angolan Trade Unions (CNTA) which organised highly successful strikes in furtherance of pay claims and improved terms of employment.

Besides the CNTA, in 1975 there were two other national centres in the country—the Union Nacional dos Trabalhadores Angolanos (UNTA) and the Central Sindical Angolana (CSA), both previously operating in exile. The UNTA was based in Brazzaville and Lusaka and had carried out clandestine activities in Angola while the country was still under colonial rule. The CSA was established following the merger of ICFTU-affiliated Ligue Générale des Travailleurs de l'Angola (LGTA) and its Christian counterpart. It was based in Kinshasa and was closely connected with the National Front for the Liberation of Angola (FLNA) led by Roberto Holden. The UNTA was more or less the industrial wing of the MPLA. By the time it moved into Angola it already had its contacts, and had a considerable following in Luanda and Lobito among railway workers.

An ICFTU mission which visited the country in 1975 reported that UNTA's policy appeared to be to try to transform the trade unions established during the colonial period rather than dissolve them. Towards that end the UNTA organised a conference in December 1974, which was attended by representatives of nine of the fourteen unions existing before the Portuguese coup. The conference discussed and drew up a programme for the establishment of a single trade union centre along the lines of the communist-dominated trade union federation set up in Portugal after the coup. The programme was believed to have been worked out on the instructions of the then Portuguese Government and was immediately denounced by the CNTA and CSA.

After the MPLA victory, UNTA remained the only trade union organisation in the country. In April 1977 its activities were suspended, its officers having been accused of complicity in the abortive coup to topple Dr. Neto's government. The trade union movement is now being restructured, and it is expected that a new organisation will be set up in 1978.

Botswana

There were eight registered unions in Botswana in 1971 representing a paid up membership of 2,150. There was no national centre, but an education committee acted as a co-ordinating body. Earlier attempts had been made with varying successes to organise unions and national centres. The first union was formed in 1947 and registered two years later, and was known as the Francistown African Employees Union led by Gabriel Mmusi. In 1959 efforts were made to improve the structure by widening its jurisdiction and making membership open to workers of all races willing to join. This led to the formation of the Bechuanaland Workers' Union, which became the Botswana Workers' Union after independence. The BWU was a general workers' union, and had branches in Mahalapye, Palapse and Lobatse.

The trade union leaders were actively involved in politics during the struggles for independence. Political differences led to the founding in 1965 of the Bechuanaland Federation of Labour (BFL) led by G. Mmusi, and the Bechuanaland Trades Union Congress (BTUC) led by K. K. Motshidisi, a Moscow-trained trade unionist, who was an active supporter of the Opposition Bechuanaland Front Party. Mmusi had attended trade union courses in England and the United States, and was an Executive member of the ruling Democratic Party led by Sir Seretse Khama. The BFL had five of the eight registered unions in the country as its affiliates while the BTUC had one.

Rivalry between the two national centres led to a great organising activity with each centre setting up general workers' unions in a number of places and claiming the membership of its opponent. This chaotic situation continued until January 1967, when the Labour Commissioner held a meeting with leading trade union officials. The meeting discussed three important topics: the basis of union organisation, trade union education and effective utilisation of trained trade unionists. It was agreed that henceforth unions should be organised on industrial basis, that three trade unionists (G. Mmusi, Miss. B. C. Tumelo and K. K. Motshidisi) who had attended advanced trade union courses outside Botswana, should be assigned to various areas of the country to undertake trade union education, and that a National Trade Union Education Committee (NTUEC) should be set up. G. Mmusi was elected Chairman and K. K. Motshidisi Secretary of the Committee.

The NTUEC was also entrusted with the responsibility of uniting the BFL and the BTUC. Three exploratory meetings ended in a deadlock before the enactment of the Trade Unions Act 1969, which dissolved existing trade unions and required them to re-register. Under the Act a national trade union centre may be established if the members of the constituent unions voted in favour. Such a referendum was conducted by the Labour Department in the early part of 1977, and the results led to the inauguration of the Botswana Federation of Trade Unions in April.

Swaziland
In 1965 there were fourteen registered trade unions in Swaziland representing about 7,000 members. By April 1970 the number of registered unions had fallen to seven representing 2,565 members. In 1975, Swazi bank employees formed a union, and it was reported in 1977 that there were only three active unions in the country. This decline demonstrates the fact that during the period 1965–75 no progress was made in the organisation of trade unions in Swaziland. The reasons for lack of progress may be traced from the weaknesses in the unions themselves, the influence of the employers' federation and the labyrinths of Swazi politics. Some of the unions were plant organisations whose members paid enrolment fees and little or no dues. Some aligned themselves with the opposition, and this seemed to have annoyed the ruling party. According to the Registrar of Trade Unions, only five of the fourteen registered unions submitted their annual returns for 1964–5. These returns showed that the five unions represented a total of 423 paid-up members. The Registrar pointed out, however, that the number was incorrect. The unions collected dues but failed to enter the receipts in their account books. But how did the Registrar arrive at the total of paid up membership quoted above? A visiting ICFTU mission found in 1966 that he merely divided the cash in hand by the rate of dues. According to the mission's report, the Registrar felt that 'all the union leaders

were a dishonest lot, and are all guilty of diverting union funds into their pockets'.[1]

The Swaziland National Movement known as Imbokodvo (grinding stone) led by the Prime Minister, Prince Makhosini Dlamini, won the last general elections before independence in 1966. Soon after that victory the Movement showed its opposition to the trade unions. Its leaders claimed that there was no need in Swazi society for such 'foreign influences' like the trade unions and that the party was capable of catering for workers' interests. In due course they modified their thinking and planned setting up a monolithic organisation on the NUTA pattern. To study how such an organisation functioned Prince Makhosini stopped over in Tanzania during one of his tours to different African countries. Before finalising the plan, the unions fought back. Some of the most militant trade union leaders teamed up with the Ngwanye National Liberatory Congress (NNLC) led by Dr. A. P. Zwane. Within a short time they made things difficult for the government and the unions which supported it. The NNLC backed certain candidates for election to the Executive Council of the Swaziland Mineworkers' Union and all of them won. This encouraged the party to try their hands at another union election, but the Labour Department could not accept the results. The Congress and their supporters in the trade union movement tried to set up rival unions to oppose the men they were trying to unseat. An observer has described their method as follows: 'If they can't take it, they ruin it,' and the resulting state of affairs forced the Government to react harshly.

In 1970, another ICFTU visiting mission reported that little or no progress had been made in trade union development in recent years. A number of unions had, for various reasons, been deregistered or ceased to exist. The only union which seemed to have any semblance of organisation was the Citrus Plantation, Agricultural and Allied Workers' Union, and this was as a result of work done in 1967 by Walter Hood of the British TUC. Attempts had been made to establish some sort of national centre, but these failed. Union officials claimed that there was no enthusiasm in official quarters for trade unions. A national centre had existed before, but the Government was responsible for its collapse. Alongside government hostility was the influence of the employers' federation. Its Executive Secretary was said to have arrogated to himself the task of advising union officials on union business. Some trade union leaders were said to be on his pay roll and 'meat for his sausage machine'.[2]

In 1973 there were political upheavals which further weakened the unions. What precipitated them was that three members of the NNLC won elections to Parliament and the ruling party did not want them there. The real object of attack was Thomas Ngwanya, a South African by birth, who had lived most of his life in Swaziland and had been active in the country's politics. Ngwanya is said to belong to that portion of Swazi territory which the British colonial administration excised in the nineteenth century and incorporated into South Africa. To date, the Swazis of South Africa still owe allegiance to King Sohbuza II, and there are rumours that negotiations are going on between South Africa and Swaziland for the return of the territory.

When Thomas Ngwanya took his seat in Parliament, a government spokesman questioned the legality of his membership, arguing that he was a refugee. In due course, the Government took the matter to court, but the case ended in Ngwanya's favour. Dissatisfied, the Government set up a special tribunal with powers over and above the courts to review the case. The decision to set up the tribunal caused Chief Justice Sir Philip Pyke who presided over the Ngwanya's case, to resign. The tribunal declared Ngwanya a prohibited immigrant, and he was deported to South Africa. South Africa rejected him arguing that he was not a South African citizen; he was therefore rendered stateless.

Deporting Ngwanya was not the end of the matter. Hatred of the Opposition and their participation in the work of Parliament made the Prime Minister, Prince Makhosini, go to King Sohbuza II and request the abrogation of the country's constitution on the ground that it was unworkable. The King reacted favourably. He suspended the constitution, declared a state of emergency and announced the dissolution of Parliament. Under the emergency workers and their organisations are denied freedom of assembly. All check-off arrangements were cancelled and systematic attempts have been made ever since to substitute trade unions with 'works councils'. Although announced earlier, the dissolution of Parliament did not actually take place until March 1977. Up until then meetings of Parliament continued to be held periodically, but only members of the ruling party attended. In the meantime, King Sohbuza dismissed Prince Makhosini and appointed Colonel Maphevu Dlamini in his place.

Mauritius

In 1975 there were fifty-nine registered unions in Mauritius representing 65,345 members. Forty unions representing 52,345 members were affiliated to the three active national centres in the country: the Mauritius Labour Congress (MLC) (22 affiliates,

24,690); the General Workers' Federation (GWF) (12 affiliates, 21,375 members); and the Popular Federation of Workers (PFW) (five affiliates, 6,280 members). The MLC is not affiliated to any political party, although some of its affiliates are; indeed, the Plantation Workers' Union (its most important affiliate and the largest union in the country) is affiliated to the Labour Party. GWF is affiliated to the Marxist Party, the Mouvement Militant Mauricien (MMM) led by Paul Bérenger, who was a frontline activist in the students' riots of 1968 in Paris. PFW is affiliated to Parti Mauricien Social Démocratique led by Gaetan Duvan, a former Foreign Minister. The MLC is affiliated to the ICFTU; the GWF to the WFTU; the PFW is unaffiliated, and holds right-wing views.

There were also unaffiliated unions. For example, the Federation of Civil Service Trade Unions, grouping the nineteen registered trade unions in the civil service, were unaffiliated, having withdrawn from the MLC the previous year because of misunderstandings and personality clashes among the leaders of the two organisations. Besides the organisations thus named, there were two moribund national centres: the Mauritius Federation of Trade Unions (MFTU), an affiliate of WFTU, and the Mauritius Confederation of Labour (MCL), affiliated to the WCL. Very little is known of their strength.

Trade union involvement in politics in Mauritius is partly historical and partly circumstantial. The Labour Party was formed in 1937 by trade union leaders who, the previous year, had organised a trade union with the help of the British TUC and on the advice of the ILO. From the outset the party committed itself to a moderate socialist policy, and drew its strength from the mass of agricultural workers and rural planters. From 1953 to the attainment of independence in 1968, the Labour Party ruled the island in coalition with the Moslem Committee for Action (MCA) and the Independent Forward Bloc (IFB) with little or no difficulties. A new phenomenon arose during and after the pre-independence general elections of 1968. The conservative Parti Mauricien (later known as the Parti Mauricien Social Démocratique (PMSD)) was opposed to independence, and the matter became an election issue. When the results were announced it became clear that PM had won as much as 44 per cent of the total votes cast with its main strength in the urban centres. That evidence underscored the fact that it could no longer be ignored in the government of the country.

Two other factors may be noted. In 1968 Mauritius was passing through an economic crisis caused by inflation and the falling price of sugar in the world markets. The crisis made it difficult for the

Government to secure a general acceptance of its policies. The Labour Party thought it necessary to invite the opposition PMSD to participate in the Government, a decision which led to the withdrawal of one of the Labour Party's traditional coalition partners—the Independent Forward Bloc. Moreover, there was opposition to the proposal from supporters of the Labour Party and the PMSD, some of them resigning and teaming up with the Union Démocratique Mauricienne, a splinter group from the PMSD. To add insult to injury, the MLC, with the active encouragement of the Government, concluded a secret agreement on wage restraint with the employers' federation without taking its affiliates into confidence. It is against this background that subsequent developments should be judged.

Mauritians have a long history of having an effective opposition in Parliament, and felt generally that that tradition had been broken and a vacuum created by what some of them described as the 'unholy alliance' between the Labour Party and the PMSD. The MMM which started as a minor students' protest movement, felt called upon to fill the vacuum. Its leader, Paul Bérenger, started organising rival trade unions in the vital sectors of the economy like the docks, transport and electricity. Inflation and the MLC's moderation played dangerously into his hands, and he showed no scruples in exploiting them. In July 1971, workers in the three sectors came out on strike in furtherance of a pay claim. The Minister of Labour referred the matter to an arbitration tribunal which awarded an increase of 15 per cent. That successful strike brought the MMM into the limelight.

In September, barely two months after the strike, a by-election was held in the Prime Minister's constituency, one of the greatest strongholds of the Labour Party. The MMM contested the seat against the Labour Party, and surprisingly won a landslide victory. Two sweeping victories within two months inspired the MMM to think that they could take over the administration of the country through the concerted action of trade unions grouped under the General Workers' Federation. A general strike was organised in December 1971, but it failed. The Government moved in quickly and banned the GWF and MMM. Bérenger and a few of his associates were arrested and detained. The ban was lifted in 1974 after a new Industrial Relations Act had been passed by Parliament. The Act provided that sole recognition could be granted to any union representing a majority of workers in a given industrial sector. Where two unions represented a sizeable number of workers joint recognition could be granted.

Bérenger's arrest and detention made him a hero. The dreams of

1971 became a partial reality in 1976. In the first general elections since the attainment of independence, the MMM, which had only one member in the previous Parliament, won the greatest number of seats, failing by only two seats to secure an overall majority. Unfortunately, it was denied the opportunity to form a government. The Labour Party and its allies formed the Government leaving the MMM in Opposition.

South Africa

In 1974, there were 181 registered trade unions in the Republic of South Africa representing a total membership of 600,000. Those with only white membership were eighty-nine in number representing 360,000. Unions for the Asians and 'coloured' numbered fifty with a membership of over 70,000. There were forty-two racially mixed unions with a membership of about 180,000. There were also some unregistered unions of black workers but these unions were small and weak, the largest being in the clothing and leather industries. Two national trade union centres existed and continue to exist to the present day: the South African Confederation of Labour—an all-white organisation representing about 190,000 workers which supports the Government's racial policies, and the Trade Union Council of South Africa (TUCSA), a racially mixed organisation representing about 200,000 workers of which about 90,000 are whites. In 1977 only two black workers' unions were members of TUCSA.

Efforts to organise black workers have been going on since the turn of the century, but they have often been thwarted by harsh and repressive laws. The racial policies of the present South African Government may be blamed for all the disabilities of the blacks in South Africa. The truth, however, is that as far as white man's treatment of the black man is concerned there is very little difference between Vorster's regime and its antecedents. Apartheid merely institutionalised what has been going on for ages, though the repression has been intensified in many respects. The plight of black workers can be appreciated by considering the following statistical information. A white mine worker earns 20 times more than his black counterpart; the ratio of black to white wages in the banks and building societies is 1 to 4; about 1 to 6 in manufacturing and the railways; over 1 to 6 in the construction industry and central government service; about 1 to 7 in electricity. Black men who constitute about 70 per cent of the population receive less than 20 per cent of all wages paid; white men who make up less than 19 per cent of the population receive about 74 per cent of total income.

There is no other country in the world where there is such an unjust distribution of income.

There is no law prohibiting the organisation of black workers, but any union they manage to set up cannot be registered nor can it be accorded normal trade union rights and freedoms. Registration is not compulsory, but only registered unions can have access to industrial councils or wages boards. In 1962, TUCSA tried to admit black unions into its membership and to help organise black workers. The Minister of Labour, Marais Viljoen, attacked TUCSA's initiative, and a good deal of white unions objected. In 1967 an extraordinary congress recommended that henceforth TUCSA's membership should be restricted to registered unions, meaning in effect the exclusion of the black unions. When a statutory congress rejected the recommendation the following year by 123,566 votes to 32,871 with 2,518 abstentions, Viljoen reacted sharply, denouncing the decision and threatening to reconsider TUCSA's registration as a trade union federation. TUCSA was thus left with the dilemma of choosing between the devil and the deep blue sea. In 1969 its annual congress decided, to exclude black unions from membership. That decision was hailed by the South African Government and the white unions, but it decided the determination of black workers to have nothing more to do with TUCSA. In the months that followed they began a clandestine campaign to organise.

Early in 1973 sporadic strikes by black workers took place in Natal. They were protesting against starvation wages and inhuman conditions of employment. Although it is illegal for them to go on strike, that restriction did not stop them. The London newspaper, *The Guardian*, gave a fillip to the strikes when, on 12 March, it published a leading news item from its Johannesburg correspondent, Adam Raphael, that the majority of British firms in South Africa were paying substantial numbers of their black workers wages which were below officially recognised levels. The paper followed that initiative with an intensive press campaign which led to the appointment of a British Parliamentary Sub-Committee to investigate the terms and conditions of employment of British companies in the Republic.

Three months later, the International Trade Union Conference Against Apartheid jointly organised by the UN and ILO roundly condemned the inhuman policies of apartheid, which it described as a crime against humanity, a flagrant violation of the UN Charter and a threat to world peace and security. It urged all workers' organisations irrespective of international, continental or religious affiliations to give, among other things, financial, moral, and material support to the workers and people of South Africa through their trade union and political organisations. After the conference the ICFTU Executive Board set up a special committee to co-ordinate aids to black workers in South Africa and to keep track of the developments there. A number of trade union delegations from some of the most important affiliates of the ICFTU in Europe have since visited the Republic to study the trade union situation and the conditions of employment of black workers. Among them are the British TUC and the joint mission of the Swedish LO and TCO. All of them, in their reports, stressed the necessity of helping black workers to set up their own unions.

Since 1973 financial and material aids have been sent to black workers in South Africa to help them to organise. By the first half of 1977, twenty-two black unions representing a total of 88,000 members had been set up. In addition, a number of institutions have been established to provide legal assistance and to train black workers in organising and collective bargaining techniques. Afraid of the growing strength of black workers' unions, South African employers began to think of how to stem the tide. The concept of 'parallel unionism' was canvassed. This meant that black unions could be set up in the same enterprise or industry with white unions, but the white unions would still dominate industrial relations since under the Industrial Conciliation Act they only have the right to bargain with employers. A law setting up industrial committees was passed by the South African Parliament in 1975. When introducing the bill the Minister of Labour announced with glee that he was striking a death blow to African trade unions. On April 1 1977 the *Financial Mail* reported that 'the Government's Bantu Labour Relations Regulation (Amendment) Bill published this week will bring tears to the eyes of African trade unionists. They won't be tears of joy. ... For the first time in SA labour history the Bill makes provision for African workers to negotiate binding wage agreements. But the way in which it has done this strengthens the existing works and liaison committee system regarded as inadequate by African unionists and even by many employers. Firstly, the Bill makes Africans eligible for appointment to the Central Bantu Labour Board. They can become chairman of that Board, or become Bantu labour officers or assistant Bantu labour officers ... but permission to sit on non-elected official bodies is hardly a substitute for full-blooded decision-making powers. As expected, the Bill makes no provision for industry-wide bargaining, unlike the draft Bill circulated over two years ago. ... It's clear that the proposal was ditched because of right wing opposition.'

Madagascar

There are three main national centres in Madagascar: the Fivondronambenny Mpiasa Malagache (FMM) affiliated to the ICFTU; the Syndicat des Travailleurs et Paysans Malagaches (STPM) affiliated to WCL; and the Fédération des Syndicats des Travailleurs Madagascar (FISEMA) affiliated to the WFTU. The FMM was closely connected to the ruling Social Democratic Party during the civilian administration of President Tsirinana and consequently became very vulnerable after the change of government. Ironically Tsirinana's Government accused the FMM General Secretary, Charles Randrianatoro, of complicity in the civil unrests which broke out in May 1972, and led to the downfall of the Government. Randrianatoro was arrested and detained, but was later released by the military administration when it was proved that the allegations against him were false. The following months, the FMM severed ties with the SDP and decided not to have any close ties again with a political party.

A national 'cartel' of Malagasy trade unions was formed in 1975. The cartel announced in May of that year that the ten point programme of the Military Directorate was in tune with the aspirations of the people, and suggested that it be implemented with the participation of trade unions, peasants and 'community cells'. The new organisation also called for the continuation of nationalisation of key sectors of the economy.

Mozambique

In 1975 the total number of the wage-earning population was approximately 406,500 made up of mining (6,500), industry (100,000), ports (10,000), railways (40,000), and agriculture (250,000). There were six racially mixed trade unions of dock workers, bank employees, employees of commerce and industry, technicians, construction workers and drivers. The membership of each of the unions and of the whole trade union movement is unknown. Before independence Africans joined the unions mainly because of the benefits they could derive through the social security system. They never benefited in any other respect. The unions catered mainly for the whites. After independence it was decided to reorganise the unions in such a way that they could benefit African members. The outcome of the reorganisation is unknown.

An ICFTU mission which visited Mozambique after independence reported that FRELIMO officials seemed to be impressed by Tanzania's trade union structure, which indicated that a NUTA-style organisation may be in the offing.

5. NORTH AFRICA

Algeria

Who should determine the leadership of a national trade union centre after a country has attained political independence—the unions themselves or the political party with which they were closely connected during the struggles against colonial rule? This was a problem which arose in Algeria shortly after that country had attained independence in July 1962, after seven years of savage warfare between the French and Algerian nationalists grouped under the umbrella of National Liberation Front (FLN). Algerian trade unions played a very important role during the independence struggles, and the ICFTU-affiliated Union Générale des Travailleurs Algériens (UGTA) was in the vanguard throughout. Thanks to the unflinching moral and financial support which the ICFTU gave during the bitter days of the Algerian war when trade unions were banned, the UGTA was able to operate from its temporary headquarters in Tunis. The headquarters was transferred to Algiers after independence. The ICFTU itself demonstrated its support for Algerian independence struggles when it made the matter one of the key issues in the agenda of its Sixth World Congress held in Tunis in 1957.

It was generally expected that independence would usher in a new era of peace and unity necessary for tackling some of the social and economic problems arising from the disruptive activities of the OAS. Unfortunately, this was not to be. Political difference arose immediately after the proclamation of independence among the leaders of the FLN creating factions which almost developed into a split. Each faction sought the support of the UGTA, but the organisation refused to be drawn. In a press release on 1 August 1962, the UGTA said that the storm raised by the personal quarrels of Algerian political leaders arose because 'these leaders have lived too long outside the country and for this reason are unaware of the preoccupations, the great needs, the ultimate aspirations of the Algerian people and the workers. ... In spite of exhortations and calls to take sides, the Algerian people and workers have maintained complete equanimity during this hard testing time. The men in whom they placed great trust have disappointed them ... they have failed to open all the doors, one by one, which would lead us to broad horizons. ... Algerian workers have taken no part in these quarrels ... on the contrary, they are in a position to demonstrate throughout the Algerian territory their attachment to the ideals of democracy, freedom and unity.'[1]

The political and military situation was stabilised when agreement was reached on the setting up of a Political Bureau, entrusted with the responsibility of organising the first general elections which led to Ahmed Ben Bella taking office in September as Prime Minister. On November 4 1962 the Prime Minister announced at a press conference that 'the UGTA, as a national trade union organisation, could be sure of having the guarantee of administrative and managerial autonomy, but not of political autonomy'. In order to avoid any possible misunderstanding as to the principles governing union–party relations, the UGTA and the Political Bureau signed an 'Agreement on UGTA–Party Relations' on 19 December. UGTA leaders had always insisted on preserving the independence of the trade union movement from the government or party, and the text of the agreement showed that it had largely succeeded in achieving that objective. But the implementation of that agreement clearly demonstrated the difference between words and deeds.

The UGTA planned holding its first congress from 17 to 20 January 1963, and had set up a preparatory committee for that purpose. After the agreement of 19 December, the committee was enlarged by the addition of representatives of the Political Bureau. These men soon established themselves, taking important responsibilities including the distribution of credentials. Invitations were sent to the ICFTU, WFTU, ILO, WAY, and several national centres in Europe, North America and Africa. The ICFTU was represented by a six-man delegation led by its General Secretary, Omer Becu. Before the conference opened it was clear that the distribution of credentials in certain regions of the country had been carried out without the knowledge of the responsible UGTA officials, and a large number of people, among them unemployed persons, had received valid credentials on no other basis besides FLN political soundness. Even then, the majority of the delegates were supporters of the incumbent officers and the concept of independence of the trade union movement from political parties.

The proceedings began with the election of officers of the congress. Ben Bella addressed the opening ceremony and emphasised that the workers could not be set up as a privileged caste in contrast to the peasants who constituted about 80 per cent of the country's population. Trade unions, he added, had to defer to the decisions of the party in power. The Prime Minister did not stop at addressing the opening ceremony. He and his Minister of Labour contributed many times to debates during the congress. Sharp disagreements followed a proposal brought up by elements opposed to trade union autonomy that the report on activities and major policy decisions be discussed *in camera*. The proposal was put to the vote and was defeated.

The third day of the congress was decisive. When the officers of the congress elected on the first day arrived, they found that their seats had been occupied by persons who had been brought to the hall as early as 6 a.m. by the Political Bureau to take over control of the congress. Efforts to regain their seats and resume their functions failed. From then henceforth attempts to give the congress a semblance of constitutionality also failed. The report on activities was rejected. A new UGTA constitution and oral resolutions were adopted. A new executive was elected, its members being die-hard FLN supporters.

On his return to Brussels, the ICFTU General Secretary issued a press statement deploring the unconstitutional procedure adopted to get rid of the leadership of UGTA. The world press reported extensively on the drama in Algiers, and editorial opinion denounced the methods used. An observer at the congress commented that 'although the methods used by Ben Bella's henchmen were not new, they were applied with a brutality and cynicism without parallel. ... The agreement signed recently between the Political Bureau and the UGTA seemed to testify that the FLN had come round to the view of free trade unionism. The congress of spoliation displayed that the FLN had signed this document merely to dupe the trade union leaders and better to ensure the success of their coup.'[2]

Six months after the congress, the UGTA disaffiliated from the ICFTU and announced its decision to adopt the same attitude towards all other international trade union organisations. A communiqué announcing the decision said that the UGTA was pursuing a policy of 'positive neutrality'. It added that three members of the national secretariat in favour of trade union autonomy had been dismissed. Contrary to its declared policy, however, the UGTA soon joined AATUF and the Confederation of Arab Trade Unions.

In 1969 the Algerian trade union movement was reorganised by the Government, and a new charter was adopted by a congress held in May. New leaders were elected. The charter emphasised the 'institutionalisation' of trade unions which were to be given a legal role to enable them play a leading role in solving the country's economic and social problems, educating workers, increasing productivity and participating in management. Foreign capital was specifically mentioned as being acceptable because it was considered as 'being indispensable to the national economy as long as it functions satisfactorily and increases production'.[3] Properly elected workers' representatives were to have the right to participate in solving the problems of organisation and management, and foreign firms were required to provide information on production, marketing costs and so on. The unions were warned, however, not to put forward extravagant claims which would produce situations in which the companies would no longer be sufficiently profitable. Union 'cells' and 'committees' were to be set up in all enterprises, and 'bad conduct and deviationist tendencies'[4] among workers were to be punished. Closer contacts were to be established between the reorganised Algerian trade union movement and the WFTU.

Egypt

Egypt had 1,456 registered trade unions in 1956 representing a membership of 480,502 (or 300 members per union). Most of them were organised on craft and plant basis. By 1962 the number of registered unions had been reduced to sixty-five representing a total membership of 1,250,000 (or 20,833 members per union). The reduction in the number of unions appears to have been in line with government policy and restrictions imposed by a law passed that year regulating the formation of trade unions. The law was probably enacted to bring the unions under firm government control. Under the law, civil servants could not be organised, and the Minister of Social Affairs could dissolve trade unions for certain reasons, for example, urging civil servants to go on strike.

An Egyptian Federation of Labour was inaugurated in 1960. That organisation soon became a vehicle for the implementation of government policies and those of Egypt's only political party, the Arab Socialist Union. Under policies promulgated in 1960, workers and their unions were to become government agents, and workers were to be represented on all company boards. Attempts were made during the following two years to organise the non-wage earners—the peasants and small farmers—so as to integrate them into a new social fabric known as 'popular forces'. A national congress of the popular forces was held in 1962 attended by 1,500 delegates of whom 25 per cent were the representatives of peasants and small farmers, 35 per cent were industrial workers, 10 per cent were business men, teachers, students and women. The Egyptian

Federation of Labour was affiliated to AATUF and the Confederation of Arab Trade Unions.

Libya
The trade union situation in Libya has to be considered against the
background of the political situation and the personal rivalries
between politicians and trade union leaders. The former Kingdom
of Libya was established by a decision of the United Nations in
1951. The political system was federal, and the three constituent
provinces of Tripolitania, Cyrenaica and Fezzan enjoyed a wide
degree of autonomy. The monarchy was absolute. Until its overthrow ministers rose and fell according to the will or intrigues of the
Court. More than 80 per cent of the population was illiterate, and
rivalry between the provinces was very lively. For a long time there
were no political parties: each parliamentary representative was
elected individually. Thus the country was fuedal in structure, and
power was in the hands of the ruling élite and foreign companies,
particularly those in the petroleum industry. In such a situation the
only organised group of relative importance which could put an
appearance of opposition or force the government to introduce some
changes was the trade union movement represented by the Libyan
General Workers' Union (LGWU) led by Salem Shita.

In 1961 two important strikes took place in the country which
had far-reaching consequences on the trade union movement. In
April about 2,000 workers in the American air base in Tripoli went
on strike in an attempt to get their employers to pay wage increases
and other social benefits provided for by the country's labour
legislation. As a gesture of solidarity dock workers in the port of
Tripoli refused to load or unload any material from or for the base.
Eventually the workers won their claims and the strike was called
off, but not until there was pressure from the ICFTU and
AFL–CIO. Later in the year, public employees received a general
wage increase because of rising cost of living. Manual and
non-manual workers in the private sector demanded an increase in
the minimum wage. One of the provincial governments, the
Government of Tripolitania, arranged a meeting of an advisory
committee provided for by the Labour Code. This committee
comprised an equal number of employers' and workers' representatives, with a government official as chairman. The committee
recommended unanimously the adoption of a graded increase in
minimum wages, but the Government of Tripolitania refused to
apply the recommendation with the exception of the lowest wage
category.

Affiliates of the LGWU were infuriated by the Government's

refusal and addressed strike notices to employers with copies to the Government. As no action was taken, about 4,000 workers went on strike. During the strike the Government of Tripolitania, which seemed eagerly to have been waiting for the opportunity, took some of the most Draconian measures to remove the trade union movement from Libyan life and these in violation of the provisions of the Libyan Labour Code. Trade union leaders, including Shita, were arrested and imprisoned without trial, the police occupied the offices of the LGWU and strike breakers were recruited to replace the strikers. In order to understand these developments it is necessary to bear in mind that the Prime Minister of Tripolitania at that time, Ali Dhili, was a political rival of Salem Shita. In 1959–60 when he was an ordinary member of Parliament, Dhili tried to break the LGWU by urging certain affiliates to withdraw and set up a rival organisation. Thanks to the implicit confidence which the unions had in Shita, that attempt failed. The tension between the two men increased after that fiasco. Observers interpreted the Government's refusal to accept the recommendations of its own advisory committee as closely bound up with the personal rivalries between Dhili and Shita.

An ICFTU delegation led by its Vice President, Ahmed Tlili of Tunisia, tried to intervene, but it was turned back at the Tripoli airport. Immigration officials told the delegation that they had received strict instructions from the Federal Government to send its members back by the same plane by which they came. A meeting of the Advisory Committee of the Trade Unions of the Maghreb was to have been held on 21 September 1961, and the members (Mahjoub Ben Seddik and Benani of the Union Moroccaine de Travail (UMT); Maachou and Djilani of the UGTA and Habib Achour and Ben Ezzedine of the Union Générale des Travailleurs Tunisiens (UGTT) had planned to intervene to secure the release of the union leaders in jail who were also members of the committee. They too were expelled by the Libyan authorities before they could make any efforts.

In October 1961 the ICFTU submitted a complaint to the ILO against the Libyan Government for violation of trade union rights. The Libyan Government invited the ILO to send a mission to make an on the spot inquiry into the situation. Lord Forster of Harray, a former President of the Industrial Court in the United Kingdom and a member of the ILO Fact Finding and Conciliation Commission on Freedom of Association, visited Libya for that purpose from 5 to 10 January 1962. His findings confirmed the facts stated in the ICFTU complaint. At its 151 Session, the ILO Governing Body adopted a number of recommendations requesting the Libyan

Government to respect trade union rights and invited the Government to amend its labour legislation accordingly. The Governing Body noted the Libyan Government's expression of regret that the ICFTU mission to Libya had been refused entry into the country and its assurance that ICFTU representatives would in future be welcome at any time.

The assurance that future ICFTU delegations would be welcome was nothing but a gimmick. A joint ICFTU/ITS mission which went to Libya in March 1962, was again refused entry. Visas granted to members of the delegation before their departure were invalidated by immigration officials who claimed to be 'acting on orders from a higher authority'. In reply to a cable that he should intervene the Libyan Prime Minister said, 'Please in future cable for another delegation stop Salem Shita's illegal activities well-known stop best attention.'[2] The Libyan Minister of Labour and Social Affairs later told a press conference that the ICFTU was propagating lies about restrictions imposed on Libyan union leaders. Although the LGWU was an ICFTU affiliate, the Minister said that the Libyan trade union movement had 'no legal ties' with the Confederation, and that its activities were aimed at instigating public unrest, meddling in the country's internal affairs and using the labour movement for imperialistic purposes. Surprisingly Radio Moscow took the cudgel in support of the Libyan authorities. In a commentary in Arabic on 21 April 1962, the mouthpiece of the 'dictatorship of the proletariat' asked, 'Whom does the so-called International Confederation of Free Trade Unions serve?' It added that ICFTU activities 'are contrary to international custom and law and threatens Libyan independence.'[5]

Meanwhile some of the trade unionists arrested in September 1961 were brought to trial. The ICFTU secured the services of an eminent British lawyer, Elwyn Jones, QC, to defend them. He was denied the right to plead, but he remained in court throughout the trial. In spite of strong Government pressure to get them convicted, justice prevailed. The twenty union leaders were acquitted and discharged. Having failed to destroy the LGWU by getting its leaders convicted of a criminal offence, the Libyan Government changed tactics to achieve the same objective. This time it was making workers sign 'the Document'—the old employer's device of making workers sign a paper pledging not to become members of a trade union as a condition for keeping their jobs. Majority of the workers who participated in the September 1961 strike lost their jobs. The Libyan Government arranged that they could be reinstated if only they could agree to leave the LGWU. A document to this effect was prepared, and employers were ordered not to reinstate any dismissed worker who refused to sign it. Moreover, the Labour Code was amended, coming into effect in November 1961; under this, public employees could not form or join trade unions and workers employed in 'public utilities' and in 'essential services' could not go on strike. The number of workers affected by these restrictions in the amended Labour Code was about 60 per cent of the total labour force. About 5,000 union members or one-third of the total strength of the LGWU were thus removed from union activities.

A split in the trade union movement, apparently encouraged by the Government, occurred in 1963. The splinter group, the Libyan National Federation of Trade Unions, joined the AATUF. Unity was eventually restored after some time, and the united movement joined the Arab Confederation of Trade Unions. When the Organisation of African Trade Union Unity (OATUU) was formed it also became a member of this.

A new labour law adopted in May 1970 by the Revolutionary Command Council (the supreme authority of the Libyan Arab Republic since Colonel Gadaffi came to power in 1969) dissolved all the existing trade unions and federations and placed considerable restraints on new unions.[6] The law banned the organisation of more than one union in any given craft or industry and the establishment of more than one national centre. A decree issued in July 1970, implementing this provision, established twenty-two trade and industrial groups, each of which was to be the basis of organising unions. Workers employed in each trade or industrial group were to be registered accordingly. No one was to be a member of more than one union at a time.

Under the new law, a branch union with a potential membership of fifty or more could be set up in each of the thirty administrative districts of the country. Each union was to have one branch in a district, but more than one branch could be set up in a district with the approval of the Ministry of Labour and Social Affairs. In addition, the Ministry could authorise a trade union committee to be set up in companies employing fifty or more workers. This committee was to represent the workers' views on the company's administration, organisation and working conditions. The law also provided for the collection of union dues by check-off. Unions were prohibited from accepting contributions or making donations without the approval of the Ministry. They could not have direct or indirect association with 'foreign trade unions' though the new national centre established by the law could 'join regional and international organisations subject to the Ministry's approval.'

Morocco

A government decree promulgated in 1957 provided that all trade union officials must be Moroccan citizens. Consequently local branches of the French national centres ceased to exist. Some joined the Union Marocaine du Travail (UMT) founded in 1955 and affiliated to the ICFTU; some constituted themselves into 'workers' associations'. From the outset, the UMT was affiliated to the Istaqlal Party, the nationalist movement which led Morocco to independence. In 1959, the party split into two rival factions. The split and the death of Mohamed V greatly reduced the UMT's effectiveness. Hitherto it had been consulted on important economic and social questions, and it had representatives on planning committees. When Hassan II took over the Government, his administration paid little attention to the UMT. By 1965, the UMT was in open conflict with the Government. Strikes and student protest demonstrations in March of that year led to the death of 100 persons, 450 others were injured and 61 trade unionists and students were sentenced to various terms of imprisonment.

The relations between the UMT and the ICFTU had taken a new turn following the establishment, in Casablanca in May 1961, of the All-African Trade Union Federation. Mahjoub Ben Seddik, UMT General Secretary, emerged from that conference as President of AATUF, whose Charter provided that disaffiliation from international trade union organisations was a condition of membership. That meant that in order to retain the presidency of AATUF, Ben Seddik's UMT must either sever connections with ICFTU or retain them and let some other person take over. It was not an easy decision to make, but eventually it was made in favour of AATUF. In 1964 the ICFTU received a letter dated 15 September and signed by UMT General Treasurer, Houssieni Hajbi, asking the Confederation 'to take note that since our Third National Congress held in January 1963, our organisation, the UMT, is no longer affiliated to the ICFTU'.[7]

The decision of the Third National Congress seems to have been misrepresented. In a resolution on international relations which that congress adopted the UMT said:

The adhesion of the UMT to the ICFTU in 1955 enabled the Moroccan trade union movement to emerge from the isolation in which it had been hitherto and to make its contribution to the international labour movement. It has more over enabled it at all times to enjoy the support of this organisation and in particular during the difficult periods through which the Moroccan working class has passed ... taking note of the fluidity of the situation and the transformations impending hereby decide on *temporary suspension* of the membership of the UMT to any *international* and *continental* trade union organisation and authorises the national council to make final pronouncement in due course on the alternatives which might present themselves.[8]

Sudan

In Sudan, trade unions were suspended and the right to strike was withdrawn after the military coup of November 1958. In 1960 a Trade Unions (Amendment) Act was passed which permitted unions to exist again where there were at least fifty workers employed, but it prohibited the formation of federations, and government and white collar workers were not to be organised. The result was that the majority of potential union members were excluded from the trade union movement. Railway workers went on strike in 1961 following the rejection by the military junta of their memorandum demanding a return to civilian administration. The strike was broken by the army. In 1964 General Abboud's Government was overthrown, and the stage was set for a new era for the trade union movement.

Between 1964 and 1971 and even before that period, the trade union movement in Sudan was under strong communist influence. The Sudanese trade union movement has the reputation of being one of the oldest and strongest supporters of the communist-dominated World Federation of Trade Unions in Africa. Developments since 1971 must be considered against the background of the abortive coup of July that year. This communist-inspired coup led to the systematic elimination of almost all known communists in the country and a reorganisation of major political and social institutions of which the trade union movement was one of the principal targets. The Government set up a special committee in August, barely one month after the coup, to review the trade union situation and make recommendations. The committee reported after three months and made three important recommendations. The first was that the trade union movement should be reorganised on industrial basis; second, that the number of existing unions (about 700 at the time) be reduced to fifty, and third, that two national trade union centres be established, one for manual and the other for white collar workers.

In line with these recommendations, the Government promulgated a new trade unions decree which came into operation in February 1972. It dissolved all the existing national centres and permitted the establishment of fifty national industrial unions and two national centres. Provision was made for the introduction of check-off and for workers to be granted paid leave of up to a week to participate in trade union courses or seminars in and outside the country. Strikes were banned. Of the fifty industrial unions established thirty-seven represent manual workers. Election of union officials was held in June/July 1972. After the elections, the manual workers unions set up an interim committee which drafted the constitution setting up the Sudanese Federation of Workers' Trade Unions (SFWTU). Abdallah Nasri Gnawi was elected President, and Al-Taieb Mohamed Ahmed was elected General Secretary. In 1974, the SFWTU had a membership of 727,932.

Tunisia

Before independence in 1956 there were two main trade union federations in Tunisia: the USTT which was an integral part of the French CGT and the Union Générale des Travailleurs Tunisiens (UGTT), an autonomous organisation of Tunisian nationals. The UGTT's watchword since its founding days has been that 'the fight against colonialism and foreign companies comes first; the fight for improving the economic situation after'. In September 1956, the USTT ceased to exist, having decided to merge with the UGTT. From the outset, the UGTT was affiliated to the Neo-Destour Party, the nationalist movement which led Tunisia to independence. Partly because of the independence struggle and partly because of its deep-rooted mistrust of non-nationals, the UGTT refused to admit workers of other nationalities into its membership and was severely criticised for doing so. Louis Saillant, the late General Secretary of the WFTU, once described the UGTT as 'a nationalist and not a national organisation; it enjoys the support of occult, religious, political and economic forces; its leaders mislead workers, indulge in demagogy and may be termed neo-fascists; the legitimate aspirations of some of its members are incompatible with the political objectives of its leaders'.[9] This was stated during the consideration of UGTT's application for membership of the WFTU. Although the application was opposed, the UGTT was eventually accepted into affiliation, but it was not a member for long. 'A UGTT leader declared that the UGTT had left the WFTU because it was denied the possibility of speaking freely and Ferhard Hached [then General Secretary of the UGTT] was prevented from expressing the views of Tunisian nationalism.'[10] The UGTT became an affiliate of the ICFTU in 1951; the following year Hached was assassinated.

Ben Selah succeeded Hached. In 1956 he refused a minor ministerial appointment in President Bourguiba's first government and attacked what he called the lack of socialist theory in the Neo-Destour, calling for a complete overhaul of the party's aims.[11]

He suggested a national economic plan which would involve a large-scale nationalisation of major industries and rapid industrialisation. His initiative brought him in conflict with the authorities and some of his trade union colleagues. Habib Achour, another veteran trade unionist, advocated the formation of a new trade union federation completely insulated from politics. This federation came into being in October 1956, but expressed willingness to unify with UGTT on the condition that Ben Selah resigned. Ben Selah resigned in December and was succeeded by Ahmed Tlili, a member of the Neo-Destour Political Bureau, who rose to that position through his trade union activities.

Unity was restored in 1957. That same year Ben Selah became a Minister. In 1961 he became Minister of Planning and Finance, and introduced a modified version of his original economic plan. In spite of that modification he was blamed for all the economic ills of the country and suffered a long term of imprisonment as a result. He eventually escaped from prison and has been in exile ever since. Ioan Davies, commenting on his resignation from the trade union movement, has remarked that 'the effect of the Tlili-Achour coup in the UGTT was to deprive the unions of an independent political role and firmly commit them to party policy. The unions were instructed to limit their attention to workers' affairs.'[12] But in spite of their Neo-Destour political soundness, both men could not escape the common fate of many dynamic trade unionists in the so-called Third World. Achour was maliciously prosecuted for alleged forgery in 1967, but was acquitted and discharged. Tlili was killed in exile by an assassin's bullet.

The UGTT has proved to be an effective trade union organisation, although its relationship with the Neo-Destour has been strained for quite some time now. The strained relationship was reflected in the election of officers of the UGTT at its congress in 1977. One of the defeated candidates was Marklouf who had been a member of the ILO Governing Body for many years. Observers at the congress believed that he was defeated because of his close ties with the party. During the second half of 1977 Tunisia was plagued by a wave of strikes. Disagreement in the cabinet over the strategy to be adopted in dealing with the situation led to the resignation of five ministers who wanted President Bourguiba to dismiss the Prime Minister, Hedi Nouira. Bourguiba refused and supported the Prime Minister. The background to the wave of strikes may be summarised as follows.

In January 1977, the UGTT concluded a 'social contract' with the Government and employers under which wages and salaries were adjusted and it was agreed that every April wages and salaries would be adjusted in relation to the cost of living and increases in productivity and production. The Tunisian Association of Industry, Trade and Crafts, the employers' organisation, undertook to keep prices down. Unfortunately this undertaking was not honoured. Prices rose considerably after the conclusion of the social contract, and the UGTT was quick to point out that the employers had not kept their part of the bargain. There was also the problem of interpretation of the contract. The Government argued that in view of the wage increases granted the unions could not claim fringe benefits which had financial implications for the employer concerned. The UGTT maintained that the contract did not contain any such provision. As prices continued to rise many individual unions organised protest strikes, and the UGTT supported them. In October 1977 textile workers in Ksar Helel went on strike, and the strike was broken by the paramilitary police. On 15 November the UGTT announced that it would hold a meeting of its National Council in January 1978 to take a decision on what it would do if workers' demands were not met. Four days later, the Political Bureau of the ruling Destour Socialist Party (of which the UGTT General Secretary Habib Achour was a member) decided to set up eight working parties to examine the demands of the unions. The UGTT was represented in these working parties, but the results of their efforts were unsatisfactory, particularly to mine and railway workers. In 1977 the wages of the workers in the Compagnie de Phosphate de Gasfa (a key sector of the Tunisian economy) were 35–45 dinars per month, with a forty-eight hour week. Their demands centred around fringe benefits to enable them minimise the effects of inflation. The most important demand dating back to 1974 was for a premium of 7.8 dinars a month for a man whose wife was not working. The company, supported by the Government, argued that it could not pay. Only a small increase was made to the night-food allowance. On 8 December 13,000 mine workers in Gasfa went on a three-day strike. In a communiqué issued the following day, the UGTT National Council stated that 'for some time now, the Government tends, in effect, to politicise the strictly trade union stand taken by the UGTT on social problems and to give a political interpretation to every union demand, all because the UGTT refuses to make any concessions as far as the right of Tunisian workers are concerned'. Railway workers also went on strike in the middle of December in furtherance of their own claims and obtained some concessions as a result, but in regard to the claims of the workers in the other sectors of the economy the Government dragged its feet.

Matters came to a head on 23 December, when the Secretary

General of the Party and Minister of Interior, Taher Belkhodja, who had agreed in principle to meet the workers' demands, was dismissed for what was considered to be his 'soft' handling of the strikes. Within three days five Cabinet Ministers resigned in protest against the dismissal. On January 10 1978 Habib Achour resigned his membership of the Political Bureau and the Central Committee of the Neo-Destour Party. At a meeting of the UGTT National Council which ended that day a resolution was adopted condemning the repressive measures taken against the workers. An eleven point statement issued after the meeting declared that the organisation did not agree with the Government's social and trade union policies and that the resignation of the General Secretary from membership of the Political Bureau and Central Committee of the party did not constitute an act of hostility towards the party. The UGTT was against the consolidation, through all possible means, of a capitalist class which identified its interests with those of foreign capital to the detriment of national interests. The statement demanded, among other things, the introduction of an incomes policy aimed at achieving social justice for workers, an employment policy which would seek the reintegration of migrant workers, readjustment of the price policy through stricter controls, and vigorous measures to end what it called 'the mismanagement of certain companies and of public funds'.

On 24 January, six regional offices of the UGTT in different parts of the country were attacked by Neo-Destour militants. The regional secretary of the Sfax region, Abderrazak Ghorbal, was arrested because, it was claimed, arms were found in his office. Achour, whose life had earlier been threatened by unknown persons but probably by the party militants, reported to the new Minister of Interior that he had received information that another regional office in Kairouan would be attacked. The Minister promised to send the police to protect the office, but he did not fulfil his promise. It was against this background that the UGTT announced its intention of organising a general strike on 26 January. The ICFTU General Secretary, Otto Kersten, visited Tunis from 22–25 January, during which time he met the Prime Minister, Hedi Nouira, twice in an effort to bring about a dialogue between the Government and the UGTT. That objective was not achieved. The general strike took place as planned and resulted in wide spread rioting. A state of emergency was declared, and the police and paramilitary forces were called in to restore order. By the time it was over official sources put the death toll at forty-two, but unofficial sources estimated it at 132. Habib Achour and ten members of the UGTT Executive Board were arrested and detained. Another ICFTU mission headed by John Vandervaken, Assistant General Secretary, visited Tunis after the strike and was informed by the Prime Minister that the detainees would be brought to trial and the confederation was free to send lawyers to defend them. In the meantime, some pro-Neo Destour members of the UGTT Executive Board resigned their positions alleging that the UGTT was being manipulated by what they called 'anarchists'. Among them was Tajini Abid, one of the Assistant General Secretaries of the UGTT. On 2 February it was announced that Achour had been removed from his post of General Secretary and Tajini Abid had been appointed in his place pending an extraordinary congress scheduled for 25 February. On 6 February it was reported that Denis Akumu, Secretary General of the Organisation of African Trade Union Unity, had visited Tunis, and that he had denounced the general strike and supported the measures taken by the Tunisian Government.

6. CASE STUDIES

In a later chapter we shall be discussing some of the factors which affect and influence union activities. In this chapter, however, we shall consider the peculiar circumstances responsible for the weakness of the trade union movement in two countries—Lesotho and Liberia. In both countries trade union development was so adversely affected by the actions of Government and government agents that complaints were filed with the ILO against the governments in question for violation of human and trade union rights. The complaints were investigated and the violations established.

Lesotho
In 1970 the Kingdom of Lesotho had a labour force of about 90,000 of which 60,000 were employed in the Republic of South Africa. The remaining 30,000 were employed in the public service and commercial undertakings of the country. There were nine trade unions representing about 20,000 members. These unions were grouped under three national centres: the Basutoland Federation of Labour (BFL) (four affiliates representing 16,808 members); the Lesotho Council of Workers (LCW) (four affiliates representing 3,200 members) and the Lesotho Congress of Trade Unions (LCTU) (one affiliate, membership unknown). All three centres seemed to be the tools of the political parties of the time—the Opposition Basutoland Congress Party, the ruling Basutoland National Party and the Marematlou Party, the weakest of the three. All the national centres were affiliated to Pan-African or international trade union organisations. BFL was affiliated to AATUF, LCW to the Pan-African Workers' Congress and LCTU to WFTU.

By 1974, only one national centre (the Lesotho Council of Workers) was in existence, and the number of registered unions had dropped to five representing less than 2,000 members. Why the decline? To answer the question it is necessary to examine the events of 30 January 1970. It is not easy to understand these events without looking at their antecedents. In 1960 the Basutoland Legislative Council was made up of eighty members, forty of whom were elected by secret ballot. The rest were twenty-two principal chiefs, four ex-officio members and fourteen persons nominated by what was then known as the Paramount Chief (now King) of Lesotho, the original name of Basutoland before British colonial administration. In the general elections of that year, the Basutoland Congress Party led by Marxist Ntsu Mokhehle won thirty-two seats and the remaining eight seats were shared by independents and other political parties. Yet in spite of its popular support the BCP was denied the opportunity of forming a government. The colonial authorities formed a government with their nominees and chiefs and this forced the victorious party into the Opposition. In the general elections of April 1965, the Basutoland National Party led by Chief Leabua Jonathan won 31 seats (108,140 votes) while the BCP won twenty-five seats (103,068 votes). BCP alleged that the elections were rigged and that it had been robbed of victory by unfair electoral practices. It appealed in vain to the UN to intervene. The most surprising aspect of the 1965 elections was that Chief Jonathan himself was heavily defeated in his own constituency by a BCP candidate. He managed to return to the legislature and retain his office of Prime Minister through a by-election made possible by the resignation of a loyal party member.

Background to 1970 and 1974 events. Lesotho achieved independence from Britain on 4 October 1966. South Africa was opposed to the idea of granting independence to Lesotho and the two other former High Commission Territories of Botswana and Swaziland. When she saw that she could not prevent the independence of the three countries, she adopted a number of tactics to ensure her dominance of their affairs. Long before independence, South Africa had tried without avail to persuade the British Government to hand over the three countries for incorporation into the Republic. Lesotho is particularly vulnerable to South African manipulations because of her geographical and economic conditions. In September 1963 the late Prime Minister of South Africa, Dr. Henry Verwoerd, outlined the Republic's intentions about the former High Commission Territories when he opened the annual conference of the ruling Nationalist Party. Dr. Verwoerd declared that South Africa would be the 'guardian' of Botswana, Lesotho and Swaziland. Guardianship here connotes control. 'Under her guardianship', Dr. Verwoerd said, 'South Africa would free them from stage to stage, just as she is doing in the Transkei.'[1] He deplored the introduction of universal adult suffrage to Lesotho and declared that 'the very small number of white people in Basutoland under the constitution now enacted, has what one would call second-class rights.'[2]

In pursuance of the 'guardianship' objective, South Africa instructed the Commissioner of South Sotho, S. J. Papenfus, a South African working in Lesotho, to fraternise with Chief Jonathan and persuade him to accept advice, assistance and political support from the Nationalist Party. The Chief agreed. In due course, three white liberals (two South Africans and one Rhodesian) were appointed to the key positions of Constitutional Adviser, Chief Justice and Economic Adviser to the Government. After independence the white liberals were replaced by Nationalist diehards, and other diehards were appointed Chief Electoral Officer, Attorney General, Legal Draughtsman, Legal Adviser to Chief Jonathan, Director of Lesotho National Development Corporation and Superintendent of the Paramilitary Police financed and equipped by South Africa. The Nationalist diehards were seconded to the Lesotho Government rather than being directly appointed apparently because it would have been inconsistent with the policy of 'separate development' and humiliating to the persons concerned for white South Africans to be the 'servants' of a black man's government. It was hoped that through these devices Chief Jonathan and his party would always be in the saddle and thus ensure continued happy relationship with South Africa.

The first post-independence general elections were held in January 1970. Chief Jonathan and his backers in South Africa believed that the BNP would not only win but that the party would also increase its majority in Parliament. But surprisingly the BCP won. Table I shows the detailed results.

Table I.[3]   RESULTS OF LESOTHO GENERAL ELECTIONS 1970

Parties and Independents	*Seats Won*	*Votes Obtained*	*%\nof Votes Cast*
1. Basutoland Congress Party (led by Ntsu Mokhehle)	36	100,642	51.39
2. Basutoland National Party (led by Chief Jonathan)	23	76,777	39.20
3. Marematlou Freedom Party (led by Tsepo Mohaleroe)	1	16,582	8.46
4. United Democratic Party (led by Charles Mofeli)	—	688	0.35
5. Independents	—	1,142	0.58
Total	60	195,831	99.98

It is against this background that subsequent events should be judged. The BCP pays Chief Jonathan's defeated Government compliments in their account of developments which followed the elections. In their 'Export of Apartheid to Lesotho' (pages 27–8) they report as follows:

Another thing that must be stated categorically is that Chief Leabua Jonathan, fully recognising the nature of the overwhelming victory of the BCP, conceded defeat and was ready to hand over power to the legal Prime Minister of Lesotho, Mr. Ntsu Mokhehle, the leader of the Basutoland Congress Party. To this effect on Thursday, 29 January 1970, when all the election results were known to the outgoing cabinet, they met and decided to hand over power and gave instructions to set afoot the process of handing over power, and what is more Lesotho's High Commissions abroad were apprised of the fact and foreign missions in Lesotho were likewise informed.

In view of this evidence, it may be asked what happened and then changed the course of events. The 'Export of Apartheid to Lesotho' itself answers the question.

On Friday, 30 January 1970, Pretoria's men and Jonathan's Legal Advisers, Judge Jacobs, Geldenhuys and Blundell attended a joint cabinet meeting in which they declared Vorster's intention that Jonathan was to rule and that all support which he required was to be given ... their mission was specific to change Jonathan from the mind of handing over power to the BCP. It was they who changed the cabinet's decision of the previous night. The state of emergency was declared in consequence of their pressures. Long before the state of emergency was declared the SA paramilitary sealed the borders and all seconded expatriates from the RSA and all whites were ordered in advance to leave the country. The SA paramilitary entered Lesotho at different times to reinforce the PMU. Vorster after having declared himself indifferent, resorted to the common anti-communist clichés and stated that he 'feels obliged to agree with Chief Jonathan that it was a communist undermining influence, because the leader of the Opposition (Mr. Mokhehle) was a Peking communist, and this was proved over and over again in the past.

Subsequent evidence seems to show that there might have been some sort of coalition between the South Africans and some officials of the Konrad Adenauer Foundation in this sordid affair, and that the state of emergency was declared on the advice of an official of the Foundation. Neil Hooper writing under the heading 'Germans Caused Crisis in Lesotho' in the Johannesburg *Sunday Times* of 17 November 1974, reported that 'the Konrad Adenauer Foundation–a German Government-subsidised organisation based in Bonn, which gives financial aid and political training to developing countries—admitted this week that it had been responsible for the constitutional crisis in Lesotho in 1970, when the country's constitution was suspended and the Leader of the Opposition arrested. The head of the Africa section of the Foundation, Dr. J. L. Entrup, told me that the Prime Minister of Lesotho, Chief Leabua Jonathan, had taken this action in 1970 on the advice of Otto Bamhawer, a constitutional expert then on secondment in Lesotho ... When Chief Jonathan realised that his party was going to lose the election he approached Dr. Bamhawer and asked him what he should do. It was on Dr. Bamhawer's advice that he suspended the constitution and had the Leader of the Opposition arrested.'

Not only was the leader of the victorious BCP arrested and detained but also members of the party's executive and leaders of the Basutoland Federation of Labour, which was closely associated with the party. When Mokhehle and his colleagues were arrested, a senior BCP official, Taekana Ramoabi, filed a writ of Habeas Corpus against Chief Jonathan, Frederich Roach, Chief of the Paramilitary Police, and two other officials to produce them or show cause why they should not be released. The case was being heard at the Maseru High Court when Chief Justice Jacobs entered the court, stopped the proceedings and suspended further sitting of the court. 'In this way', says the BCP Appeal to the UN Human Rights Commission in Geneva (Part 7, page 2) 'a peaceful and constitutional effort by the Basutoland Congress Party officials to resolve the election crisis in court was frustrated by the Judge of the High Court himself.'

As a result of unprovoked attacks and mass killings of BCP members and supporters by the police, the BNP's so-called 'peace corps' (Lebotho la Khotso), police reservists and home guards, other BCP members took up arms in self defence and widespread riots ensued. Police chiefs and two other senior government officials visited Mokhehle in the Maximum Security Prison and asked him to issue an appeal to his supporters to stop fighting, claiming that Chief Jonathan had done the same. He accepted the suggestion and acted accordingly. His appeal was recorded and broadcast over the radio and police public-address vans. In fact Chief Jonathan made no such appeal. The police chiefs and senior government officials merely deceived the BCP leader whose supporters laid down arms in response to his appeal. Thereupon BNP 'peace corps' had a field day, and they killed and maimed their opponents with reckless abandon.

Reconciliation efforts. Between April and June 1970, a conference of leaders of the main political parties was held in Maseru to find a solution to the election crisis and the resultant lawlessness and bloodshed. During that conference the BNP representatives made no secret of their intentions as to the type of society they would like to have in Lesotho. 'We, the Council of Ministers, and I (Jonathan) who are also representatives of the BNP declare (*a*) that there is in fact no room in the political life of the Basutho for the existence of rival parties. The concept of divisions along party lines may work very well in other countries and among other nations where political and cultural backgrounds are particularly suited to that kind of system, but it must be clear to all that it cannot work in Lesotho. (*b*) We ... firmly believe ... that we too must rid ourselves of the party system; while it exists there seems to be no hope of attaining our ideal of one culture, one custom and one nation.'[4] The BCP reports that what was agreed was that 'only for the sake of resolving the disastrous crisis, for the sake of restoring peace, law and order, and for the sake of stopping the shedding of blood of innocent people, the results of the 1970 normal and, in law, valid elections be set aside, provided an interim coalition government could be formed.'[5] Chief Jonathan misrepresented the agreement when announcing it to the world. According to the BCP he merely said that agreement had been reached by all the political parties that the 1970 elections be nullified, ignoring the important proviso that an interim coalition government be set up. It was apparently on the understanding that agreement had been reached by all the political parties on the 1970 elections that inspired leading industrial nations like Britain, West Germany, the United States and others to grant Chief Jonathan's Government economic aid. When the prospects of receiving aids became clear Chief Jonathan and his colleagues abandoned the idea of setting up an interim coalition government.

During the state of emergency workers were denied freedom of assembly. They could neither hold committee nor general meetings to discuss their problems. Employment was based on political inclinations, and workers known or suspected of being anti- or not pro-Government were dismissed from their jobs and forfeited their entitlements. The dismissals were not limited to public servants: private employers were also instructed to dismiss their employees known or suspected to be anti-Government. This state of affairs continued until January 1974, when some frustrated BCP members and supporters attacked some police stations in an attempt to overthrow the Government. History repeated itself. The police and BNP 'peace corps' went on a rampage, killing BCP supporters in a manner that would make even the devil to blush. The BCP reports that a total of 1,125 of its members and supporters were known to have been killed and the number unreported could be higher. Property estimated at R 1,082,640 was destroyed.[6]

As a result of the 1974 riots, thirty-two BCP members were arrested and charged with treason, sedition and conspiracy, among them was Shakhane Mokhehle, General Secretary of the BFL. Shakhane and four others were acquitted and discharged on a no-case submission, but fifteen of the accused persons were convicted of treason, and two of sedition. Those convicted received various terms of imprisonment ranging from eighteen months to nine years. Some of the remarks of the Chief Justice who tried the case are a great indictment of Chief Jonathan's regime. Mr. Justice Mapetla took judicial notice of the widespread rumour and fear among BCP members and supporters that drastic actions were to be taken against their leaders if a second state of emergency were declared and a one-party state introduced. The previous state of emergency had been lifted, but the experiences of those days were still fresh in the people's memory. The Chief Justice said that 'these fears must have been increased and given substance by the apparent alliance between the Parliamentary Group, led by Ramoreboli, and the Government, the attempt of the former to persuade the Government to take more stringent measures against the BCP and perhaps even more pointedly by the undertaking given by the Prime Minister to eliminate the BCP altogether should Ramoreboli and his group so suggest. This is what motivated these disturbances.' The Chief Justice went on: 'The plan was as rash and reckless as it was ill conceived, rather pathetic and doomed to failure. That it fizzled out and went off like a squib is no fault of the accused. ... What I find most unfortunate is that the custodians of law and order, namely, the police themselves, showed little if any respect for law and order in dealing with these disturbances and unleashed such violence against the perpetrators of these offences as to throw the public sympathy on them and overshadow the enormity of their crimes. The real point is that any salutory effect which sentences might have had has, to a large extent, been neutralised by the unbridled violence of retaliatory measures taken by the police against the perpetrators of these offences.'[7]

In March 1974, the Lesotho National Assembly passed the Internal Security (General) Amendment Act which officially was intended to kill terrorism in Lesotho. Journalists covering events in the country at the time commented that 'the trouble is that it kills a lot of other things too—such as the right to protest, the right of redress and the right of appeal to the courts'. The law gave frightening powers of detention and interrogation to law enforcement agencies at a time when the way and manner law enforcement was being carried out in the country was already suspect. It indemnified the Government and its agents against any attempt to seek redress by a citizen for any action they had taken since 1970. Under the law no proceedings could be taken against a policeman, government official, civil servant or any persons acting on their orders who were deemed to have acted in the interest of the state to discourage internal disorder or maintain public safety in essential services. People could be held for sixty days, released and immediately rearrested and held for another sixty days *ad infinitum*. No one could visit detained persons without ministerial permission.

The 1970 killings, harassments and persecution compelled the Lesotho General Workers' Union, an affiliate of the BFL, to file a complaint with the ILO against the Lesotho Government for infringement of trade union rights. Further information in support of the complaint was submitted in March 1971. The complaint was first examined by the Committee on Freedom of Association which reported in November 1971 to the ILO Governing Body. In their report the Committee observed that the allegations called in question some of the standards laid down in the Freedom of Association Convention as well as the generally recognised principles on the subject. These principles were: (*a*) Freedom of assembly for trade union purposes, and the right to express opinions through the press constitute one of the fundamental elements of trade union rights. (*b*) Workers should have the right, without discrimination whatsoever—and particularly without discrimination of any kind on the basis of political opinion—to join the union of their choice. (*c*) No person should be discriminated against in his employment by reason of his trade union activities or membership. Not only dismissal but also compulsory retirement or termination of services would be contrary to this principle if the activities, in respect of which action was taken against an employee, were in fact lawful trade union activities. (*d*) In all cases, in which trade unionists are charged with political and criminal offences which the government considers have no relation to their trade union functions, the persons in question should receive a prompt and fair trial by an independent and impartial judiciary.

Fact Finding and Concialiation Commission. Special circumstances arose before the report was ready, and this necessitated a further investigation of the complaint. Lesotho ceased its membership of the ILO in July 1971, having given notice two years earlier in accordance with procedure. Under a special arrangement between the UN and the ILO, when a complaint is filed against a government which is not a member of the ILO but is a member of the UN, such a complaint is referred to the UN Economic and Social Council. This was done in the case of the complaint against the Lesotho Government, and led to the appointment of a three-man Fact Finding and Conciliation Commission made up of: Andreas Movrommatis of Cyprus, a former District Judge and Minister of Labour, Chairman; H. S. Kirkaldy of the United Kingdom, former Professor Emeritus of Industrial Relations at the University of Cambridge and Member of the Committee of Experts on the Application of ILO Conventions and Recommendations; and Dr. F. A. Ajayi, former Attorney General of the Western State of Nigeria. It took a long time for the Commission to begin work mainly because it had not received the observations it expected from the Lesotho Government and the complainant organisation. When these observations were eventually received it was agreed that the Commission should visit Lesotho, and the mission should be undertaken by the Chairman accompanied by a member of the ILO secretariat in Geneva. The Chairman and the ILO official visited Lesotho in January 1975, and received written and oral evidence from the Government, the BFL, the LCW, employers' federation and members of the public. They later prepared a report which was unanimously adopted by the other members of the Commission.

Findings. The Commissioners found that in the months following the declaration of the state of emergency the Government set about eradicating what it considered to be subversive elements in the opposition Basutoland Congress Party. There followed a wave of arrests and dismissals of persons said to be actively plotting the overthrow of the Government by force and even persons who were simply supporters of the Congress Party. These arrests gave rise to the submission of the complaint. As regards the allegation that trade unionists had been arrested and detained, several persons including those named in the complaint and other members of the public gave evidence to substantiate it. In the course of the hearings it became clear that the BFL which claimed a membership of about 12,000 in January 1970, identified itself with the BCP, and the 'evidence showed that it was almost exclusively for this reason that members of this organisation or its affiliates found themselves victims of the measures taken by the Government during the state of emergency.' The Commissioners went on: 'Significantly, every witness who had been arrested stated that his sympathies lay with the Congress Party and that, when interrogated, they had been asked about their political activities and their involvement in acts considered by the authorities to be subversive. No witness was able to say that his trade union activitives contributed to his arrest and detention apart from stating that the authorities appeared to take the view that any person connected with the BFL or one of its affiliates was necessarily anti-government and possibly involved in a plot to overthrow the Government.'

Many persons, including trade unionists, were detained on one or several occasions, sometimes for periods of two years without being formally charged or brought to trial. The Government admitted the charge, but explained that the delay was due to a shortage of magistrates and a backlog of cases to be tried. The Commissioners found the explanation unacceptable, and pointed out that although the courts never ceased to function normally throughout the emergency, a number of persons, including trade unionists, were 'preventively detained' for as long as the Government considered them to be a threat to its stability. On the question of arrests and detention, the Commissioners concluded that the measures taken against workers in general and against trade unionists in particular were not connected with their trade union activities as such, and that the members of the BFL who were arrested and detained were subjected to such measures because of the very close association of the Federation to the Congress Party. While refraining from expressing an opinion on the political aspects of the state of emergency, the Commissioners nevertheless pointed out that measures of preventive detention were liable to involve serious restrictions on the exercise of trade union rights and should be accompanied by adequate judicial safeguards applied within a reasonable period, and that all detained persons should receive a fair trial at the earliest possible moment. Certain persons had suffered ill-treatment while in detention or during interrogation. Trade unionists, like other persons, should not be arrested except in accordance with the ordinary criminal procedure and rights enshrined in the Universal Declaration of Human Rights should be guaranteed. The authorities should issue special instructions prescribing effective penalties to guarantee protection against all forms of pressure during detention. As a result of the events which followed the emergency situation declared in January 1970, the safeguards required for the enjoyment of these rights 'were impaired and fundamental human rights and freedoms were violated in a number of cases'.

The Commissioners noted that dismissals took place mainly in the civil service where about 300 persons in various departments lost their jobs. All the civil servants interviewed by the Chairman of the Commission were members of the Civil Service Association which the Commissioners described as 'neither a registered trade union nor was it considered by any one to be performing trade union functions'. The Commissioners were told that the Association was more of a consultative body than an occupational organisation and its meetings were held at irregular intervals. Most of the civil servants were dismissed summarily in March or April 1970, and dismissal involved the forfeiture of gratuity and pension rights. The Government admitted that the normal procedure through the Public Service Commission on the matter of dismissals was not followed. None of the civil servants interviewed by the commissioners had in any way been active in party politics, but all seemed to have sympathies for the Congress Party. As for dismissals in the private sector, the commissioners found that 'it seems likely, from the evidence obtained, particularly from the employers, that there were cases in which pressure was brought to bear upon employers to terminate the contracts of workers who supported the Congress Party'. The dismissal of workers was part of the Government's policy of purging both the public and private sectors of the economy of political elements who were not favourable to it. While they were not in themselves a violation of trade union rights, nevertheless dismissals encountered in the case were not in conformity with the generally accepted principle that any form of discrimination in respect of employment on the basis of political opinion should be eliminated.

The commissioners also found that enough convincing evidence was given to prove the allegation that the issuance of employment cards to workers by the Labour Department was based on whether or not the persons applying for them were pro-Government. Although the Labour Commissioner denied the allegation, the commissioners found that 'this practice did exist and it affected workers who were members of organisations affiliated to BFL and hence thought to be supporters of the opposition party'. Acts of this kind, the commissioners declared, were discriminatory and not in keeping with the principles they had outlined earlier. Restriction imposed on the right of assembly constituted the most serious aspect of interference in the normal running of trade union affairs following the emergency. Unions required special permissions to hold meetings, and the evidence obtained showed that the BFL and its affiliates experienced much greater difficulty in obtaining permission than its counterpart, the LCW, which was founded in 1963/4 by T. Lepole, son-in-law of the Prime Minister, and had a membership of about 1,500. The commissioners pointed out that the right of trade unions to hold meetings freely in their own premises, without the need for previous authorisation and without control by the public authorities is a fundamental element in the principle of freedom of association. The trade unions should be given the greatest possible freedom of action in the occupational sphere which was compatible with the maintenance of public order, and it was hoped that the Government would consider the situation in the light of these principles.

In a situation such as that of Lesotho where part of the trade union movement had experienced serious difficulties because of its close association with a political party, the commissioners considered it desirable to draw attention to the distinction between trade union freedom and the performance of essential political activities. They referred to a resolution on the independence of the trade union movement which the ILO Annual Conference adopted in 1952 which says that 'the fundamental and permanent mission of the trade union movement is the economic and social advancement of the workers. When trade unions, in accordance with the national law and practice of their respective countries and at the decision of their members, decide to establish relations with a political party or to undertake a constitutional political action as a means towards the advancement of their economic and social objectives, such political relations or actions should not be of a nature as to compromise the continuance of the trade union movement or its social or economic functions, irrespective of political changes in the country.' The commissioners then added: 'In the same resolution it was stated that governments should not attempt to transform the trade union movement into an instrument for the pursuance of political aims nor should they attempt to interfere with the normal functions of the trade union movement because of its freely established relationship with a political party.' Difficulties might arise, they pointed out, if there existed a general prohibition on trade unions from engaging in any political activities because of the interpretation given to the relevant provisions, but states should be able—without prohibiting, in general terms, political activities of occupational organisations—to entrust the judicial authorities with the task of repressing abuses which might, in certain cases, be committed by organisations which had lost sight of the fact that their fundamental objective should be the economic and social advancement of their members.

The commissioners noted that the trade union movement in Lesotho was weak and disunited. Both the two main organisations, however, appeared to be fully conscious of their weakness and appreciated that added strength, as well as a more dynamic and constructive approach to trade union matters, could be obtained through the voluntary amalgamation of the BFL and LCW. They noted with interest the move then being made by the BFL to hold discussions with the LCW, and expressed the hope that the Government would encourage the two organisations to merge voluntarily rather than impose unification by legislation. A decision to merge voluntarily was eventually taken in 1977 not as a result of Government encouragement but in consequence of a trade union course organised by the ICFTU.

Liberia

The Republic of Liberia is inhabited by two main groups of people: the Americo-Liberians, descendants of the slaves freed in the United States after the abolition of slavery; and the indigenous Liberians from the various ethnic groups commonly referred to as 'the native people' or 'the natives'. The Americo-Liberians are a minority of the total population, but they dominate practically all the main activities of the country including politics, the public service, commerce and industry and agriculture. In the foreign-owned plantations of Firestone and Goodrich, they occupy most of the key positions in the administrative, financial and technical divisions. Until 1965 they also dominated the trade union movement. To a large extent, the history of the Liberian trade union movement is both a history of the struggles of the so-called 'native people' to play a leading role in it and the efforts of the Americo-Liberians to maintain the *status quo*. Shad Tubman, son of the late President Tubman, and Lawrence Sawyerr, two prominent Americo-Liberians, held the positions of President and General Secretary respectively of the Congress of Industrial Organisations (CIO) from its founding congress until early 1965. Shad was succeeded that year by another Americo-Liberian, J. B. McGill, generally acknowledged as the founder of the trade union movement in the country.

Although Liberia is one of the oldest independent countries in Africa, trade union development in that country is a comparatively new thing. Only a small percentage of industrial workers is organised, and the vast majority of the labour force in agriculture and the plantations remains unorganised. Two laws passed in February 1966 (of which more will be said presently) gave the country's President sweeping powers to declare a state of emergency in the event of strikes, and forebade industrial workers from organising or helping to organise agricultural labour. Before the introduction of that law, the domineering influence of Firestone and other interest groups had effectively destroyed every effort to organise plantation workers.

The emergence of the CIO. In the early part of the twentieth century, several efforts were made without much success to found trade unions in Liberia. The present unions owe their origin to the successful launching in 1957 of the Labour Congress of Liberia. Dissatisfaction with its operation led to a split and the subsequent inauguration in 1959 of the Congress of Industrial Organisations, a monolithic body which served both as a general workers' union and a national centre. There were good reasons for adopting that structure. Liberia is a small country with a small labour force. The workforce in commerce and industry as well as in the public service was considered inadequate to warrant organising on a craft or industrial basis, particularly as agricultural and plantation workers could not be organised for the reasons stated earlier. Moreover, Liberia was, and is still, considered a high cost area. The cost of operating an effective union underscored the importance of organising on a broad basis. From a humble beginning in 1959 the CIO developed rapidly in membership and income, and by 1963 its average monthly income from entrance fees and dues was US$3,000. So promising was its growth that Lannart Kindstrom, then the ICFTU representative in Liberia, felt that the organisation needed no financial assistance, and advised his principals accordingly.

Although its field activities were commendable, its administration left much to be desired. Its staff strength was top heavy (forty-five in 1964) and the principal officers spent money recklessly. Members soon realised that the leadership was equally guilty of the same weaknesses which formed the basis of the 1959 split. Moreover the leaders were accused of lacking guts and of being more interested in the prestige of office than in servicing the membership. These factors determined the decision of junior officers like James Bass, Amos Gray, J. O. Jomah and Victor Seton to organise for the removal of the President and General Secretary. In 1964 'the natives' won the first round of the fight against Americo-Liberian dominance when James Bass defeated Lawrence Sawyerr in the election of the General Secretary of CIO. McGill was re-elected President, and Sawyerr became Vice-President. It would appear that the Americo-Liberians were unhappy about the result of the elections, so efforts were made to turn the scale at the earliest possible opportunity.

Natives versus Americo-Liberians. A few weeks after his re-election, McGill reported sick and began gradually to transfer his functions to Sawyerr. As Acting President Sawyerr set up what was known as a 'Presidential Commission' ostensibly to examine the ways and means of strengthening the CIO already weakened by 'decentralisation' (an agitation inspired by certain ITS respresentatives in 1964 to change its structure from a general workers' union to a federation of industrial unions) and to look into allegations of financial mismanagement; but actually the intention was to pave the way for his re-election as General Secretary at the next CIO Convention. The Tubman administration was more favourably disposed towards Sawyerr and his supporters than the militant Bass group. The Presidential Commission appears to have failed in their primary responsibility of finding ways and means of strengthening the CIO. Rather than making tangible suggestions to this effect, they spent much time and energy accusing their opponents of engaging in subversive activities against the state. Consequently Bass and his supporters were subjected to severe investigation by the National Bureau of Investigation, and for months lived under constant fear of being arrested and thrown into jail without trial. There being no evidence to substantiate the allegation, the investigations were discontinued. A good deal of bad blood was created among union leaders by this false allegation, and the bitterness inspired the anti-Sawyerr group to strengthen their campaign to ensure his defeat. In the national union elections which preceded the CIO Convention, 'the natives' won a decisive victory J. O. Jomah defeated Sawyerr as President of the Mechanic and Allied Workers' Union; Amos Gray defeated Robert Ben as President of the Petroleum Workers' Union; and Francis Wolo defeated W. B. Tugbeh as President of the Maritime Workers' Union. Their crushing defeat forced Sawyerr and his supporters to change tactics.

The CIO was to hold its Convention on 3 February 1965. Three days before then, McGill issued a statement published in the press announcing its postponement. No tangible reason was given to justify the postponement, and this provoked a sharp controversy among the union leaders. Could the President, some asked, validly postpone a Convention summoned by the Executive Board? There was no provision in the CIO constitution covering such a situation. Bass and his supporters argued that he could not, and proceeded to hold the convention as planned. The Convention elected Foulton W. Yancy, President; Percy Williams, Vice President; James Bass, General Secretary; and Amos Gray, Assistant General Secretary. McGill condemned the Convention and declared the elections null and void. He appealed to the Secretary of Commerce and Industry, the Hon. A. Romeo Horton, who also held the responsibility for labour matters, to intervene. The Secretary duly intervened, and in doing so threw his whole weight and influence in favour of McGill.

He declared the Convention unconstitutional, set aside the elections, and ruled that all persons holding office before the Convention should continue to function in their respective positions pending a Convention summoned by the CIO President and supervised by Government officials. He then issued a circular letter to all employers not to recognise or deal with any faction of the CIO.

The Convention ordered by the Secretary of Commerce and industry was scheduled for 23 May 1965. A few days before then McGill again issued a statement postponing it. Like the previous one, no reasons were given for the postponement, and this caused a great embarrassment in official quarters and generated bitterness against him. McGill later denied authorship of the statement, and claimed that it had been written by Sawyerr who persuaded him to sign it. He did so, he said, on the understanding that it would be submitted to the CIO legal adviser for approval before being released to the press. It would appear that Sawyerr did not do so. Sawyerr himself denied responsibility, and to strengthen his case produced a copy of the statement signed by McGill. McGill's reaction was sharp and bitter. He declared that he would from then have nothing to do with Sawyerr, and Sawyerr retorted that he too would have nothing to do with McGill. Comrades in arms thus fell apart. In that atmosphere, the Convention ordered by the Secretary of Commerce and Industry was held according to schedule. During the elections which ended the meeting, McGill and Sawyerr were voted out, and all the persons elected in February were returned.

The Americo-Liberians were still unhappy about the results. In an attempt to tip the scale other tactics were employed. Pressure was brought to bear on Foulton Yancy to resign his position of President of CIO; he was succeeded by Mrs. Susan Berry, another Americo-Liberian. L. B. Jacobs, a former CIO employee, was encouraged to accuse CIO leaders again of engaging in subversive activities against the state. Such an accusation would normally be referred to the National Bureau of Investigation, but for reasons best known to the Secretary of Commerce and Industry the accusation was referred to a Labour Inspector, another former CIO employee who left the Congress with a grouse. The investigation was postponed twice because the accuser could not come forward to substantiate his case. Whether the allegation was eventually proved is unknown. Yet, in spite of the doubts surrounding the allegation, Bass, Gray, Seton and Patricia Hill were removed from their positions in the CIO by government order and banned from holding any trade union office because of the findings of the investigator.

1966 labour unrests. In 1966, two major labour unrests changed the trade union situation in Liberia. In January, the tappers of Firestone Plantations went on strike in protest against starvation wages, deplorable terms of employment and the management's decision to introduce an incentive scheme limited to certain divisions. At that time, according to UN sources, the cost of living in Liberia was one of the highest in the world. Yet the minimum wage of industrial workers was merely US$1.25 per day while their counterparts in agriculture and the plantations earned only US$0.64 per day. The great difference between the minimum wage of industrial and agricultural workers was considered by Liberian trade union leaders as an injustice brought about by the absence of a trade union catering for the interests of agricultural workers. In 1965 the Firestone management came to the conclusion that the productivity of their tappers was low and ought to be increased. They therefore decided to introduce an incentive scheme. Under the scheme tappers' tasks were increased from 300 to 450 trees per month. In addition they were to collect latex and earth scraps, ring-weed three times a year and apply fungicide twice a week. Surprisingly, the increase in tasks was not matched by an increase in wages. The Labour Practices Review Board, a government agency which adjudicates labour disputes, commented on the scheme as follows:

The difficulty with this plan is that it does not promise the workers anything specific. ... The tapper seems to want to know what he can expect at the end of each month for specific work done. Firestone alone determines this. Firestone determines how much extra is paid to the tapper for each DRC pound. This varies according to clone and season. Firestone determines how many DRC pounds are required for each clone and during each season under the incentive system in order for tappers to acquire the minimum earnings.[8]

Reaction to the scheme varied. In some divisions the tappers wanted to know what monetary reward they were entitled to before accepting the scheme. Firestone management was not prepared to disclose this. They just wanted the workers to accept and trust their sense of fairplay to work out reasonable wages later. That condition was unacceptable to the workers. In some divisions where it would appear that the tappers had some measure of confidence in the management's fairplay, the scheme was accepted without much difficulty. In consequence the average earnings of tappers who had accepted the scheme rose to US$1.08 per day as against US$0.70 in other divisions. When the difference was known, tappers not covered by the scheme could not understand why people doing the same type of work were not being paid the same rate. This grievance was dovetailed in a number of other grievances like overtime pay, poor housing and insanitary conditions in the company's premises and workshops, and a decision was taken to go on strike. The strike began peacefully, but later got out of hand when the strikers clashed with strike breakers. Troops were called in. In the disturbances which followed, one striker was killed and several others were wounded. Management accused the strikers of damaging company property and man-handling non-strikers, but those conversant with Firestone's tactics on such occasions told a different story. They said that the company's agents deliberately poured latex on the ground in order to find a justification for inviting the Government to send troops to break the strike, a common occurrence during the Tubman era. After the strike, the Liberian Parliament passed the Emergency Powers Act.

Five months following the Firestone strike, another strike of mine workers took place at the LAMCO Joint Venture Mining Company in Yekkepa, Nimba County. The background to that strike may be summarized as follows. In March 1964 a general wage increase was granted to Liberian workers following a petition which the CIO submitted to the legislature. This brought industrial workers' minimum wage to 15 cents per hour and agricultural workers' minimum wage to 64 cents per day. While other employers paid the new minimum wage, Messrs Vianini (Liberia) Limited, one of the contracting firms attached to LAMCO when the mines in Nimba were being constructed, failed to do so. The workers complained to the CIO which took up the matter with the Department of Commerce and Industry. At first the CIO estimated the amount involved at US$40,000. The company admitted liability to the tune of US$30,000. Since no agreement could be reached on the amount involved, the matter was referred to a tripartite body for investigation. The body comprised two Government representatives, two representatives of LAMCO, and a representative of the CIO. During the investigation Vianini explained certain irregularities and the reasons for their failure to pay the new wage rate. LAMCO representatives exonerated Vianini from any liability and said that their company accepted full responsibility for what happened. The investigators found that the total amount owed to the workers was US$175,000. In a unanimous report accepted by the Department of Commerce and Industry and adopted by the Labour Practices Review Board they recommended that the amount be paid as early as possible.[9] Unfortunately, the money was not paid. Usually when the Labour Practices Review Board makes a decision on an industrial dispute the Department of Commerce and Industry puts pressure on the employer to comply if he fails within a reasonable time to do so. The Department failed to do this in the Vianini case.

In July 1966 the Vianini arrears (as they became popularly known) and other grievances were the cause of a spontaneous strike of LAMCO employees which lasted seven days. During the strike the Government tried to use the President and Treasurer of the Liberian Mineworkers' Association (as the union was then known) to persuade the workers to return to work. When they failed, President Monger and Treasurer Rufus Murray were arrested and jailed without trial for organising what the Government called 'illegal strike'. Alexander Kawah, the Association's Secretary, was also arrested and detained for allegedly destroying company property, but he was later released for want of evidence. That same day, 23 July, 500 soldiers and 150 police men were deployed to break the strike. LAMCO management asked all the company's supervisors to submit the names of those believed to have masterminded the strike or supported it. In consequence, thirty-two workers were summarily dismissed and forcibly evicted from the quarters they were occupying in the company's premises.

A Swedish television team then visiting Liberia filmed the event. 'Black Week in Nimba' is a testimony of that sordid episode. The film was later shown on Swedish television and the television services of other European countries, and generated a great resentment among trade unionists in those countries. Swedish mine workers contributed money which they sent to the ICFTU to administer as relief assistance to their counterparts in Liberia. An ICFTU representative was in the country to carry out that assignment when a warrant of arrest was issued against him. But he left the country before the warrant was executed. In another development, James Bass, Secretary General of the CIO, was arrested and detained for criticising the Government for violation of trade union rights. Later he was charged with sedition.

Restrictive laws. Earlier in the year (9 February 1966) the Liberian legislature had passed the law 'to restore, supplement and enlarge emergency powers granted to the Liberian President.' Section 1 (*r*) of that law empowered the President 'to ban any unions where there is evidence that they receive any financial assistance or other benefits from any outside source unless such financial assistance or other benefits are approved by and channelled through the Government.' Sub-sections (*f*), (*u*), and (*v*) of Section 1 enabled the President to consider as illegal, and threatening the security of the state, all strikes instituted or staged contrary to Liberian law, and to deem guilty of a criminal offence all persons aiding, abetting, encouraging or participating in such strikes and to deal with them summarily. They also enabled the President to pronounce guilty of an attempt to overthrow the Government and endanger the safety of the state the leaders of any strike staged without first complying with the laws of Liberia, to suspend the writ of Habeas Corpus for a period of up to one year, and to arrest, imprison and detain all violaters of the laws of the country and have them tried summarily before a commission set up by the President. On 11 February 1966, the legislature also passed the Act to Amend the Labour Practices Law under which 'no industrial labour union or organisation shall exercise any privilege or function for agricultural workers and no agricultural labour union or organisation shall exercise any privilege or function for industrial workers.'

Complaints. These laws and the repressive measures taken against Liberian union leaders as well as the harsh treatment meted to representatives of international trade union organisations then on various assignments in Liberia formed the basis of complaints filed in January 1967, by the ICFTU, the International Federation of Plantation, Agricultural and Allied Workers (IFPAAW) and the Miners' International Federation (MIF) against the Government of Liberia for violation of trade union rights. Before then Liberia had ratified ILO Conventions 87 and 98. The complaints covered five main points as follows: (i) the Emergency Powers Act, (ii) the Act to Amend the Labour Practices Law, (iii) strikes, (iv) arrest and detention of James Bass, and (v) the Rubber Tappers' Association. Both the ICFTU and IFPAAW criticised Section 1 (*r*) of the Emergency Powers Act as infringing Article 5 of Convention 87 which provides that national trade union organisations shall have the right to affiliate to international trade union organisations. This right, the complainants contended, implied that national trade unions were entitled to seek the advice and assistance of international trade union organisations in all fields which are relevant to the exercise of trade union functions and to the promotion of genuine trade unionism. The complainants also argued that Section 1 (*s*) was incompatible with Article 5 of the Convention because the right of international affiliation implied that national trade union organisations were entitled to receive the services and benefits of their affiliation for the furtherance of trade union activities and programmes which, in accordance with the provisions of Article 3 they had the right to establish without Government interference. IFPAAW made the striking point that sub-sections 1 (*r*) and (*c*) had been used to prohibit meetings between international trade union representatives and Liberian trade unions, and that it had become obligatory for the unions to obtain specific permission from the Government before their representatives could leave the country to participate in meetings and conferences outside the country held by international trade union organisations to which they were affiliated and of which, in some cases, the leaders were elected officials.

Since 1960 the IFPAAW has been trying to help set up a union of plantation workers, but every effort had been frustrated by the hostile attitude of Firestone management and the encouragement the latter received from the Tubman administration. In September 1966, Ed Colbert was granted an interview in Zurich by President Tubman, the object being to obtain permission pursuant to Section 1 (s) of the Emergency Powers Act to assist the plantation workers to organise.[10] According to IFPAAW, during the interview President Tubman referred to the LAMCO strike as indicating the need for Liberian trade unions to receive help and guidance from international trade union organisations like IFPAAW, and assured Colbert that he approved IFPAAW's plan. IFPAAW apparently took oral assurance as a formal approval, and on 1 November 1966 reported the outcome of the interview in letters to Dash Wilson, then Under-Secretary for Labour, and the Hon. Romeo Horton, Secretary of Commerce and Industry. Colbert later arrived in Liberia, and together with C. P. N. Vewesse, an official of IFPAAW's affiliate in Cameroun, and W. B. Tueh, a former official of the Rubber Tappers' Association, began contacting officials of the Association after working hours with a view to constituting them into an Organising Committee of the proposed Liberian Plantation, Agricultural and Allied Workers' Union, the appropriate government officials and Firestone management being fully informed of their activities. On 11 November an official of the Labour Bureau, accompanied by two policemen, handed to Colbert and Vewesse a letter from the Secretary of Commerce and Industry asking them to report at once to the residence of the Attorney General, the Labour Bureau official assuring them that they were not under arrest. In fact the policemen took them to police headquarters where they were told that they were under arrest. The following day they appeared before a special commission as provided for in the Emergency Powers Act. They were not allowed legal representation nor were they told of any offence they had committed or any complaint against them from the Firestone management. But they were ordered to cease forthwith their activities until they had obtained written permission from the Government.

Jim Roberts of MIF came to Liberia in October 1966 to assist the Liberian Mineworkers' Union in their negotiations with the management of the Liberian Mining Company. On arrival he reported to the Department of Commerce and Industry and told them the purpose of his mission. He was told that he could proceed, but as he set about his task he was warned by the Secretary of Commerce and Industry that he was violating the laws of Liberia and was forced to leave the country.

With regard to the Act to Amend the Labour Practices Law, both the ICFTU and IFPAAW contended that the provision denying industrial unions the right to organise agricultural workers was contrary to Article 5 of Convention 87 and had prevented the existence of a single national centre embracing all organised workers. The amendment, they added, also destroyed whatever organisation and membership the CIO had been able to achieve in the rubber industry and precluded the plantation workers then and in the future from drawing on the experience and facitilities of the CIO.

Investigations. The ICFTU, IFPAAW and MIF complaints were referred to the Special Committee on Freedom of Association and the Right to Organise for examination. In accordance with procedure the complaints were forwarded to the Liberian Government for comments. The Government's observations may be summarised as follows:[11]

(a) Emergency Powers Act. The Act must be considered as a whole and in the light of the conditions existing at the date of its enactment in February 1966. It deals with such matters as increasing the National Guard, mobilisation for defence and other measures in case of threat of invasion, moving the seat of government, monetary arrangements, setting up of emergency hospitals, etc., so that labour is dealt with only as one of several factors composing the national fabric. When it was enacted an uneasy state of affairs existed in Liberia and in Africa as a whole, and the Government had ample reasons to believe that its existence was threatened. The Act was a temporary measure to deal with a particular situation and it expired on 8 February 1967. (In fact the Act has remained in the Statute Book ever since then, having been periodically renewed after its first expiry date.)

(b) Right of International Affiliation. The Freedom of Association and Protection of the Right to Organise Convention 1948 (No. 87) is not a licence for a union to become a tool or an agent of a foreign power or external force to work against the security and existence of the state in which the union is located. (The Government did not produce any evidence to support the allegation that Liberian unions were tools or agents of a foreign power working against the security and existence of the state.)

(*c*) Strikes. The Labour Act did not make strikes 'usually illegal'. On the contrary, it recognised the right to strike. But strikes must be executed in a legal manner. By accepting the provisions of Convention 87 the Government did not abandon its right to enforce the laws of the country and to prevent their wilful and deliberate abuse. Whether a particular machinery was functioning properly in dealing with labour problems was a question of judgment and not of law. 'Even if there exists a snag in the process of administering labour laws in Liberia so as to cause delay in its appropriate execution, this cannot in any way justify illegal activity.' It was generally recognised that a state in the exercise of its duty to protect the inhabitants and their property might use the amount of force necessary to subdue hostile persons, and that the use of troops and police in restoring order in cases involving labour unrests could not be regarded as inappropriate. The Nimba and Goodrich (another protest strike of plantation workers) strikes were illegal. They 'were not in furtherance of any legitimate demands or grievances' and 'were not directed by the union itself or its legitimate leaders'.

(*d*) Arrest and Detention of James Bass, CIO Secretary General. Bass was arrested on 25 November 1966, and was later charged with sedition in accordance with Section 52 (*a*) and (*b*) of the Penal Law. He was detained to await trial, he himself having refused bail. Subsequently he wrote a letter of apology to the President who ordered his release. Bass filed a six-month good behaviour bond.

(*e*) Ed Colbert, IFPAAW Representative. Colbert's case was nothing but an attempt to blackmail the Government, and the Government would not submit to blackmail. President Tubman granted him an interview in Zurich, and they discussed many aspects of trade unionism in Liberia. Because Colbert could not, on his return to Liberia in October 1966, obtain an immediate audience with the President, he presented the President with an ultimatum stating that if he could not have an audience by 18 December, he would leave the country and report the matter to the ICFTU. This was blackmail, and the contention had been rein-forced by the subsequent submission of the ICFTU's complaint.

(*f*) Jim Roberts, MIF Representative. Roberts was granted per-mission to make contacts with the local mine workers' union. But he 'took it upon himself to substitute himself for the local union in its negotiations on miners' terms and conditions with the Liberian Mining Company, a right which no foreigner could arrogate to himself pursuant to any ILO Convention.' The Government asked Roberts to withdraw from the negotiations, and did not force him to leave the country. (The truth, however, is that the Mine Workers' Union asked Roberts to become their spokesman at the negotiations. The union leaders felt they lacked the skill and experience to do the job themselves. The Liberian Government challenged the union's right to do so, and argued that 'the right of the union to elect its representatives for the purpose of negotiating a pay rise, etc., with the employers must legally be limited to members of the local union itself: the international representative can advise but not to substitute himself for the local union representatives.')

(g) The Act to Amend the Labour Practices Law: Government did not consider itself precluded by Article 5 of Convention 87 from separating industrial unions from agricultural unions. It recognised the right of industrial and agricultural unions to affiliate, but it could 'not accept a situation in which agricultural and industrial workers could function in a single union which would not only be dangerous but could undermine the existence of the state.' (The Government did not elaborate on how the existence of a single union embracing industrial and agricultural workers could undermine the existence of the state, but the general conclusion which some observers drew was that the law was motivated by fear of the combined strength of industrial and agricultural workers on the economic interests of most of the people in government who were themselves owners of big plantations.)

Findings. The Special Committee on Freedom of Association and the Right to Organise found that the Emergency Powers Act and the cases of Ed Colbert and Jim Roberts raised a number of aspects of the application of the principle of the right of international affiliation of trade unions and called for examination of their compatibility with Article 5 of Convention 87 and to some other Articles of the Convention. Since the Government stated that the Emergency Powers Act expired on 8 February 1967, the Committee hoped that any further emergency powers legislation would not contain provisions similar, in their relation to trade union rights, to those in the Act which had expired. The Committee also expressed the hope that the Liberian Government would be good enough to confirm this and furnish the text of any such legislation.

With regard to the Act to Amend the Labour Practices Law, the Committee stressed that it had always attached the greatest importance to the principle that workers should have the right to form and join organisations of their choice without previous authorisation. This right, it pointed out, was guaranteed by paragraph 2 of Article 8 of Convention 87. The CIO was a national confederation of which the occupational unions were constituents. Plantation or agricultural workers had in fact been organised to some extent by the CIO, but such degree of organisation that had been achieved had been negated by the amendment of the law. The law as it stood prevented the CIO from directly seeking to further the interests of plantation workers and to assist them in organising in a union or unions under its own aegis and as a constituent union of this national trade union centre and also prevented the existence of a single national trade union centre including all the trade unions of the country. The Government did not deal with these aspects of the matter in its observations, and the Committee expressed the hope that it would be good enough to specify what forms of trade union organisation might be adopted by plantation workers and to furnish its observations on the specific allegations made in the complaints.

On strikes, the Committee found that the Government did not directly reply to the point that 'when a dispute is reported the Board takes an unreasonably long time to give a decision or never gives a decision or is never even convened' though it had stated that even if there were delays in the administrative process in resolving disputes this was not a justification for calling an illegal strike. The Committee then emphasised the point it had always made in similar cases that the right of workers and their organisations to go on strike as a legitimate means of defending their occupational interests was generally recognised. In exercising the right to strike workers and their organisations must have due regard to temporary restrictions placed thereon, e.g. the cessation of the strike during conciliation and arbitration proceedings in which the parties could take part at every stage. When restrictions of this kind were placed on the exercise of the right to strike, the ensuing conciliation and arbitration proceedings should be adequate, impartial and speedy. The Committee also emphasised the importance which the ILO Governing Body had always attached to the right of all detained persons, including trade unionists, to receive a fair trial at the earliest possible moment. As the Government did not comment on the Rubber Tappers' Association, which the complainants alleged had been set up at Firestone's Harbel Plantation as a substitute for a trade union and its officers appointed by Government officials, the Committee requested the Government to be good enough to do so. It recommended the ILO Governing Body to note that James Bass, Secretary General of the CIO, had been released and no useful purpose would be served in pursuing that aspect of the complaint.

Post-Tubman Era. The Tubman administration ended in July 1971, when President Tubman died. To a certain extent, the end of the Tubman era also marked a new lease of life for the Liberian trade union movement. Amos Gray had succeeded James Bass as Secretary General of the CIO. In 1971 the CIO showed promise once again of being a growing and effective organisation. Its membership had risen from about 6,000 in 1966 to over 10,000, and it was receiving an average income of US$16,000 per month. A multi-purpose secretariat estimated at US$110,000 was planned. The greater part of the cost was to be paid by the African-American Labour Centre and the balance by the CIO. In due course, however, a series of problems arose, which not only had an adverse effect on the existence of the CIO but also put the building project in difficulty. The problems were not only many but also complex. Some were caused by the union leaders themselves, while others were either created or encouraged by the Government and some of the employers. The situation in LAMCO is a case in point.

It would appear that the company had never been happy with the CIO since the Vianini underpayment affair, and had been trying as best it could to destroy CIO influence among its employees. Alexander Kawah, Benjamin Duncan and Thomas Wablo are but a few of several employees of the company who had lost their jobs because of their loyalty to the CIO. LAMCO management seemed to be interested in individuals and local union leaders whose loyalty to the CIO was either suspect or non-existent. In 1972 they appeared to have been successful in getting the type of union leaders they had been looking for when Joseph Toweh and his associates were elected chairman, secretary and treasurer respectively of the National Mineworkers' Union (NMWU), Local 3, which was made up of the company's employees. Local 3, and its parent body, the National Mineworkers' Union, were important in the Liberian trade union movement for a number of reasons. The NMWU was the largest of the five national unions which made up the CIO, and Local 3 was also the largest of the four locals which constituted the NMWU. John T. Pratt, President of the NMWU was also the President of the CIO. In 1972, Local 3 had a membership of over 2,000 and its average monthly income was a little over US$2,000. What happened in Local 3 could easily have a snow-ball effect in other mining areas, as would be seen in later events.

Before 1972 there had been some disquiet over the financial arrangements of the CIO but no one had been bold enough to raise the matter at the appropriate organs of the organisation. Under the financial arrangements, 80 per cent of the monthly dues and all entrance fees were paid to the CIO, 10 per cent went to the national unions and 10 per cent to the locals (branches). Dues were collected mostly by check-off, and the proceeds were paid to the locals which deducted their entitlements and remitted the balance to the national unions and CIO. The CIO took the greatest percentage of the dues because it was responsible for the payment of all salaries and social charges of the staff of all the constituent unions and also for organising expenses. When Toweh and his colleagues assumed office they addressed a letter to LAMCO management asking them to put all the proceeds of monthly dues under escrow. But while the dues were under escrow they could go to management and withdraw any amount they liked.

Under the collective agreement between 'LAMCO and the National Mineworkers' Union Local 3 represented by the CIO', LAMCO was to provide buses to take workers to and from work. To meet that obligation, LAMCO initially financed a transport company, the Mount Nimba Transport Company, said to have been formed by certain LAMCO officials and some Ministers of State. The company concluded an agreement with Toweh and his colleagues under which it undertook to provide transport to take Toweh and members of Local 3 Executive Board to and from lunch. For that service Local 3 was to pay US$500 every month, and the amount was to be deducted from the proceeds of dues. The agreement was made without the consent of the CIO or the NMWU. When the fact was known, the CIO reported the matter to the Ministry of Labour, Youth and Sports, requesting investigation and an order that all monies collected and so far withheld be remitted to its banking account. The Ministry appointed a team of auditors to audit the accounts of Local 3. The auditors found that between July 1969 and August 1972, a total of US$82,103 was collected from check-off. Of this amount only US$14,214.20 was transferred to the CIO. As much as US$11,382.21 was unaccounted for. The former chairman of the Local, one Gbatu, was responsible for US$1,161. At the time of the audit, i.e. August 1972, Local 3 had assets of US$3,852.89 and liabilities of US$30,508 made up as follows: remittance to CIO US$24,518; remittance to the National Mineworkers' Union US$3,260 and Jos Hansen & Co. for a vehicle US$2,730. Later the

CIO reported that up to 31 March 1974, it had been deprived of a total of US$40,000 by Local 3. Three members of the Executive Board of Local 3 who felt that the administration of the Local's finances left much to be desired demanded an account. The chairman reacted sharply. He wrote to LAMCO management demanding the dismissal of the men, and management acted accordingly. A meeting of Local 3 attended by national leaders of the NMWU and the CIO suspended the chairman, secretary and treasurer. In an attempt to raise anti-CIO feelings in Yekkepa, Toweh organised an abortive strike for which he and his colleagues were arrested and jailed.

Split. Local 3 eventually withdrew from the NMWU and the CIO, alleging that the two organisations had failed to look after the interests of their members. This was in spite of CIO's victory in a case involving about US$300,000 which was then under appeal. The Ministry of Labour, Youth and Sports conducted a referendum to test the workers' views on the question of disaffiliation. Under the law, a union or a local wishing to disaffiliate from its parent body must obtain the support of two-thirds of the workers concerned. According to the CIO, only one-third of the workers concerned voted in the referendum conducted by the Ministry. Yet this was accepted by the Ministry as valid authority for Local 3 to withdraw. The developments in LAMCO soon spread like wild fire to other mining companies. Leaders of Local 1 at the Liberian Mining Company who were alleged to have misused a total of US$7,200 building fund followed the same procedure as their counterparts in Yekkepa and left the NMWU and the CIO. In Bong Mine, the referendum was conducted twice. In none of these exercises did those seeking disaffiliation obtain the necessary two-thirds majority. Yet the result was accepted as a valid authority for the local to disaffiliate. To understand what happened and why it happened it is necessary to bear in mind that there was no love lost between the Minister of Labour, the Hon. Jenkins Peal, and the principal officers of the CIO, J. T. Pratt and Amos Gray. Pratt himself was facing stiff opposition from certain leaders of some of the locals of the NMWU. Some wanted to stand against him for the Presidency, but the conference at which the election was to have been held was postponed at the last minute. According to James Bass, the Minister of Labour told a CIO delegation which met him in September 1974, with a view to normalising relations, that everything was possible 'provided the CIO got rid of the Secretary General, Amos Gray, and the President, John T. Pratt, by removing them from office'.[12]

Between 1973 and 1974 other sad developments helped to weaken the CIO and bedevil the situation in the mines. Wellington Ross, an Assistant Secretary General of the CIO, was relieved of his position for allegedly selling the Congress's vehicle without authority and failing to account for the proceeds. Frank Walker, whom he brought to the organisation, was elected as his successor. Ross remained unemployed for some months. Out of sheer sympathy Pratt employed him as an organiser to reorganise the mines. Ross and Walker had a masterplan unknown to Pratt and Gray. This plan was to prepare the ground for Walker to be elected Secretary General and Ross Assistant Secretary General at the next CIO Convention. To enable it to work Ross was to set the mine workers against Pratt and Gray. The plan failed for two reasons. First, the developments in the mines moved so fast that only one of the four locals of the NMWU was still in the CIO at the time of the Convention. Second, Walker's Domestic and Allied Workers' Union had, like Local 3 of NMWU, been putting their own dues under escrow apparently to make things difficult for the CIO. During the convention, the Steering Committee ruled that no person would be eligible for election unless he was a member or an official of a union whose dues had been paid up to date before the beginning of the convention. So by putting their dues under escrow, the leaders of the union had unknowingly disqualified themselves from standing for election.

Early in 1974 the Domestic and Allied Workers' Union announced that it and other unions (unnamed) had disaffiliated from the CIO 'because of corruption in the organisation', a claim which was quickly denied by the CIO. Later it was also announced that the union and the Liberian TUC—a paper organisation headed by Emmett Harmon, one of the principal shareholders of LAMCO and the company's Legal Counsel as well as being Liberian Ambassador at Large—had founded a new national centre called the United Workers' Congress (UWC). The new centre received immediate recognition from the Government. Government recognition paved the way for the various mine workers' locals which had disaffiliated from the NMWU and the CIO to affiliate to the UWC. But before accepting them into affiliation each of the locals had to be registered as a separate mine workers' union bearing the name of the company in which the members were employed. So from a national industrial union, Liberian mine workers moved back to house or company unionism. By May 1976, UWC claimed a membership of 7,000 made up as follows: the three mining companies (Bomi Bills, LAMCO and Bong Mine) 4,900; Domestic and Allied Workers' Union 1,700; and Wood and Timber Workers'

Union 400. The CIO claimed a membership of 4,500 made up as follows: Mano River Mines 1,400; Mechanic and Allied Workers' Union 2,000; Maritime Workers' Union 500; Petroleum Workers' Union 400 and Transport and General Workers' Union 200.

Under Liberian law, a union cannot engage in collective bargaining with an employer until it has won a representation election and has been duly certified by the Ministry of Labour, Youth and Sports as the sole representative and collective bargaining agent of the workers concerned. In 1974 a representation election was held in LAMCO. During the arrangements for the election the CIO requested that the names of three of its affiliates—the National Mineworkers' Union, the Mechanic and Allied Workers' Union and the Transport and General Workers' Union—be placed on the ballot. The Ministry of Labour, Youth and Sports refused, arguing that in the case of the NMWU the workers had already rejected representation by that union, a conclusion apparently drawn from a referendum of doubtful validity. In the case of the Mechanic and Allied Workers' Union and the Transport and General Workers' Union no reason whatsoever was given. The request was apparently turned down in order to eradicate CIO influence in LAMCO.

In 1976 President Tolbert urged the CIO and UWC to unite in response to the appeal for trade union unity at the national level made by the OATUU. Leaders of the two organisations expressed willingness to heed the President's appeal. Exploratory talks were held, followed by full scale negotiations in which the CIO, UWC and the one-member Liberian Confederation of Labour participated. The negotiations later ran into difficulty, both the CIO and the UWC blaming each other for lack of progress. The lack of progress apparently inspired the UWC to hold its first congress in April 1977. That congress elected Emmett Harmon, President; Esmael A. Sherif, Executive Vice President; and Frank Walker, Secretary General. It decided to reconvene in four years' time. The following month the CIO and LCL merged and formed the Liberian Federation of Trade Unions. The Hon. A. B. Tolbert, son of President Tolbert, was elected President; J. T. Pratt, Executive Vive President; and Amos Gray, Secretary General. The elected officers and members of the Executive Board of the Federation were formally installed by President Tolbert on 12 October 1977.

These two case studies illustrate some of the difficulties facing the trade union movement in many African countries. On the one hand they show the extent to which an unpopular government could go to perpetuate itself in power and victimise workers because of political belief. On the other hand they show the extent to which some governments can go in support of foreign companies against their own nationals in the name of maintaining law and order, economic development and protection of private property. The Tubman administration is now history but the law forbidding industrial workers to organise agricultural labour is still there. Since agricultural workers cannot benefit from the experience of their colleagues in industry and vested interests cannot allow them to organise themselves, will President Tolbert be good enough to tell the world what can be done to organise agricultural and plantation workers in Liberia?

7. CONTINENTAL TRADE UNION ORGANISATIONS

AFRO

The ICFTU African Regional Organisation (commonly known as AFRO) is the oldest continental trade union organisation grouping national trade union centres in English, French and Portuguese-speaking Africa. It was founded in 1960 following resolutions adopted to that effect by the First (Accra, January 1957), Second (Lagos, November 1959) and Third (Tunis, November 1960) African Regional Trade Union Conferences organised by the International Confederation of Free Trade Unions. Although a regional organ of an international organisation, AFRO enjoys a reasonable degree of autonomy. Constitutionally, a national trade union centre cannot become a member without being an affiliate of the ICFTU.

At its founding conference in 1960, AFRO had twenty affiliates from twenty countries representing about three million workers. By 1977 the membership had dropped to eight representing less than half a million workers. AFRO's pathetic decline in membership and influence is due to a number of circumstances some of which are beyond its control or the control of the trade union movement in Africa. The organisation came into being at a most inauspicious moment in African political and trade union history. Many African countries achieved political independence in 1960, and preparations for the inaugural conference of the All-African Trade Union Federation (AATUF) were then under way. Indeed, the Preparatory Conference held in Accra in November 1959 had recommended that the inaugural conference be held in May 1960. That conference was postponed until May 1961, mainly to reconcile some of the differences which had arisen from the decisions of the Preparatory Committee. One of these differences was that in order to become and remain a member of AATUF a national trade union centre must sever links with any international trade union organisation to which it was affiliated. It was argued that international affiliation was contrary to the policy of non-alignment which almost

120

every independent African country had adopted as the corner stone of its foreign policy.

At the Third African Regional Trade Union Conference held in Tunis in November 1960, delegates recognised the danger likely to arise if the proposed All-African Trade Union Federation were to be dominated by the national centres of what was then know as the Casablanca Group of African States. They therefore adopted the recommendations of the conference's Organisation Committee that 'the idea of a Pan-African trade union federation is not basically inconsistent with the free trade union movement of Africa, and that it would be injudicious to ignore the spiritual and emotional appeal which Pan-Africanism generates in the political and social institutions of twentieth-century Africa. But there is reason to be concerned that unless the free trade unions participate in its creation and direction, it may quite easily fall into the hands of other forces and be used for political ends by certain African states and thereby cause a split in the African labour front. With this consideration in view, the Committee recommends that the free trade unions should not take a back seat in the projection, direction and policy-making of a proposed Pan-African trade union federation, provided that the principles of free trade unionism are not compromised.'[1] It was precisely the inability or unwillingness of the promoters of AATUF to recognise and guarantee these 'vital principles' that led to the failure of the founding conference of AATUF in May 1961. Attempts to guarantee these principles by the formation of a rival Pan-African trade union organisation in January 1962 also failed, partly because the African Trade Union Confederation was an amorphous grouping of various tendencies which talked glibly of trade union freedom but lacked the capacity and resources to give meaning to its professions and partly because no government in the so-called Monrovia Group of African States was prepared to do for ATUC what the Nkrumah Government did for AATUF.

Could AFRO have been a more effective organisation for safeguarding free trade union principles and in defence of trade union rights if steps had been taken immediately after the Accra conference of January 1957, to constitute the organisation? Obviously this is a question on which views are bound to differ and have been differing since 1960. Some people have blamed AFRO's ineffectiveness on the failure or refusal of the ICFTU to set it up in 1957. It has been argued that had this been done, AFRO would have been firmly established before the emergence of AATUF, and having been so established it would have been difficult, if not impossible, for AATUF to make any significant inroad to its strength and influence. Those who belong to this school of thought readily point out that it was not until 1964 that a full-time Regional Secretary was elected.

Against these arguments stand certain salient facts which cannot be ignored in an objective analysis of the situation, and tend to show that the problem was not as simple as that. There was undoubtedly a certain amount of hesitation in ICFTU about the establishment of AFRO. Even now it can hardly be said that that hesitation has been completely overcome.

Much more is involved in setting up a regional organisation than the mere passing of resolutions. At least the constituent organisations must show some willingness to support the organisation morally and financially and be prepared to shoulder the responsibilities of office. Between 1957 and 1960 most ICFTU affiliates in Africa were struggling for existence which is itself a *sine qua non* for maintaining a viable organisation. Most had no funds of their own since their affiliates were not paying dues. A good deal were existing because of financial support given by the ICFTU. It was against this background that the ICFTU was eventually persuaded to provide the funds with which AFRO took off the ground. Having done that, it was naturally expected that the responsibilities of running the organisation, determining policies and programmes would have been taken over by the affiliates. It is a sad commentary on ICFTU African affiliates that these responsibilities have hardly been discharged creditably. Declarations supporting ICFTU actions have often been made, but no affiliate has ever fulfilled its financial obligation to AFRO.

Between 1960 and April 1964, AFRO was run by two interim administrative officers mainly because no trade union leader from ICFTU affiliated organisations was willing to come forward to serve as a full-time regional secretary. At the fourth African Regional Conference held in Addis Ababa in April 1964, it appeared that the organisation had been given a new lease of life and a certain degree of dynamism by the election of Mamadou E. Jallow, General Secretary of the Gambia Workers' Union as Regional Secretary. Unfortunately things did not work out that way. 'The administrative abilities of the new Regional Secretary did not match his undoubted verve and capacity for trade union negotiations.... While time was given to him to loosen his bonds with his own country, the Gambia, he continued to devote a considerable amount of his time to that country and not for trade union affairs alone. Nor have his other frequent and long absences been conducive to the efficiency of the work of AFRO head office. ... In short, it has been found that the Regional Secretary's handling of funds entrusted to him on stringent conditions has nevertheless been such that a thorough inquiry has proved indispensable. This inquiry is still going on, but preliminary findings indicate that a considerable sum (approximately £2,750 or US$7,700) entrusted to him for expenses arising out of his functions as Regional Secretary has not been accounted for and there is grave suspicion that in fact it cannot be accounted for.'[2]

The ICFTU Executive Board reacted sharply to these alleged irregularities. At its meeting in Amsterdam in July 1965, it decided to put 'the accumulated body of constitutional rules and regulations in regard to the African regional machinery in latent existence' and directed that henceforth all activities in Africa be carried out from Brussels under the supervision of the General Secretary. In taking that decision, the ICFTU Executive Board made one serious mistake. It did not give AFRO Executive Board, a supposedly autonomous body in relation to its own affairs, an opportunity to examine the conduct of its chief executive officer and suggest what disciplinary action should be taken. Years later, some trade union leaders claimed that their national centres disaffiliated from ICFTU partly because of the way AFRO Executive Board was treated in what became known as the 'Jallow affair' and partly because of the political climate in Africa.

In the seven years which followed the Amsterdam decision of the ICFTU Executive Board, several national centres affiliated to the ICFTU pressed for the reactivation of AFRO. Two problems bedevilled every effort to achieve that objective. The first was an insistence by the ICFTU secretariat that the affiliated organisations should state in writing what they thought a reconstituted AFRO should be doing. The other was a written statement committing the affiliated organisations to supporting AFRO morally and financially. Such committal statement could not be made without creating some sort of forum where the affiliates could meet and discuss matters of common interest. That forum was created in 1967 after a fact-finding tour which the writer undertook following a consultative meeting in Geneva between the ICFTU and representatives of ICFTU affiliated organisations attending that year's ILO conference. A preparatory committee was formed in September charged with the responsibility of preparing the ground for the Fifth African Regional Conference tentatively scheduled for the first quarter of 1968. The Committee held a meeting in Addis Ababa, and made useful recommendations not only on what a reconstituted AFRO should be doing, but also how to finance the organisation. The recommendations covered such matters as defence of trade union rights, stimulation of trade union organisation, training of trade unionists who could be assigned to various areas to assist affiliated organisations in some of their activities and trade union participation in economic and social development of their countries. The area of participation included making proposals regarding the formulation and execution of economic and social development plans, research to aid collective bargaining activities and assisting workers to set up thrift and credit societies in urban and rural areas.

The committee worked out a three-tier organisational structure for AFRO and suggested that because of the precarious financial situation of most affiliated organisations, the existing rate of affiliation dues should be maintained and dues payable to ICFTU be shared between the Confederation and AFRO as follows: ICFTU 25 per cent; AFRO 75 per cent. The arrangement was to come into effect immediately after the Fifth African Regional Conference. In order to encourage affiliates to pay dues the committee recommended that (*a*) only affiliates in good standing or in arrears of dues payment for less than six months should be considered for financial assistance from the ICFTU International Solidarity Fund; (*b*) the existing practice of deducting affiliation dues from ISF grants should be stopped as soon as the arrangement came into operation; (*c*) henceforth AFRO officers should be elected from among candidates sponsored by affiliates in good standing.

Although these recommendations seemed to have met the conditions demanded by the ICFTU secretariat, they did not advance the prospects of reactivating AFRO. It took another four years for that objective to be realised. But by that time developments in the African trade union scene had changed remarkably, so that rather than thinking of how to support and finance AFRO attention was devoted to how to preserve the concept of free and democratic trade unionism in Africa . Since 1972 when AFRO was reconstituted almost all of its meetings have been devoted to the consideration of the best possible strategy to be adopted by ICTFU affiliates at meetings of the Organisation of African Trade Union Unity. Very little, if any, thought had been given to how to build AFRO as a true representative and spokesman of African workers who believe in the principles of free and democratic unionism.

AATUF

The All-African Trade Union Federation (AATUF) was founded in Casablanca, Morocco, in May 1961. The founding conference was marred by the extremely undemocratic procedures adopted by the organisers and their insistence that disaffiliation from international trade union organisations like the ICFTU, WFTU and WCL, must be a condition of membership of AATUF. A meeting of the Preparatory Committee held in Conakry in April 1961, decided that the national trade union centres of Algeria (UGTA), Egypt, Ghana, Guinea, Mali, Morocco, Tunisia and UGTAN should act as 'sponsors' of AATUF, and each sponsoring organisation should be entitled to six delegates at the founding conference. The meeting also decided that 'a mandated commission be established in Casablanca before the opening of the conference to decide on the position and number of representatives of other trade union organisations which might be present at the conference and compile a list of organisations which should be invited and provided with tickets to Casablanca'. That was the basis of giving two delegates to each bona fide trade union organisation not belonging to the Casablanca Group and the same number to such unrepresentative and largely paper organisations like Uganda Federation of Labour, Kenya TUC, Mogadishu TUC, Nigerian Trade Union Congress, Sudan Workers' Trade Union Federation, Liberian Labour Congress, Union of Free Workers of Ethiopia and the Union of the Populations of Angola. Several organisations known to be affiliated to the ICFTU were denied delegate status: their representatives participated as observers.

The Preparatory Secretariat had arrogated to itself the responsibility of determining how the conference was to be run, of verifying the credentials of delegates, of drafting resolutions and determining what should or should not be included in the draft constitution of AATUF. As soon as debate opened on the first item on the agenda (evolution of African trade unionism), Lawrence Borha, General Secretary of the Trade Union Congress (Nigeria) took the floor and challenged the arbitrary manner in which the agenda had been drawn up, standing orders imposed, list of delegates and observers established, and the way in which the Preparatory Secretariat had substituted itself, rather than the Steering Committee, as the governing body of the conference. Mahjoub Ben Seddik, Chairman of the conference, made criticial remarks on Borha's intervention and ruled that no further reference to the points raised by him would be tolerated. His ruling was greeted with wild acclamation, and the conference was, from then on, run by the self-appointed Preparatory Secretriat.

In his report on doctrine and orientation, Mahjoub Ben Seddik strongly advocated 'positive neutralism' and the international solidarity of workers. He criticised 'foreign interference' in African trade union affairs, emphasised the unique and revolutionary character of African trade union movement and made a strong plea for trade union freedom and independence of trade unions from governments and political parties. He stressed the point that the workers of Africa, Asia and Latin America were tied together by special bonds, and rejected the notion that trade unions should be non-political. He also stressed the importance of trade union unity at the national and continental levels and advocated 'free co-operation' with 'foreign organisations'. On the controversial question of international affiliation the report was surprisingly silent. Observers interpreted the silence as Ben Seddik's anxiety that the issue should not be raised in a manner to divide the conference.

Diallo Seydou, the Guinean Ambassador to Cairo and one of the two General Secretaries of UGTAN, presenting a report on joint action, suggested that AATUF should establish a training centre and an organ of propaganda. The report was referred to a committee for detailed consideration, but that committee never met.

The report on activities of the Preparatory Secretariat prepared by John Tettegah, Secretary General of the Ghana TUC, contained several attacks on the ICFTU. Whether by coincidence or design that report was presented at a time when leaders of several ICFTU affiliates were not present as they were attending a meeting of the Committee on Charter (the only committee meeting held while the conference itself was in plenary session). Delegates received copies of the report while Tettegah was speaking, and the report was adopted without debate.

The Committee on Charter, which was presided over by Tom Mboya, General Secretary of the Kenya Federation of Labour, reached agreement on all points except the question of international affiliation. It appeared that the advocates of disaffiliation were ready to make every concession provided they won on that issue. The committee reported on its deliberations whereupon a debate ensued. It lasted a whole day (30 May). Adherents of international affiliation were allowed to speak in the morning, ably defending the principle; some said they were proud of their affiliation to ICFTU. They made passionate appeals that international affiliation should be freely decided upon by each autonomous national centre and warned of the unpleasant consequences which forcing the issue was likely to have on African trade union unity. In the afternoon only those who favoured disaffiliation were allowed to speak. There being no agreement several meetings of heads of delegations were held. Later the chairman asked leaders of delegations to state the position of their organisations. The response varied from those who were strongly in favour of international affiliation, to those who were opposed to the idea, and there were those who declared themselves to be unable to express an opinion without first consulting the governing bodies of their organisations. Tettegah's attempt to interpret the procedure as a vote against international affiliation was rejected by the chairman. Thereafter most of the supporters of international affiliation did not attend the final session of the conference. In their absence it was decided that international affiliation was incompatible with membership of AATUF. National centres affiliated to international trade union organisations were given ten months to terminate such affiliations. This provision was then adopted by acclamation at the final session of the conference.

The Casablanca conference proclaimed the inauguration of the All-African Trade Union Federation, but failed to adopt its constitution which was the last item on the agenda. That item was never discussed. Wide differences surfaced during committee discussions on structure and character of AATUF. The national centres of Egypt, Ghana, Guinea and Mali pressed for a centralised federation with wide powers. Others led by the Senegalese national centre, UGTS, called for a loose federation. No agreement was reached by the committee and no proposals were submitted to the conference. Before the conference was adjourned, Mahjoub Ben Seddik was elected President and John Tettegah and six others were elected secretaries.

An ICFTU delegation which attended the conference as an observer reported that 'there can be no doubt that a vast majority of the conference participants other than those from the organisations of Ghana, Guinea, Mali, Egypt, Morocco and Algeria sharply reacted to the manner in which the conference was conducted and used by a group of organisations for their purposes. There was a general condemnation of the undemocratic and non-representative character of the conference and a desire to counteract propaganda, which had to be expected, that the conference was the expression of genuine views of African labour organisations.'[3] The ICFTU report was confirmed by press statements made by leaders of some of the most important ICFTU affiliates in Africa.

Tom Mboya said that the composition of the Steering Committee was such that non-sponsors were not given an opportunity to direct the conduct of the conference. Secondly, he said that the sponsors invited a lot of splinter and non-existing unions from various African countries and not only gave them prominence out of proportion with their influence in their own countries but also tried to use them to intimidate and demoralise national trade union centres which the sponsors knew would not subserve their aims.

Thirdly, many delegates felt that the chairman conducted the meetings partially and in a way calculated to promote certain ideas and decisions. Fourthly, the conference was packed with members of the public who were neither delegates nor observers and whose main aim was to jeer and heckle some delegations. In that type of atmosphere no decisions could be reached, and the conference reached deadlock on almost every issue. Denying that he and others who left in disgust deliberately wrecked the conference, Mboya declared, 'We have some basic principles which we hold and are not willing to be bullied or coerced out of them ... one point that we must pose and which many leaders still ask is—who will finance AATUF especially now that two political blocs are emerging among the African states, and whether if financed by either bloc, AATUF would be used as a political weapon against some states in Africa.'[4]

Ahmed Tlili, General Secretary of the Tunisian trade union federation, UGTT, referred to delegates 'who have lost touch with African workers and who for most part live in Eastern countries ... some have no independence at all and are rather leaders imposed by their governments. They came to the conference to make the views of their governments prevail, thus accentuating the already existing divisions between African states, divisions which do much to foment the cold war.'

Lawrence Borha, General Secretary of the Trades Union Congress (Nigeria), described the Casablanca conference as a complete failure, the decisions reached being the opinion of three countries—Ghana, Guinea and the United Arab Republic (Egypt), and Ghana having spent much money and effort to make them possible. It was obvious, he continued, that the decisions were not taken by bona fide African trade union representatives but by splinter groups, individuals representing no body but themselves and hired hooligans. That was why credentials were not checked. Under no circumstances would Ghana, Guinea and the UAR who represented not more than 300,000 workers impose their thinking on the rest of African workers. The TUC(N), he declared, endorsed the statement recently attributed to Tom Mboya that African trade union centres would not be obliged to abide by the decisions of the conference.

Six days after the Casablanca conference (6 June 1961), Tettegah issued a press statement in which he declared a 'total war' on African trade unions which refused to disaffiliate from international trade union organisations. 'We shall isolate them, break them, enter their countries and form AATUF unions there,' he said; 'It's simple as that—total war.'

AATUF held its second conference in Bamako, Mali, in June 1964. That conference made significant changes in the Charter adopted by the Casablanca conference and for the first time adopted AATUF constitution. Under Chapter IV, 'The Role of African Trade Unionism in the Building of a New Africa', it was stated that 'our role is first of all political.' Article VII provided that 'AATUF shall be independent of all governments and of all political or religious bodies.' But how did AATUF abide by the provisions of its Charter and Constitution? Eight days after the Bamako conference, Tettegah, AATUF's newly elected General Secretary, addressed a secret memorandum to President Nkrumah saying 'although the AATUF on the surface must appear to be an international organisation subservient to no single government, my election as Secretary General enables Ghana to manipulate the whole organisation by subtle means. I am no independent Secretary General, but a mere instrument of the Convention People's Party and the Osagyefo's [Nkrumah's] policy. Methods of work can be devised to achieve Ghana's political manipulation of the AATUF without other countries discovering our designs.'[5] The memorandum outlined the methods of work as follows:

(a) An announcement would be made at a most convenient time and the most psychological moment that AATUF was a non-governmental international organisation, and the Ghana Government, in response to AATUF's secretariat request, would grant the organisation an international status as had been done to the FAO, UNESCO and other international organisations then having their regional offices in Accra. The necessary protocol would be signed, and AATUF's name would be included in the Diplomatic List.

(b) Tettegah would be granted a three-year leave of absence during which time he would devote his 'full-time and energy to creating an apparatus of an international organisation which must compare in efficiency and status to the ICFTU and WFTU'.

(c) Responsibility for national trade union affairs must be put firmly into the hands of J. K. Ampah as National Secretary of the Ghana Trades Union Congress.

(d) The National Secretary must forget about international politics of the TUC and leave that responsibility to the Director of the International Department who would head my 'Ghanaian underground outfit' operating in the name of Ghana TUC.

(e) During Tettegah's absence from Ghana, the Director of International Department should replace him on the African Affairs Committee and other Government bodies or Party Committees where Ghana's African policy were formulated and executed. 'He reports directly to me as the instrument of Osagyefo's African policy.'

(*f*) In order to avoid any misunderstanding with particular reference to the functions of the Director of International Department, the position should be made very clear to the new leaders of the TUC.

(*g*) Ghana's underground outfit should continuè to be financed from the allocation already made to AATUF of £G30,000 per annum.

The document concluded as follows: 'I am only a humble and most obedient soldier of the Osagyefo's revolution who executes every assignment with fanatical loyalty and I can swear on oath by the shrines of my ancestors that life for me will be meaningless if it cannot be spent in the service of Osagyefo and by his side.'[6] In due course Tettegah became Minister Plenipotentiary and Ambassador Extraordinary of the Government of Ghana.

In February 1965, the AATUF Executive Bureau approved a budget of £G246,540. Of this amount only £G54,000 was to be derived from affiliation dues. Tettegah was authorised by the Bureau to try to obtain the difference of £G192,540 from 'friendly socialist governments and friendly socialist organisations'. In his *Trade Unions in Chains* (p. 33), B. A. Bentum asks, 'Where now are even the vestiges of the façade, so carefully maintained by Tettegah, that AATUF was non-aligned? What friendly socialist government or friendly socialist organisation would provide this kind of money without a commitment in return?'

The same day that Tettegah addressed his memorandum to Nkrumah he also addressed another entitled 'The New Phase of AATUF in Africa' to the Presidential African Affairs Committee outlining plans to subvert African trade unions. The memo said that there could be no doubt that Ghana would give AATUF its political direction. 'Our Accra based headquarters', it continued, 'will only serve as a subterfuge apparatus subservient to the will of Osagyefo, but this must be kept secret.' To achieve that objective AATUF was to rely not only on the financial subscriptions of member organisations, etc., but, more important, on grants from the Governments of Ghana and the Soviet Union. In July 1965, President Nkrumah approved £G10,000 from his Contingency Vote for AATUF activities in Congo (Brazzaville), Dahomey (now the Republic of Benin), the Gambia, Senegal, Sierra Leone, Togo and Upper Volta. Part of this allocation was to be transferred to dissident groups in the countries concerned and part to Ghana Diplomatic Missions for onward transmission to the appropriate groups.

A rumour that Milton Obote's Government was about to seize the ICFTU African Labour College in Kampala was received with glee in Accra. Nkrumah promised AATUF £G20,000 to help defray administrative expenses. Tettegah himself was reported as promising Uganda's former Minister of Labour, George Magezi, more funds from the WFTU if the alleged intention to sequestrate the college was carried out. This sequestration did not take place, however, until four years later. Reports of the emergence of a splinter organisation in the Uganda trade union movement inspired Tettegah to send a monthly subsidy of £G500 to sustain the split. Even when the FUTU could no longer exist, Tettegah continued the subvention for another three months hoping that Magezi would grant FUTU affiliates compulsory check-off.

In Kenya, AATUF offered the splinter Kenya Federation of Progressive Trade Unions (KFPTU) 50 motorcycles, 6 typewriters, 4 duplicating machines and paid office rent of £120 per month for several months. In addition £2,000 was transferred to an official of the Ghana High Commission in Nairobi to channel to the KFPTU.

In February 1966, the Nkrumah Government was overthrown by a military coup. The effect of the coup on AATUF was tremendous. Not only did the reconstituted TUC of Ghana withdraw from it, but it also lost its greatest financial supporter. At its extraordinary congress in May 1966, AATUF decided to shift its headquarters to Dar-es-Salaam, capital of Tanzania. Mahjoub Ben Seddik was re-elected President and Famady Sissoko of Mali succeeded Tettegah as Secretary General. Tettegah himself turned volte-face and denounced Osagyefo the President as one of the greatest crooks he had ever known. Journalists and other members of the public who attended his press conference in Accra soon after Nkrumah's fall from power later commented on the two Tettegahs in Ghana—Tettegah the fanatical Nkrumaist who was the 'instrument of Osagyefo's African policy' and Tettegah the public relations promoter painting his master black in order to save his own skin.

In March 1969, AATUF and WFTU held a joint conference in Conakry, Guinea, to develop a joint struggle against 'imperialist monopolies'. The conference resolved to set up a 'WFTU/AATUF Liaison and Coordination Committee' the functions of which were to promote the common struggle, to ensure a wide exchange of information and experience, to promote bilateral contacts between national centres and to reinforce indispensable trade links. AATUF held two other conferences before it ceased to exist following the inauguration in 1973 of the Organisation of African Trade Union Unity.

ATUC
Convinced that the Casablanca conference was a dismal failure,

certain trade union leaders, notably Ahmed Tlili of Tunisia, Tom Mboya of Kenya and Lawrence Borha of Nigeria, decided to explore the possibilities of setting up a genuine Pan-African trade union organisation in response to the decision of the All-African People's Conferences of 1958 and 1960. In June 1961 they held an exploratory meeting with African workers' delegates attending the 45 Session of the ILO Conference. That meeting agreed to convene a Pan-African trade union conference in Dakar, Senegal, in August, at which the African Trade Union Confederation was to be inaugurated. It was also agreed that all national trade union centres were to be invited, that the agenda, programme of work as well as other matters of procedure be determined at a meeting of heads of delegations. The conference was to consider the draft consititution of the organisation, examine the social, economic, political and trade union problems of African states and try to reach agreement democratically, avoiding as much as possible questions likely to create divisions.

Plans to hold the conference in August failed owing to certain difficulties. When it eventually convened in January 1962, forty national centres from thirty countries were represented. They included affiliates of the ICFTU, International Federation of Christian Trade Unions, the Pan-African Congress of Believing Workers (CATC) and several unaffiliated organisations. In spite of differences in orientation, they shared one thing in common: adherence to the principles of free and democratic unionism. None of the national centres from the Casablanca Group of African States attended the conference. Indeed, before and during the conference the AATUF secretariat was busy attacking its sponsors as imperialist stooges trying to divide African workers.

The founding conference adopted the ATUC's constitution and a series of resolutions pledging the ATUC's support for the total liberation of the African continent from colonial rule and white minority rule in Southern Africa. The conference declared itself in favour of creating socialist societies in Africa and of democratic systems of government. Stress was laid on the need for unity among the working peoples of Africa, and the Executive was mandated to do all it could to attain trade union unity in the continent. Ahmed Tlili was elected President and David Soumah of CATC, Senegal, was elected General Secretary.

The emergence of ATUC signified an open split in the African trade union movement. In the months and years that followed one question dominated the thinking of union leaders in almost every African country and that was how to achieve trade union unity in the continent on a basis acceptable to everybody and safeguarding the autonomy of national trade union centres. The problem was complicated by the division in the political scene with the Casablanca and Monrovia Groups of African states peddling Pan-Africanism and each group trying to impress public opinion that solution to African problems could only be found through its own devices. Exploratory talks held between ATUC and AATUF in October 1963 on trade union unity broke down because of AATUF's intransigence on the question of international affiliation. An ATUC circular letter reporting on the outcome of the meeting said that 'there was a distinct feeling that what was preoccupying the Casablanca group was purely and simply the desire to come out of the meeting with a statement on formal disaffiliation from the international confederations.'

Following the breakdown of the October 1963 talks, ATUC sent a three-man delegation to the Second Summit conference of Heads of States and Governments held in Cairo in 1964 to explain the Confederation's activities and its stand on the question of African trade union unity. Members of the delegation were Ahmed Tlili, President; L. L. Borha, Vice President; and Bassirou Gueye, Administrative Secretary of ATUC. During the meeting Ghana tried to get the Heads of States and Governments to accord recognition to AATUF as the only Pan-African trade union organisation to represent African workers. That manoeuvre failed thanks to the strong case made by the ATUC delegation and the intervention of several friendly delegations.

ATUC held its second congress in Lagos in October 1965. One of the most important subjects discussed by that congress was Pan-African trade union unity. Several speakers stressed the importance of unity particularly since the problem of political disunity had been solved by the founding of the Organisation of African Unity (OAU). While agreeing that unity was desirable and indeed imperative, many others pointed out that in order to be effective and lasting, African trade union unity must be founded on the recognition of the independence and autonomy of the con-stituent organisations. The congress expressed the view that continental trade union unity ought to be founded on the indepen-dence and liberty of each affiliated organisation to determine its own destiny in keeping with ILO Convention 87 and the provisions of the OAU Charter forbidding interference in the domestic affairs of member states. The congress then mandated its Executive Board to negotiate Pan-African labour unity on the basis of the principles outlined above. Before it ended the congress elected the following officers: L. L. Borha, President; Bechir Bellagha of the UGTT, Vice President; and David Soumah, Administrative Secretary.

Very little is known of ATUC activities after the Lagos congress. Apart from periodical statements declaring its stand on Pan-African labour unity, very little was done in furtherance of its aims and objects. The reasons are not far to seek. Affiliates did not pay dues. Most of them were merely trying to exist. Some owed their continued existence on the sufferance of international labour organisations and aid agencies interested in trade union development. ATUC came into existence with the aid of these organisations, and it was expected that having been set up the affiliated organisations would take over the responsibility of running and financing it. As none seemed interested and as the cry for labour unity grew wider the original backers developed cold feet. Moreover, a powerful lobby had emerged in the international trade union movement and among some of the powerful national centres in Europe and North America which felt that the Africans should be left alone to develop whatever type of trade union movement they thought was suitable to the realities of the African situation. In the circumstance financial assistance was withdrawn. One other factor may be considered. As had been stated earlier, no government in the Monrovia Group of African states was prepared to do for the ATUC what the Nkrumah Government did for the AATUF mainly because none had the same ambitions as Nkrumah. A few governments which were sympathetic to the ATUC could not help because they believed that such an assistance would subvert its independence.

Following the founding of the OAU, governments and union leaders felt that unity ought also to be attained in a similar manner in the trade union movement. Aiding one organisation against the other no matter how likeable that organisation might be, would be perpetuating disunity. In February 1966, the African Labour Ministers' Conference discussed what role the trade unions should play in the development of African states. It was agreed that member states should study the question closely so that concrete proposals could be presented to the next meeting scheduled in February 1967, in Nairobi. Since the founding of OAU, African governments have been thinking that a parallel organisation should be set up in the trade union field so that it could work 'co-operatively with the OAU' in developing the continent. It was in pursuit of that objective that the OAU, through its Administrative Secretary General, took a series of initiatives which culminated in the founding of the Organisation of African Trade Union Unity in April, 1973.

OATUU

The founding in 1973 of the Organisation of African Trade Union Unity (OATUU) is the crowning event of a nine-year effort made by the OAU to create a 'non-aligned' trade union organisation which could co-operate with it in developing the African continent. When the question was first discussed by the Council of Ministers in Lagos in February 1964, AFRO submitted a memorandum pointing out that 'the key question which complicates negotiations for trade union unity concerns respect for the right of each national centre to decide for itself what its international affiliation should be. In short, is membership of an international trade union federation extending beyond the borders of Africa inconsistent with or contrary to the idea of African unity?' That question was unanswered and was not answered by subsequent conferences (Cairo, July 1964; and Accra, October 1965) which stressed the necessity of trade union unity.

In September 1967, a resolution on labour adopted by the Council of Ministers and Heads of States invited the OAU Administrative Secretary General to service previous resolutions of the Conference of Labour Ministers by sending invitations to national trade union centres to attend a unity conference, preparing if necessary and desirable, any documents in connection with the agenda and co-ordinating the activities of the conference, 'it being understood that the expenses incurred in connection with the above-named points as well as the physical organisation of the conference will be at the expense of the host organisation.' The resolution urged the Administrative Secretary General to continue his activities aimed at organising a meeting, before 30 April 1968, for the unification of the African trade union movement.

On 22 October 1969, *Marchés Tropicaux et Méditerranéens* published a news item reporting a meeting between the AATUF and ATUC at which unity was discussed. It was stated that agreement had been reached, and a document to that effect was signed in the presence of Diallo Telli, OAU Administrative Secretary General, by Bissarou Gueye (Senegal) and Faye Malik (Mauritania) on behalf of the ATUC and Oumezaine (Algeria), Techtali (Morocco) and Melangwen (Tanzania) on behalf of the AATUF. The document said to have been signed stated, among other things, that 'the delegations give their total support to the achievement of a united African trade union movement and the constitution of one Pan-African trade union centre, independent, anti-colonialist and anti-imperialist, grouping all the national trade union organisations disaffiliated from all the non-African international centres'. It was also reported that both delegations agreed to call, in July 1969, a meeting of the preparatory committee which was to be composed of the representatives of the secretariats of the AATUF and ATUC. The preparatory committee was to draft the programme, constitution, doctrine and orientation of the new organisation which was to be inaugurated in Dakar in March 1970.

It became clear later that the meeting at which these decisions were made had not been discussed by the governing bodies of the organisations; that the gentlemen who claimed to be representing the ATUC had no authority to commit the organisation in the way they did. Apparently unaware of these irregularities the African Labour Ministers meeting in Algiers in March 1969 adopted yet another resolution on labour unity. The resolution 'noting with satisfaction the agreement reached in Algiers on 12 March between the duly empowered delegates of the AATUF and ATUC, invited both organisations and all African trade unionists to exert every effort to implement the agreement'. It did not advance the prospects of unity. Many more efforts were made without success until November 1972, when the Preparatory Committee eventually met in Addis Ababa. That meeting was attended by the representatives of the AATUF and unaffiliated national trade union centres. The ATUC was not represented. An exploratory meeting held in Geneva earlier had agreed that the AATUF, ATUC and unaffiliated organisations should be represented at the Preparatory Committee meeting by four delegates each. The meeting elected the following officers: Lancine Sylla (Guinea), head of the AATUF delegation, Chairman; Dennis Akumu (Kenya) representative of the unaffiliated organisations, Vice Chairman; and Satougle Defith Moise, (Cameroun), Rapporteur. The meeting had only two items on its agenda: consideration of the draft constitution submitted by the OAU secretariat and any other matters.

Speaker after speaker regretted the absence of the ATUC delegation and appealed to the OAU secretariat to send an urgent messege urging them to come. It was agreed to suspend session for some hours pending the outcome of the message. When the meeting resumed differences arose over the old question of international affiliation. According to the report of the meeting prepared by the OAU secretariat, 'the committee agreed to condemn double affiliation which is incompatible with the aim of unity.' However, a representative of the Confederation of Ethiopian Labour Unions expressed reservations on the committee's stand on international affiliation, and added that his organisation was proud of its affiliation to the ICFTU. Some members wondered whether in the light of the position taken by CELU the founding congress should still take place in Addis Ababa as was originally planned.

ATUC representatives comprising Mohamed Ezzedine of the UGTT and Robel of the Christian outfit in Madagascar eventually arrived on the third day, and were elected Second Vice Chairman and Assistant Rapporteur respectively. Ezzedine blamed their lateness on communication breakdown between OAU secretariat and the ATUC. The ATUC, he said, received only one letter that the meeting would be held in November 1972. Having finally arrived the ATUC delegation would do its utmost to make a positive contribution to the work of the committee. Members welcomed the speech, and it was agreed that the ATUC delegation could propose amendments to the preamble, aims and objectives of the Charter, which had already been adopted. Unfortunately no amendments were proposed, and the draft Charter as prepared by the OAU Secretariat was endorsed. The draft Charter was more or less word for word adoption of the Charter adopted by AATUF at its second congress in Bamako in 1964.

A few national centres reacted sharply to the report of the Preparatory Committee. The CIO of Liberia said that the Committee exceeded its powers by (a) accepting a draft charter prepared by the OAU secretariat which is not a trade union body; (b) changing the venue of the founding congress from Addis Ababa to Yaounde without prior consultation with national trade union centres and (c) starting the Preparatory Committee meeting in the absence of ATUC delegation. The Sierra Leone Labour Congress pointed out that African Governments and employers had their international affiliation with the UN, ILO, the Commonwealth and multinational companies. Moreover the OAU Charter permitted African states irrespective of their leanings to become members of the OAU. While governments and employers were allowed to enjoy the right of international affiliation that right was being denied to trade unions.

The inaugural congress was eventually held in Addis Abada in April 1973, under the auspicies of the OAU. The draft charter and constitution were adopted, but it was agreed that the question of international affiliation be put off for consideration at another congress. That other congress was held in Tripoli, Libya, in April 1976. Delegates assessed OATUU activities since the founding congress and what it planned to do in the future. One question which took much time and generated a lot of heat was, once again, international affiliation. Several delegates including those whose organisations were affiliated to international trade union organisations as well as those from unaffiliated organisations maintained that Article 8 of the OATUU Charter infringed trade union autonomy and violated the principles enshrined in ILO Convention 87. The Sierra Leone Labour Congress suggested that Article 8 be amended to include a provision that the OATUU 'shall be composed of African trade union organisations whose autonomy, national and international policies, shall not be prejudiced by virtue of their membership.' The proposal was accepted by the Preparatory Committee and later by the General Council, and included in the agenda.

What promised to be a good congress was marred by the decision of the Credentials Committee to deprive certain organisations, including some of the founding members of OATUU, of the right to vote or to stand for election to the Executive Board on the ground that there were more than one national trade union centre in their countries. The 'problem of plurality' as it was popularly known, was discussed at length, and the Steering Committee, basing its argument on that provision of the constitution which said that the OATUU shall recognise one national trade union centre in each country, decided to draw a set of principles which should be adhered to when considering the case of the countries involved: the Gambia, Lesotho, Liberia, Madagascar, Mauritius, Morocco, Sierra Leone, Sudan and Upper Volta. These principles were:

None of the countries with plural organisations would be allowed to stand for election as a member of the Executive. If the plural organisations in each country could agree among themselves to have a single spokesman, they would be permitted to exercise their right to speak and vote but not to stand for election as a member of the Executive.

Those which agreed to come together and have a single spokesman would exercise their voting right only if they had paid their dues, and it would be their responsibility to agree in whose name the dues should be paid.

The Mediation Committee should discharge its responsibility of effecting unity where there are plural organisations and the Executive should provide the necessary facilities to enable it to accomplish its task. Within a year, the Mediation Committee should present a progress report to the General Council.

Where the Mediation Committee found it difficult to get plural organisations to unite, it should recommend in its report that the most representative organisation be admitted as a member of the OATUU.

Guided by these principles, the Steering Committee made what certain observers described as a fair decision in some cases and a harsh and unjustified one in respect of Lesotho, Liberia and Sierra Leone. Lesotho has two national centres: the Basutoland Federation of Labour founded in the late 'fifties with a paid up membership of a little more than 6,000, and the Lesotho Council of Workers founded in 1963 with a paid up membership of about 3,000. The General Secretary of BFL was then in exile in Botswana, but the other officers were operating in Lesotho. OATUU sent invitation to the congress to Lesotho Council of Workers but BFL was not invited. Its representative came nevertheless mainly to state the Federation's case that it was the more representative organisation. In spite of this the Steering Committee recommended that the Council of Workers be recognised arguing that it would have created a dangerous precedent if one of the two organisations was not recognised.

The CIO of Liberia and the Sierra Leone Labour Congress were founding members of OATUU. At the time of the founding congress in 1973, only one national centre existed in Liberia and Sierra Leone. The rival organisations which emerged in both countries before 1976 were not members of the OATUU and there was no evidence that before the Tripoli meeting they had sought membership. In the circumstance it would appear to be rough justice for the Steering Commitee to deprive the CIO and SLLC of their right to vote and be voted for. The decision was particularly reprehensible in the case of SLLC because the splinter organisation, the Sierra Leone Council of Labour, was not even present at the meeting and no invitation was extended to it. It was no surprise therefore that shortly after the Tripoli meeting the SLLC decided to disaffiliate from the OATUU. The decision caused a great surprise in OATUU secretariat and forced the General Secretary, Dennis Akumu, to make a hurried visit to Freetown in an effort to persuade the Minister of Labour to pressurise the Congress to rescind its decision. The trip was a failure, the Minister telling his guest that he had no power to compel the organisation to change its decision.

A. E. O. Nyyueque, OAU Assistant Secretary General, addressed the Tripoli meeting. Noting proudly that the number of affiliates had increased from twenty-eight to forty-six including five liberation movements, he expressed the hope that the eight national centres which still maintained international affiliation would take steps to sever the connection as it compromised OATUU's independence. OATUU Secretary General, Dennis Akumu, expressed the same hope when speaking on the report on activities and named the organisations concerned. If naming the organisations was intended to embarrass them, he seemed to have failed as the delegates of the organisations concerned felt proud that they were the only organisations in the continent which enjoyed the right to determine their policies freely and without intimidation or coercion from governments, political parties or the armed forces.

The greatest joke of the second congress came during the election of officers. Immediately after the last item from the Resolutions Committee was disposed of, the chairman declared the existing Executive Committee dissolved, and the members left the rostrum. He called upon members of the OAU secretariat to conduct fresh elections. The returning officer than called upon S. E. Doudou Ngom, Senegal's Minister of Labour, to make a proposition. Ngom made a long speech and later proposed Nefishi of Libya as the new President of OATUU. This was greeted with applause, and Ngom smilingly said that he had been encouraged to go on. He then named Dennis Akumu as General Secretary and E. O. A. Odeyemi of Nigeria as Treasurer. He went on to name the countries from which Vice-Presidents and Assistant Secretaries were to come from and to complete his list he named Uganda and Central African Empire as Auditor and Assistant Auditor respectively. Mali was to provide the chairman of the newly created Conciliation Committee. After completing the list the OAU returning officer called upon Alfred Tandau, Tanzania's Minister of Communication, to say a few words, which were merely seconding Doudou Ngom's propositions. Two delegates, one from Guinea and the other from Mali, spoke, after which the OAU presiding officer declared all the persons and the countries named as duly elected. Thus ended the second OATUU congress. The third congress was scheduled for 1980.

PART 2

Promise and Performance

8. AFRICAN TRADE UNIONS AT WORK

Organisation

Trade Union organisation has changed remarkably in pattern and style since the attainment of independence by most African states. The old pattern of organisation on a craft or plant basis during the early development of trade unions has largely given away to organisation on an industrial and general workers' basis, though there are a few countries (Ethiopia, Mauritius, and the Seychelles for example) where the old pattern still exists. Similarly, the traditional method of recruitment—approaching workers, trying to persuade them to join the union and eventually convincing them to do so by paying their entrance fee and obtaining their membership cards—has been replaced in many places by merely giving the prospective members check-off authorisation forms to complete and sign. Three factors would appear to be responsible for the change. The first is the law, which we shall be considering in greater detail later. Before independence, the Trade Unions Ordinance of certain countries (Kenya, Malawi, Tanganyika, Uganda and Zambia for example) empowered the Registrar of Trade Unions to refuse the registration of a new union if he was satisfied that the workers to be represented were adequately represented by an existing registered union. That provision has become a common feature of most trade union laws passed or promulgated since independence. Its omission in the Trade Unions Ordinance of other countries (like Ghana and Nigeria) coupled with the small number of persons required to register a union were often blamed for the multiplicity of trade unions in these countries before the introduction of Ghana's Industrial Relations Act 1958.

The second factor responsible for the change appears to be sound judgment and expatriate advice. In those countries where the law empowered the Registrar of Trade Unions to refuse registration in the circumstance outlined above, the unions, acting partly of their own volition and judgment and partly on the advice of expatriates sent by the international trade union movement to assist in organising and collective bargaining, adopted industrial unionism as a pattern of organisation so as to minimise the incidence of poaching and jurisdictional disputes. Another reason was to increase their membership potential. In the Gambia and Liberia the workers adopted a general workers' pattern of organisation because of the special circumstances of the two countries—the size of the countries and the workforce.

The third, and probably the most important factor, appears to be Ghana's controversial Industrial Relations Act 1958, which created the Ghana Trades Union Congress and replaced the ninety-four craft and house unions representing a total membership of 71,149[1] with twenty-four national industrial unions. Addressing the Ghana Parliament in December 1958, the Minister of Labour and Co-operatives said that the main reason for introducing the law was to create 'a strong centralised trade union, whose central body is recognised by the Government and is given certain powers and duties, and over which the Government would be able to exercise some supervision and to ensure that these powers were not abused'.[2] The Act is divided into six parts covering such things as the TUC and its constituent national industrial unions, collective bargaining by certified trade unions, settlement of industrial disputes involving certified unions, strikes and lock-outs, and unfair labour practices. No specific provision is made regarding union recognition, though it is implied in the provisions in Part II covering collective bargaining by certified trade unions. The law introduced check-off and gave legal recognition to union shop. Under section 40 (2) of the Act check-off was applicable to employees who were members of a union, and an employee could contract out of it. An amending Act of 1965 removed that right, and made check-off virtually compulsory.

Politicians and governments of newly independent states who claimed to be interested in securing trade union co-operation in the economic and social development of their countries, particularly the working arrangement which enabled the ruling parties and governments to exercise a domineering influence and control over the trade union movement, found the 'new unionism' in Ghana and the law which created it an object of emulation. At that time Ghana had a tremendous influence in Africa. Being the first black African country to achieve independence and the venue of a number of Pan-African conferences which had stressed the importance of 'African Personality' in various fields of human endeavour, she was considered in many things to be a pattern setter for Africa. The developments in Ghana had their greatest impact on East and Central Africa whose leaders were great admirers of President

Nkrumah and his Government. In 1964 Tanzania followed Ghana's example by creating NUTA by an Act of Parliament. The following year Zambia established ZCTU by law. In 1966 the Kenya Government followed the examples of its neighbours by creating COTU in a similar manner. Uganda completed the process in East Africa by establishing a Uganda Labour Congress on the NUTA style, although the military take over in 1971 prevented the enforcement of that law. (In 1974, however, President Amin's Government promulgated a new trade union law which established the National Organisation of Trade Unions (Uganda) with sixteen national industrial unions.)

In the course of research for this work, questionnaires were prepared and sent to individual unions and national centres in English-speaking Africa and also to international trade secretariats with a view to ascertaining from the unions themselves what they have been doing in the various fields of trade union activity. Interesting disclosures were made in the replies received. Most of the unions which replied reported tremendous increases in their membership during the decade 1965–75. Among them are the United Food and Allied Workers' Union of Rhodesia (600 in 1965; 9,803 in 1975) and the National Union of Plantation and Agricultural Workers of Zambia (2,500 in 1965; 10,000 in 1975). Some others like the Zambia Railway Workers' Union, the National Union of Clerical, Commercial and Technical Employees of Uganda, and the African Timber and Plywood Workers' Union of Nigeria suffered a decline in membership during the period owing to redundancies, retirements and reorganisation. According to the replies most unions do not require a pledge of fidelity from their members and officers. In some unions office-bearers constitute the majority at the national, district and branch executive: in others non-office-bearers constitute the majority. Some unions devote between 10 and 25 per cent of their annual budget to organising. Of all the unions which replied only one had a provision in its budget for benefit schemes for its members. No union made a provision for strike fund, and only three made provisions for research, ranging from 1 to 6 per cent of the budget. All made provision for audit, and a few for reserves.

While encouraging progress has been made in the development of individual unions, the same thing cannot be said of the national trade union centres. This is probably due to the degree of solidarity among the workers, the financial position of individual unions and the role which the national centres play or are expected to play in the various countries. The only viable centres in Africa at present are either those created by law and whose sources of income are guaranteed by check-off and direct remittance from source or those which are closely tied to the ruling parties or governments and in consequence receive regular subventions from them. Centres created by the unions themselves either exist only on paper because of lack of financial support from their affiliates or owe their existence to grants made by the international trade union movement or 'aid' agencies interested in helping African trade unions.

Education

Workers' education—or, to be more precise, trade union education—has long been recognised as an effective tool for the building of strong and viable trade unions. Workers will form or join trade unions, support them morally and financially, and render service according to their abilities if they have a sound knowledge of what unions are, how they operate and how they help to protect and promote their economic and social interests. How do African trade unions utilise this tool in developing their organisations? In considering this question, a distinction must be made between educational activities organised and financed by the unions themselves, those organised by the unions in co-operation with other organisations and jointly financed by the co-operating parties, and those organised and wholly financed by international trade union organisations, inter-governmental agencies and international development agencies created by certain governments in Europe and North America.

There are very few educational activities that come within the first of these categories. The majority of the unions which answered the questionnaire of 1975 claimed they had their own education programmes which they organised and financed by themselves. Education took between 3 and 20 per cent of their annual budget. Since less than 25 per cent of the unions replied, the information given here must be treated with caution. The low level of self-financed educational activity among African unions is due largely to the fact that most unions are yet to accept trade union education as an integral part of normal trade union activity. There are, however, a few countries where individual unions and national centres recognise the importance of education and have been doing something in that field mainly with the financial assistance and expertise from the international trade union movement and international development agencies. Botswana, Ghana, Gabon, Ivory Coast, Kenya, Mauritius, Nigeria (up until 1975), Sierra Leone, Zaire and Zambia are examples.

In Botswana, the African–American Labour Centre built a trade union education centre in 1971 which is being used to conduct basic trade union education for members, branch officials and shop stewards. The AALC finances the courses and pays the salaries and social charges of the secretary, organiser and secretarial staff of the centre. On the founding of the Botswana Federation of Trade Unions in April 1977, the centre was donated to the Federation for its educational work. The ICFTU, the Friedrich Ebert Stiftung and the Norwegian trade union federation, LO, have also carried out educational programmes in Botswana.

After the overthrow of the Nkrumah Government, the AALC helped the Ghana TUC to establish the Ghana Labour College, and for some years provided tutorial and administrative staff. The TUC has now taken over tutorial and administrative responsibilities, but financial support is still being received from the AALC. In order to secure adequate financial resources for its educational activities, the Gabonese national centre, FESYGA, requested the Gabonese Government to legislate for a compulsory check-off. The request was granted, and since 1975 FESYGA has been financing most of its education programmes, although occasionally courses and seminars are jointly organised with the international trade union movement. Ivory Coast and Central African Empire are reported to have followed FESYGA's example, but details of their own arrangements are unknown.

In Kenya, COTU signed an agreement with the AALC in 1975 under which the Americans undertook to help it implement its education programme for five years. Under the agreement the AALC is to finance most of COTU's education programme during the period, and pay the salary and social charges of the Education Director and his staff. In addition the Americans will help COTU build a labour college in Kisumu, which the unions hope to maintain from the proceeds of an education levy (probably the first of its kind in Africa) which the Kenya Government has authorised by an administrative order. The education levy is operated like check-off, but the worker is not required to sign an authorisation as a condition of making the deduction. The proceeds of the education levy are paid into a special fund administered by the Government.

The Mauritius Labour Congress has an active Education Committee which determines policy and programmes, selects candidates for scholarships and participants for courses and seminars organised in and outside the country. Education is carried out on a continuing basis, and programmes include courses for rural workers, women, branch and national union officials. Most of the programmes are financed from external sources, but the courses and seminars are usually conducted by the ICFTU, ITS, FES representatives and local union officials. Occasionally there is an input from the academic staff of the University and senior Government officials.

Until 1965, workers' education in Nigeria was organised and financed by the ICFTU, ITS, the Federal Ministry of Labour and the Extra-Mural Departments of some of the older universities. In 1966 the United Labour Congress of Nigeria, concluded an agreement with the AALC which led to the establishment, later that year, of the Trade Union Institute for Economic and Social Development popularly known as the TUI. Later, the WFTU helped its affiliate, the Nigerian Trade Union Congress, to establish the Patrice Lumumba Academy. Both institutions existed until 1975 when they were closed down on the orders of the Nigerian Government. In 1972, Nigerian representatives at the Pan-African Seminar on Trade Union Education Policy (Lagos, 7–11 February) reported that 351 trade unionists had attended TUI's residential courses of three and four months' duration and 3,800 others had participated in short courses of one week's duration organised by the Institute's staff in various parts of the country.

A workers' education association existed in Sierra Leone in the early 'sixties and became moribund following the split which occurred in the trade union movement in 1963. When unity was again achieved no attempt was made to revive the association. At present, the Sierra Leone Labour Congress has an Education Department headed by a director, who has two assistants. All three are honorary officers. Individual unions like the Clerical, Mercantile and General Workers, the United Mine Workers and Railway Workers, have their own education programmes which are financed and conducted by the unions. The greater part of educational activity is carried out by the ICFTU, ITS and other agencies as aids for the Sierra Leone Labour Congress.

Zaire and Zambia are two countries where the unions devote a good deal of their financial resources to education. In Zaire, the national centre, UNTZa, has a comprehensive education programme covering the training of trade union educators, full-time national officers, organisers, shop stewards, committee members and the rank and file membership. Between June 1967 and December 1971, the UNTZa organised 247 courses attended by 7,852 participants.[3] In Zambia, workers' education took a positive turn following a policy decision which the ZCTU General Council made in December 1970. That decision was reinforced by a provision in the Industrial Relations Act 1971, requiring the provision of workers' education as one of the main aims and objects which must be included in the constitution of every union. In 1970 Mindolo Ecumenical Foundation established a Commerce and

Industry Division whose main functions were to conduct training courses for workers and management representatives. The Foundation requested the ZCTU to nominate a workers' educator to join their staff whose salary and social charges were to be jointly paid by the Foundation and the ZCTU. The Congress nominated Herbert Silungwe of the National Union of Local Authorities Workers. The ZCTU then decided that provision be made in the budgets of its affiliated unions to finance workers' education. Silungwe worked with the Mindolo Ecumenical Foundation for a year and left to take up a fulltime appointment as Director of the ZCTU's Department of Workers' Education. The Department runs courses and seminars for shop stewards and branch officials, committee members and national officers. It pays all expenses including compensation for loss of wages incurred by participants who are released by their employers without pay. In its 1977 budget, the ZCTU provided as much as K85,000 for workers' education.

The bulk of trade union educational activities in Africa falls under the third category. The greatest part of it has been done and continues to be done by the ICFTU and the ITS associated with it. The WFTU and WCL have made some contributions though on a very small scale. For ten years (1958–68) the ICFTU maintained a residential college in Kampala, Uganda, which offered training courses to trade union leaders from English-speaking Africa. A total of 625 union leaders from twenty-two countries attended its general and specialised training courses. Some of the products of the ICFTU African Labour College are now holding key positions in their unions, national centres, commerce and industry and public service. When the college was closed in 1968 the ICFTU developed a new approach to trade union education, which involved dividing Africa into zones for operational purposes and appointing field representatives to service each zone. Their educational responsibilities included visiting the countries within their zones, discussing with the national centres the problems facing the trade union movement and how education could be help to solve them. On the basis of their report and recommendations, the ICFTU planned a suitable education programme. Since the closure of the African Labour College many other organisations have been involved in workers' education in Africa. The ILO, AALC, FES, the national centres of the Nordic countries and the Canadian Labour Congress are a few examples. The OATUU made a contribution in 1976.

The intensification of trade union and workers' educational activities in Africa, welcome as it is, has brought in its train several problems. The cost of education has been increasing not necessarily because of inflation but because of inducements paid by competing agencies. There is a tendency to duplicate courses and seminars in certain places and about the same time. A common feature in these events is that the participants tend to be the same. Whether the desire to gain knowledge or the wish to benefit from the financial inducements offered is the motivation to attend is anybody's guess. Consequently a large number of union leaders and functionaries spend more time attending courses and seminars and little in actually building and running their organisations or putting into practice what they have learned. Courses and seminars organised by internationl trade union organisations, inter-governmental and international development agencies as aids to national centres and their affiliates are usually referred to as 'ICFTU, ITS, WFTU, WCL, ILO, FES, AALC' events rather than 'our activities' organised in co-operation with such bodies. As a result there is a tendency among some union leaders to expect from these 'aid' organisations certain things they would normally not expect from their unions or national centres if these activities were organised by them. Lecture fee is a typical example. Should union leaders be paid lecture fees when they come to address their members attending courses or seminars organised by an international organisation or aid agency? The Zambian Congress of Trade Unions is a noted example where union leadership has taken exception to what appears to be a habit of some trade union leaders to do this. At its General Council meeting in December 1970, Wilson Chakulya, then General Secretary of the ZCTU, deplored the K12 per day allowance being paid to national union leaders and ZCTU officials travelling out of the Copperbelt to give lectures at training courses or seminars. 'It will be appreciated', he said, 'that we are given financial assistance sometimes by an outside organisation. Would it not be creating a bad impression and defeating the object for which the aid is given if such aid is mainly spent on paying allowances to union officers organising seminars. ... The ICFTU gave us £750 for seminars this year. If it were not for the high rate of allowances, we would have organised about three seminars out of this.'[4]

There are other problems which are not necessarily the outcome of the rivalries among competing organisations and agencies. For example, workers are often released by their employers without pay to attend courses and seminars organised by their national centres in co-operation with an international trade union organisation or international development agency. In such a case who should pay compensation for the wages lost—the worker's own union or the national centre or the international organisation? One African country has taken the stand that international organisations or aid agencies coming to organise courses or seminars for workers in that country must guarantee payment of lost wages before permission could be given to them to proceed. It has been said that the reason is to ensure that course participants do not suffer financial hardship as a result of their attendance. Although the reason may be appreciated, it must be noted, however, that that stand has the ultimate effect of encouraging the unions and the employers not to accept some responsibility in workers' education.

Finance
Financial weakness is one of the most intricate problems facing the trade unions in Africa. Union leaders tend to blame it on the alleged unwillingness of members to pay dues regularly. A thorough examination of the problem shows that the matter is not as simple as that. Financial instability is closely linked with the level of industrial activity in the country, the number of people in wage earning employment, the jurisdiction of the union, the number of union members, the level of wages, the rate of enrolment fees and monthly dues, method of dues collection, accounting and general administration of union funds. As was indicated earlier, industrial unionism has become a common pattern of organisation in most African countries, but the size of the average union in most countries remains comparatively small. Furthermore, the potential membership of a union is largely dependent on the level of industrial activity, and most African countries are still very backward in this respect. The rate of entrance fees and monthly dues is a crucial factor in any consideration of the financial situation of a union. Entrance fees themselves constitute a very small percentage of the income of a union since they are usually charged once, on enrolment. Many unions, particularly those operating check-off, are no longer charging it, so its significance to the overall financial situation has been considerably reduced. In view of the precarious financial situation, however, it is very doubtful whether the decision of many unions to abandon it is wise and well considered. But assuming that entrance fees should be retained as a source of union income, the question arises whether rates fixed many years ago should continue to be the same in these days of galloping inflation. The same question may be raised in connection with monthly dues.

Within the last decade wages in most African countries have increased by more than 100 per cent and prices have also increased much more than that. Many unions have increased their dues rate by between 50 and 100 per cent, yet this has not very much improved the financial situation because of the size of the unions and rising administrative costs. In many of the increases made, the flat rate contribution has been abandoned in favour of sliding scales. In 1974, Ghanaian trade unions set a pattern for increasing dues rates by deciding that union dues must not be less than 40 peswas per member (equivalent of the old 4s. and representing an increase of 100 per cent) and not more than 1 per cent of a member's wages or salary.

The second factor responsible for financial weakness is the method of dues collection and remittance to the union's head office. The traditional method of collection by shop stewards or specially designated collectors still prevails in certain countries: in most countries the unions, aided by sympathetic governments and employers, have been trying to replace it by check-off. Check-off arrangements vary from country to country. In some countries remittance is made by the employer directly to the union's head office or banking account; in others cheques are issued to the responsible official at the branch or enterprise level for onward transmission to the union's headquarters.

In French-speaking countries there are two systems of check-off in operation. One is the voluntary check-off in which the worker is required to sign a written authorisation before it could be operated, and this exists in Senegal, Tunisia and Madagascar. Tunisian trade unions were probably the first unions in French-speaking Africa to introduce the check-off, having started the experiment in the early 1950s, when the UGTT fixed the rate of monthly dues at 1 per cent of a member's net wages or salary. The proceeds of check-off are sent to the UGTT, which retains 40 per cent and sends 20 per cent to national profession federations, 20 per cent to the regional unions (trades councils), and 20 per cent to the base unions (branches based on the enterprise). Check-off is now widespread in the country, the only unions not operating it being the dock workers and agricultural workers because of the seasonal nature of employment in the two industrial sectors. The second system is the compulsory check-off which operates in the Cameroun, Gabon, Ivory Coast, Mali, Mauritania, Togo and Zaire. Under this system every worker, except probably those in managerial positions, is obliged to contribute to the union whether or not he is a member. The distribution of the proceeds varies from country to country, but a common feature is that the greater part of the proceeds is sent to the national centre and the rest divided among the professional, regional and base unions.

There is no check-off in Central African Empire and Upper

Volta. In Upper Volta, an effective system of dues collection exists in only two unions—the postal workers and teachers—which dominate the Confédération Syndicale Voltaïque (CSV), one of the five national centres in the country. In the CSV and CNTV all the proceeds of dues are remitted to the national centre: the CSV returns CFA 10,000 every month to each of its affiliates. In OVSL 50 per cent of the dues goes to the centre, while the USTV collects 75 per cent of all dues. In Upper Volta the sources of union income are membership cards, monthly dues and subsidies from international trade union organisations. It has been reported that as many as 85 per cent of the union members do not pay dues; the only occasion when the unions compel their members to pay dues is when they have a grievance. The most important source of union income is the membership card which is renewed annually, and the price varies from CFA 200 to CFA 300.[5]

How do the unions spend their money? Information about union finances is sketchy and not easy to come by unless one attends executive council meetings or conferences where financial reports are discussed, or visits union headquarters and meets an official willing to co-operate, or visits the office of the Registrar of Trade Unions and is permitted to examine the annual financial returns filed by the unions. Very few governments ever publish figures relating to trade union finance. The Kenya Government is an outstanding exception. Not only does it publish the income and expenditure of all registered unions and the national centre but it also publishes their book and paying membership. Table II shows the paid-up membership, income and expenditure of eighteen of the largest unions in Kenya for the period 1969–73. From it we learn that between five and ten unions every year spent more money than they earned; one union overspent its income during four of the five years concerned; seven overspent during three of the five years, while others overspent once or twice. The greatest over-expenditures were made by the Union of Kenya Civil Servants (£K11,840), the Plantation and Agricultural Workers' Union (£K11,267), the Railway African Union (£K5,891), the Commercial, Food and Allied Workers' Union (£K4,514), the Local Government Workers' Union (£K3,796), and the Chemical Workers' Union (£K2,636). These over-expenditures suggest that the unions either borrowed money from their reserves, or they obtained overdrafts, or they earned more income than was reported in the annual financial returns to the Registrar of Trade Unions.

To what extent do the unions support their national centres financially? The amount differs in the various countries. In Ghana up till May 1966, the TUC collected all the proceeds of check-off

Table II. STRENGTH, ANNUAL INCOME AND EXPENDITURE OF THE 18 LARGEST UNIONS IN KENYA 1969–1973

		1969	
	M*	I* £K	E* £K
1. Transport and Allied Workers' Union	10,242	10,063	9,362
2. Tailors and Textile Workers' Union	5,510	10,792	10,760
3. Domestic and Hotel Workers' Union	120,000	18,935	16,880
4. E.A. Federation of Building and Construction Workers Union	8,833	16,293	15,067
5. Kenya Local Government Workers' Union	22,457	27,044	30,383
6. Railway African Union	13,360	16,194	16,468
7. The Dockworkers' Union	7,142	15,622	15,264
8. Kenya Electrical Trades Workers' Union	3,422	4,606	4,242
9. Kenya Chemical Workers' Union	3,460	7,028	7,014
10. Union of Kenya Civil Servants	35,911	30,016	31,261
11. Kenya National Union of Teachers	23,929	29,598	33,649
12. Kenya Engineering Workers' Union	3,891	4,914	4,885
13. Kenya Motor Engineering and Allied Workers' Union	3,133	5,758	5,698
14. Kenya Union of Sugar Plantation Workers	3,030	3,680	3,968
15. Kenya Plantation and Agricultural Workers' Union	40,000	36,599	35,541
16. Kenya Union of Commercial, Food and Allied Workers	23,248	38,736	35,252
17. Union of Posts and Telecommunication Employees	2,656	7,960	8,362
18. Kenya Timber and Furniture Workers' Union			

*M = membership; I = income; E = expenditure.
Source: Annual Reports of the Registrar General, Government of Kenya.

| | 1970 | | | 1971 | | | 1972 | | | 1973 | |
M	I £K	E £K	M	I £K	E £K	M	I £K	E £K	M	I £K	E £K
1. 7,968	13,850	13,731	8,018	13,715	13,846	17,690	14,662	14,474	20,356	14,948	15,024
2. 5,628	10,092	10,139	7,280	11,157	11,244	8,513	13,172	13,424	9,689	14,761	15,056
3. 15,471	30,058	29,045	17,000	33,034	31,872	20,424	32,860	35,538	23,175	38,049	35,109
4. 9,547	21,207	19,939	9,900	24,758	22,186	14,386	26,736	27,756	10,330	26,131	27,193
5. 16,919	38,463	37,002	17,894	36,950	37,407	19,034	31,352	30,374	20,460	44,742	35,433
6. 13,309	15,924	15,689	13,299	15,663	19,421	15,465	22,326	17,815	15,575	20,835	22,694
7. 7,284	16,024	13,511	7,458	13,948	15,887	7,608	21,063	17,826	7,818	20,207	16,695
8. 2,875	5,254	4,651	2,175	4,935	4,466	2,070	4,254	4,262	2,207	4,066	4,186
9. 3,932	7,711	7,476	3,739	7,441	9,948	3,957	8,840	8,969	4,011	9,551	9,160
10. 33,903	35,262	34,303	39,372	32,913	39,019	39,217	34,303	33,812	44,140	51,926	56,415
11. 27,336	82,968	72,584	45,144	107,651	98,353	50,148	127,335	112,944	50,217	183,459	181,203
12. 4,136	10,724	9,526	4,621	11,346	12,022	6,189	11,091	11,338	6,394	12,363	12,973
13. 3,451	6,226	5,942	3,818	6,784	6,010	4,020	7,953	7,898	4,210	10,592	11,021
14. 4,843	4,388	5,359	4,425	4,526	3,827	5,000	3,474	3,080	5,130	3,753	3,749
15. 40,575	35,101	36,238	33,864	33,651	39,403	33,864	33,386	37,764	25,289	29,316	27,439
16. 19,746	31,673	32,035	21,296	35,303	35,907	22,459	33,079	36,627	24,807	37,589	31,707
17. 3,052	7,569	8,052	3,574	9,062	8,939	3,448	5,306	5,175	4,284	6,128	6,731
18. 3,067	5,158	4,888	3,530	6,342	6,247	4,106	5,509	5,590	4,003	5,436	5,303

and paid a given percentage to the national unions. At the extraordinary congress in June 1966 it was decided that 30 per cent of the proceeds of dues be paid to the TUC, 50 per cent to the national unions and 20 per cent to their branches. In Kenya 15 per cent of dues goes to COTU and the balance to the unions and an investment fund approved by the Government. In Zambia 30 per cent of monthly dues is paid to the ZCTU and the rest to the national unions. Although Nigerian unions were required to pay less than 10 per cent of their dues to the national centres to which they were affiliated very few unions ever paid. In 1976 the Adebiyi Tribunal found that only twenty-five of the 300 or more affiliates of the United Labour Congress of Nigeria ever paid dues; some of the leaders of its affiliated unions demanded 'gratification' as a condition for dues payment: when this was not forthcoming they reduced the strength of their unions on which dues payment was calculated; the WFTU-affiliated Nigerian Trade Union Congress did not collect more than £N100–150 per month from its 200-odd affiliates—even this, the Tribunal pointed out, was an exaggeration; dues collected by the WCL-affiliated Nigerian Workers' Council amounted to 'little or nothing in comparison with the amounts required to keep the organisation going', while throughout its eleven years' existence the unaffiliated Labour Unity Front collected only £N110 as dues and special levies from its affiliates.[6] The ULCN, NTUC, and NWC existed as a result of financial aids from the ICFTU, African–American Labour Centre, WFTU and WCL.

In the Gambia and Liberia the national centres are general workers' unions and so receive all the dues except the percentage due to the branches. In Sierra Leone affiliation dues are 5 cents per member per month. The Sierra Leone Labour Congress has sixteen affiliated unions representing 40,000 paid-up members. In Mauritius, the twenty unions affiliated to the Mauritius Labour Congress pay a total of about US$ 800 per annum,

Administration

Union administration may be considered under three main headings: the local or branch union, the national union and the national trade union centre. Administrative arrangements vary depending on whether the union is enterprise- or company-based or a craft, industrial or general workers' union. If it is an enterprise- or company-based union it may or may not have an office depending on its size and financial resources. In Nigeria most enterprise- or company-based unions had no office. They were run by a group of men whom certain writers have described as 'trade union promoters' or 'trade union entrepreneurs'. One man may be General

Secretary of up to ten unions collecting 'allowances' every month from each, the total of these allowances far exceeding what he could have been paid per month were he employed by a company or in the public service.

Branch unions are usually required by the union's constitution to hold meetings periodically, say once a month, to transact branch business. Some branches do, but many others do not. Meetings may not be held for months, and members may never know what their union or the branch committee has been doing. The standard of administration in the national union depends to a large extent on the quality of its leadership, the extent of membership participation in the decision-making process, and the accountability of union officials. There are many able and dedicated trade union leaders in both the English and French-speaking areas, but there are many others whose capability, integrity, commitment and dedication to the union leave much to be desired. Both types of union leaders abound in the small and big unions. In the well-run unions the General Secretary comes to his office punctually and sometimes earlier than his subordinates. He remains there as long as necessary attending to business deserving his attention and referring others to his colleagues for appropriate action. In other words, there is a division of labour, and the good example is emulated by others. In the badly run unions there is little or no division of labour. Mr. General Secretary wants to do everything and often does them badly or secretly. He does not trust anybody and therefore cannot delegate authority to any one. He may not be available most of the time he may be required, and considers criticism of his performances as a plot to oust him from office.

How do members know their rights and obligations to their union? Very few unions have their constitutions in a printed form. Most unions which have printed constitutions sell copies at a reasonably cheap price, but it is rare to find unions giving copies of their constitutions to members free of charge. Most union constitutions are mimeographed, and made available to officers and executive committee members. In some unions branch officials also receive copies, but in many others they do not. A branch secretary told me in 1976 that he had never seen the constitution of his union before that year although he had been an executive member for five years and branch secretary for three. A copy of the union's constitution which he brought to a trade union course was made available to him on the express condition that it be returned to the General Secretary after the completion of the course. (The course organisers had requested participants to bring along their union's constitution for comparative study.)

It is difficult in many countries to know who are, and who are not, union members, particularly in unions operating check-off. Before the introduction of check-off it was comparatively easy to identify union members because they had membership cards in which their monthly dues were recorded. Since the introduction of check-off most unions collecting dues by that method have abandoned the issuance of membership cards. Failure to issue membership cards, though open to question, may not be altogether a bad idea if it is motivated by economic considerations, provided the unions keep proper records of their members and dues payment. Some do, but the majority do not. There seems to be two reasons for the failure. In many countries, except where they are obliged by law to do so, most employers operating check-off do not supply the list of members from whose wages and salaries deductions are made. The few who do supply merely quote numbers and not the names of the individuals concerned. In such a case it could be assumed that there must be an understanding between the employer and the union that the numbers are known by the representatives of both sides. Secondly, most union officials seem to be more interested in getting the money rather than discharging some of the responsibilities involved, like proper record-keeping. A fundamental weakness in this attitude is that the unions may not even know whether they are getting what they should from the employers. This is particularly true in those countries with compulsory check-off.

Collecting the dues from workers is one thing, transmitting the proceeds to the union's head office and administering the funds properly is quite another. Budgeting and keeping track of the budget, applying union funds strictly to the things they are meant for and in keeping with laid down procedures, rendering proper accounts periodically to the union's governing bodies and submitting financial returns regularly as required by law—these are some of the measuring rods of efficiency and effectiveness. But it is in this important area of efficient financial administration that most African trade unions are weakest. It is not uncommon to hear that remittance has not been received from branches for several months, or that failure to make a remittance is simply because the money, though collected from workers, is not available. A story has been told of a branch treasurer who collected union dues for nine months and failed to remit the proceeds to the union's head office. During that period he was a virtual money lender to local traders and collected 50 per cent interest!

The treasurer's report often provokes one of the most heated debates in union conferences either because of critical remarks from auditors or because audited accounts are not presented. One of the commonest devices adopted by many union leaders to avoid controversy over financial administration is to delay consideration of the treasurer's report until very close to end of conferences or executive meetings. At the appropriate time someone rises and moves a motion that the report be remitted to the Executive (in the case of conferences) or deferred to another meeting (in the case of Executive meetings) because delegates or members are tired. Most of the time such a motion is carried. At the Executive the report would be considered only when majority of the members likely to vote in favour would be present.

A common problem noticeable in many countries is the failure of unions to submit their annual financial returns to the Registrar of Trade Unions. In consequence, several union officials have been prosecuted and fined. In extreme cases the defaulting unions have been deregistered. In some countries the law states not only that the unions must file returns, but that national and branch treasurers may be prosecuted for failure to produce their account books for inspection by the Registrar of Trade Unions. Kenya is a typical example, and its law enforcement agencies have been very vigilant in administering this aspect of the Trade Unions Act. Between 1965 and 1973 thirty-seven union secretaries were prosecuted for failing to submit their unions' financial returns and thirty-three were fined. One secretary received what the Registrar General's Annual Report for 1966 called a 'deterent fine of 700s. for being a persistent defaulter'. In 1968 the Minister of Labour stopped the check-off order in respect of the Kenya National Union of Teachers for precisely the same reason. Between 1967 and 1971, forty-five national treasurers and branch treasurers were prosecuted for failing to submit their account books for inspection. In Nigeria, after many years of hesitation, and prompted more by sympathy than by neglect, the Registrar of Trade Unions began to take drastic actions against unions which failed to submit their annual financial returns. On one occasion before 1975 he deregistered twenty unions in one day.

Certain bureaucratic problems may be noted in connection with the submission of financial returns. Trade unions in many English-speaking countries argue that the problem is not just filing the returns, but getting them accepted and approved by the Registrar of Trade Unions. There are complaints against fees charged by certain auditors and the insistence of certain registrars that only members of certain professional associations can be considered fit and proper persons to audit trade union accounts. During the Adebiyi Tribunal in Nigeria, Samuel U. Bassey, former General Secretary of the Nigerian Trade Union Congress, alleged that returns submitted by unions were not checked for months. When they were eventually checked, the Registrar raised a number of queries and sometimes demanded that receipts be forwarded. This might have dragged on for months before the returns were finally approved. He suggested that since auditors must be approved by the Registrar before they could audit union accounts, any accounts audited by them should be accepted without further queries.[7]

In 1974, participants in a trade union course organised by the ICFTU in the Seychelles complained bitterly about a letter written to the unions by the Registrar of Trade Unions. The letter advised them that henceforth their financial returns would no longer be accepted as being in compliance with the provisions of the Trade Unions Ordinance unless they were audited by members of the Seychelles Society of Auditors. Fourteen members of the Society were listed in the letter as persons whom the Registrar would consider as fit and proper persons to audit trade union accounts. The participants alleged that members of the Society were charging exorbitant fees, and quoted an example where a small union was charged R500 (£37·50) for auditing an account which showed assets of R1,000 (£75). During the discussion on labour legislation an opportunity was taken to examine the provisions of the Trades Union Ordinance and it was found that the law merely required the accounts to be audited by 'fit and proper persons' and not by members of any particular professional association like the Seychelles Society of Auditors. That knowledge prompted one of the participants to declare—and his statement was greeted with wild applause—that 'by obliging trade unions to use only the services of members of the Seychelles Society of Auditors the Registrar of Trade Unions was creating a business monopoly for his friends'.[8] The Registrar who sat as an observer during the discussion later addressed the class and promised to reconsider his letter.

If the administration of national unions leaves much to be desired, that of the national centres is not better, and in certain respects it is even worse. The main reasons appear to be the financial situation of the national centres and the fact that most of the best trade unionists and the most able administrators are not usually found in the centres but in the individual unions where the prospects of security are comparatively better. There are broadly two kinds of national centres in Africa. One consists of those which were voluntarily created by the constituent unions themselves: the others are those created by law on the initiative of the ruling parties or military regimes ostensibly to give a new image and sense of direction to the trade union movement but actually to enable the authorities to secure greater control and sometimes domination of the trade union movement. The former suffer from a perpetual lack of financial support from their affiliates: the latter are generally in receipt of regular contributions through check-off arrangements which oblige the employers to pay directly from source. With adequate income assured it is possible to attract able and dedicated trade unionists to work on full-time basis for the national centre. This is the situation in Ghana, Kenya, Tanzania, Zambia and Zaire, to mention only a few cases.

Nigeria is an example of how some national centres are badly administered in Africa. This conclusion is reinforced by the findings of the Adebiyi Tribunal of Inquiry and the decision of the Nigerian Government to ban some of the leaders of the former four national centres from holding any trade union office. The Tribunal found, in respect of the United Labour Congress of Nigeria, that 'the affairs of the congress, especially between 1969 and 1975, were run in a most haphazard and careless manner ... the leadership of the congress exhibited very little, if any, sense of responsibility and accountability in managing congress affairs ... for the most part they were preoccupied with intrigues and counter-intrigues to ensure that they remained at the helm of affairs.' In respect of the distribution of financial and material aids made available to the Congress by the ICFTU and the AALC 'there seemed to be a tacit understanding among the officers of the Congress of adopting a policy of "what you have you hold". The result was that each officer kept to himself/herself what came to him/her be it money, car, or scooter, and provided that he acknowledged receipt of it to the donating organisation that virtually was the end of the matter.'[9]

In connection with the Nigerian Trade Union Congress the Tribunal found that between 1967 and 1973, the Congress received a total of £N30,971 10s. 11d. This amount did not include the value of goods and materials received from Soviet and other Eastern European trade unions which the Congress was expected to sell to raise funds to finance some of its activities. Although so much money was received during the period—and in particular the sum of £N11,306 received from the Soviet Embassy in Lagos when the Congress's President and General Secretary were in detention from 1971 to 1973—the Treasurer created the impression of 'artificial scarcity of money', in consequence of which the staff could not be paid. In order to raise funds to meet staff salaries the Congress's Acting President sold some of the goods received. In the thirteen years of its existence the only time its financing, assets and liabilities were discussed fairly exhaustively and meaningfully was as a result of an internal inquiry set up by its Executive popularly known as the Bamgbala Commission. The Tribunal also found that 'all funds coming from abroad were sent to the President and the position was that only he could tell what sums, if any, were received. The circumstances of the receipt of the funds ruled out any proper accounting because, as has been pointed out, the sources of the funds themselves did not wish to be publicly identified. Therefore no proper books of account were kept.' Under the 'secret cult' method of operating the Congress not all officers knew the details of funds received. The Bamgbala Commission itself found that a large sum of the amount received was unaccounted for and recommended that the Treasurer and the Administrative Secretary be relieved of their positions and be made to repay the unaccounted monies. Although the two officers were removed no action was taken by the secretariat to give effect to the recommendation approved by the General Council that the unaccounted funds be recovered.[10]

In relation to the Nigerian Workers' Council, the Tribunal found that during the period 1970–5 the Council virtually ceased to function as a national trade union centre. No meetings or conventions were held where the leaders could give account of their stewardship. Six of its leaders were 'irresponsible and inexperienced men who had no knowledge of how to run an organisation in the interest of its members ... and were unworthy of holding any office of trust'.[11]

Grievance handling
Grievance handling and collective bargaining are two important trade union activities which give the union a meaning to the workers. Workers form and join trade unions because they have certain problems at workplace which they think the union can help to solve. They may be individual or group problems. They have certain hopes of improvement in their wages and terms of employment which they think the union can help them to achieve. They have certain dreams of a better future which they think the union can help them to attain. Members will support their union according to its success, or efforts to succeed, in achieving these objectives. The ability of the union to discharge the primary responsibility of protecting the workers from the errors and mistakes of the employer and his representatives depends to a large extent on the relationship existing between the union and the employer, and the procedure—established either by collective agreement or by law—for settling grievances.

In Africa generally, one problem that has often bedevilled industrial relations is the reluctance of employers to recognise and deal with registered trade unions and their representatives. The question raised is whether an employer should recognise and deal with any registered union, or whether he should recognise and deal with the registered union which enjoys the support of majority of his employees. Supporters of the former argue that registration as a legal requirement would be meaningless if it does not imply automatic recognition by the employer. They readily point out the number of man-days lost in many countries through strikes organised to achieve recognition, and maintain that such trial of strength is unnecessary and damaging to the economy. Supporters of the second question argue that the trade union is a group activity: employers deal with union leaders because of their representative capacity. Representative capacity, they point out, means that the union has at least a simple majority of the workers as its members. We shall return to this matter later. In the meantime, it should be noted that since independence there have been many changes in the law relating to trade unions. Some laws make recognition of a registered union mandatory on the employers; some allow employers and trade unions to negotiate and conclude a 'recognition agreement' as a basis of establishing their relationship. Liberia appears to be the only country to have adopted the North American system of conducting representation elections. A union which wins such an election is eventually certified by the Ministry of Labour, Youth and Sports as the sole representative and collective bargaining agent of the workers concerned.

The procedure for handling and disposal of grievances is usually laid down in the collective agreement between the employer and the union or in company rules or staff regulations where no collective agreement exists. A slightly different procedure applies in the public service. Grievance procedures generally provide the steps through which grievances should be handled until they are finally disposed of. Two complaints have often been made against grievance procedures in many African countries. The first is that the steps are too numerous: the second is that there is no time limit within which management ought to make a decision or the aggrieved worker to file an appeal if he is dissatisfied with management decision. In consequence much time is wasted before minor grievances can be settled.

Some countries in English-speaking Africa (Kenya, Uganda, Tanzania, Nigeria, and Sierra Leone) have established industrial courts or industrial arbitration tribunals for the settlement of industrial disputes. These bodies adjudicate on issues referred to them by the Ministry of Labour on the request of the unions and employers including the application and interpretation of collective agreements. While these bodies have done remarkably good jobs in settling disputes, two aspects of their work have often been criticised. The first is that it takes too long to dispose of a case. The delay may be due to the number of cases requiring attention, legal arguments or the complexity of the cases. The second is the effect of their decision on free collective bargaining. Although cases should normally be referred to industrial courts or tribunals after the unions and the employers have tried through collective bargaining to reach agreement and failed, this is not generally done. In Kenya, which has the oldest industrial court, it has been reported that little or no bargaining ever takes place before cases are referred to the court. One employer has been quoted as saying, with reference to union claims, 'We don't pay any attention to them: we just refer the matter to Industrial Court'.[12] Apparently because of employers' attitude and the fact that the court has established a reputation for justice and outspokeness, union leaders tend to spend most of their time in the court in an effort to obtain social justice for their members. Both sides of industry tend, therefore, to lose sight of the importance of free collective bargaining and training their representatives for the responsibility of policing collective agreements.

What are the unions' own arrangements for handling grievances and how well do they discharge that responsibility? Practices vary in the various countries and in different unions within the same country. Those involved in receiving and processing members' complaints range from the shop floor representative to the President or General Secretary, depending on the grievance procedure, the nature of the grievance and its complexity. Where the shop steward system exists, the grievance will first be handled by the shop steward of the particular section or department from which the grievance originates. If the matter is not settled to the satisfaction of the person concerned it is referred to the next step of the grievance procedure and so on until it is finally disposed of. Unfortunately, the shop steward system is not well developed in many countries in English-speaking Africa and in some countries it does not even exist. A branch union official who attended a trade union course in 1973 organised by the ICFTU wrote an essay captioned 'The Missing Link'. That missing link, he said, was the absence of the shop steward system in most Nigerian trade unions. He argued that had the system existed many of the problems of the trade union movement in the country could have been solved or considerably minimised. It should be noted, however, that the absence of the system does not necessarily mean that the normal functions of a shop steward are not being performed at all. They are, but they are performed by branch officers like chairman and secretary. Thus the responsibilities of branch officials tend to increase greatly in branches where there are no shop stewards.

In French-speaking Africa grievances are handled by the *délégué du personnel* who is elected by the entire workers in the enterprise. In some countries he is an entirely different person from the *responsable syndical* who is a trade union representative elected by members of his union. In certain countries both functions are carried out by the same person.

It has often been alleged that some union officials demand and collect bribes from their members as a condition for handling their grievances. In some unions members' grievances may not be handled until they have paid their dues up to date. It has also been alleged that some companies try to defeat workers' demands by making deals with their union leaders. There seems to be no conclusive evidence as to the extent of corruption among union leaders. But the testimony of a witness at the Adebiyi Tribunal in Nigeria indicates what may be happening in certain unions. Emmanuel U. Ijeh, a former Assistant General Secretary of the ULCN, told the Tribunal that a few years ago information was received that a textile company in Kaduna was giving a bale of cloth every month to certain leaders of the Congress to sell and support themselves. At the time the information was received in Lagos a bale of cloth was said to be worth £N200. When the allegation was made, he added, the ULCN secretariat did not take it seriously because there was no evidence to substantiate it. Eventually, a copy of a letter dated 2 February 1971 was produced. The letter, which was addressed to the director of the company through its personnel manager, was alleged to have been signed by a vice-president of ULCN, and read: 'I am directed by the National President of the above Congress ... to inform you that he shall be meeting you by 9 p.m. at Hamdalla Hotel today to enable a private discussion on how to subdue the workers' housing demand. Because it is not the policy of our Congress to go against the improvement of foreign investors in this our poor nation. At any rate the meeting shall put us into light as to how to bow down the entire workers.'[13]

Allegations of bribery and corruption have also been made against union leaders in other countries. The division which occurred in the Liberian trade union movement in 1974 is not unconnected with it, though the leaders of the CIO quickly denied it.

Publicity

How do the unions inform their members of their activities, and how do members express an opinion or influence union activities?

Very few individual unions have their own journals in which they publicise their activities. Those which exist appear irregularly and most times when there are important developments about which the leaders think that members ought to be informed. Publicity as an on-going activity is not within the thinking of many union leaders. Besides three house unions in Nigeria the only national unions which appear to have their own journals are the Union of Kenya Civil Servants, the Teachers' Unions in Ghana, Mali, Mauritania, Sierra Leone and Zambia. A small house union in Nigeria, the African Timber and Plywood Workers' Union, seems to have done an impressive work in this field. Its *Voice of Labour* not only carries stories of the union's activities, but also contains detailed information about the activities of its multi-purpose co-operative venture. The union has a handbook for its executive members which contains information about the composition of the Executive, the responsibilities of executive members, union policies, finance, grievance procedure and the union's benefit schemes.

Publicity by most national unions consists in occasional press releases and circular letters to branches. The bulk of trade union publicity is undertaken by some of the national trade union centres, the OATUU, the ICFTU African Regional Organisation, and the Regional Economic Research and Documentation Centre, a branch of the African-American Labour Centre. Even then, some of the publications appear irregularly. A survey conducted by the Regional Economic Research and Documentation Centre in 1976 showed that there were thirty-two trade union journals published by African trade unions. Two have since ceased publication. Sixteen are published in French and fourteen in English. Of the thirty journals, fourteen are monthly publications, two are weeklies and two quarterlies. Of the monthly publications as many as nine appear irregularly. Trade union journals which appear regularly are the *African Labour News*, a monthly organ of the ICFTU African Regional Organisation; the *Voice of African Workers* published by OATUU; the *African Trade Union News* and *Labour and Development*, published by the Regional Economic Research and Documentation Centre (RERDC). The main obstacles to trade union journals in Africa are undoubtedly financial constraints and lack of technical know-how.

Collective Bargaining

Collective bargaining in Africa, as in other parts of the world, depends for its success on the provisions of the law, the attitude of the employers, the strength of the trade unions and the skill of the parties engaged in the bargaining process. We shall examine the legal framework later. Meanwhile we shall examine what has been happening in the bargaining process in a few countries in English-speaking Africa. Collective bargaining in the sense that it is carried out in Europe and North America and the practice of concluding and signing collective agreements are a comparatively new development in many African countries. There are several unions which have no collective agreements with employers. This does not necessarily mean that some sort of bargaining never takes place: it means that the method and practice have not been well developed.

Practically all English-speaking countries but one (Liberia) inherited the British model of industrial relations which implies the creation of joint negotiating machineries and well-defined procedures for holding meetings, and details of what these meetings may discuss. Generally the constitution of these negotiating machineries provide that the chairman shall be a representative of the employer and the vice-chairman a representative of the workers. There are joint secretaries, one from the employer's and the other from the workers' side. The Joint Industrial Councils, or JICs, as they are commonly called, consider claims presented by the workers through their trade unions. During meetings of the JICs minutes are usually taken by a secretary provided by the employer. Although the joint secretaries are expected to vet the draft minutes before final production, this is not generally done. More often than not the joint secretary from the employees' side fails to carry out his responsibility, trusting too much the integrity of the secretary from the employer's side. The result has often been that the minutes are prepared to suit the employer's interpretation. Over the years, and in many countries, a good deal of time, effort and money has been wasted in arbitration proceedings in an effort to find out whether the minutes of JICs are a true reflection of what the employer and the union had in mind when they were discussing. One question has often been asked in connection with another aspect of interpretation and that is, assuming both parties agree as to the correctness of minutes, is such a record a 'collective agreement'? Opinion differs on the matter. Industrial relations specialists say no; another school of thought argues that in so far as collective agreement is understood to mean the decision voluntarily arrived at by both sides in the bargaining process such minutes could be said to be collective agreements. It is only in recent years that workers and their leaders have come to realise that minutes of JICs are not collective agreements but record of proceedings of discussions; that after discussing the union's claims, agreements reached with the employer ought to be produced in the form of a written and binding contract and signed by the representatives of both sides.

In the following pages an attempt will be made to examine some of the most important clauses of collective agreement in certain English-speaking African countries. We shall begin by taking a look at the clause on recognition—the basis on which the union and the employer establish their relationship. Under the British model of industrial relations a union cannot deal with an employer until it has been recognised by him. This also applied in the former colonial territories. The law did not compel recognition, so most employers took undue advantage of the situation to refuse recognition. In most countries strikes were organised to obtain recognition. In certain countries hardly a single union secured recognition without resort to the strike weapon. Some countries have now made union recognition mandatory on employers. Others take the view that workers and employers should negotiate and conclude 'recognition agreements'. If they fail to reach agreement, particularly, if the employer fails without just cause to recognise the union, then the state, through a Ministerial Order, could compel recognition. The basic problem with recognition agreements is not necessarily the conditions which the employers demand, but what they cover. This raises the question which observers have sometimes asked, namely, whether there is any limit to what may be covered by collective agreements. Furthermore, recognition has several meanings in Africa. In some countries it means having the right to negotiate with employers on certain topics stated in the recognition agreement; in some it means the right to participate in negotiations subject to the fulfilment of certain conditions; in others it means the right of sole representative and collective bargaining agent of the workers concerned.

The Recognition Agreement and Collective Agreement between the Nigerian Bank (Employers') Association and the Nigerian Union of Bank, Insurance and Allied Workers, dated 27 August 1971, states that the union has bargaining right on eight subjects: salaries and wages, hours of work, overtime and overtime rates, leave and leave conditions, medical and sickness benefits, principles of termination of service, principles of redundancy, uniforms and protective clothing. The union was recognised subject to the following conditions: (*a*) that the terms of the agreement were observed in full; (*b*) that it is the sole negotiating body to represent the employees of those members of the Association whose staff the union could substantiate its claim to represent; (*c*) that recognition would operate as long as the union continued to be representative of the employees; and (*d*) that terms and conditions of member banks whose staff the union had not claimed authority to represent would continue to be negotiated between the individual member bank and the 'house union' or employee representatives as the case might be.

Two agreements, one dated 20 November 1975 between the National Iron Ore Company Limited and the National Mine Workers' Union of Liberia (Mano Branch) and another dated 1st January 1974 between the State Shipping Corporation and the National Union of Seamen, Ghana, recognise the unions as sole representative and collective bargaining agent. In the recognition agreement between the Government of the Republic of Kenya and the Union of Kenya Civil Servants (UKCS) the union is recognised as the 'only properly constituted representative body competent to represent employees of all grades in the service of the Government in respect of matters listed in Appendix A of this Agreement.' The matters listed are nine in number and include rates of pay, overtime and allowances, hours of work, method of wage payment, leave, duration and termination of contract, principles of redundancy, medical expenses and sick pay, retirement and other terminal benefits and any other matter by mutual agreement. Certain employees are excluded from coverage and these include confidential staff, directive and administrative personnel and supervisory staff. The UKCS seems to have recognised the inadequacy of the coverage of the recognition agreement. At a meeting of the union's Central Council held in 1977 an eight-member Social; Economic and Legal Committee was appointed to deal with, among other things, 'such matters which are not adequately covered by our Recognition Agreement.'[14]

In two agreements concluded in Botswana in March and July 1973, between De Beers Mining Company, the Bamangwato Concessions Limited and the Botswana Mine Workers' Union, Selebi-Pikwe and Orapa Branches, recognition is accorded subject to the conditions that (a) the union represents at least 25 per cent of the companies employees; (b) it does not represent senior staff or employees who have access to confidential information relating to management policy or personnel affairs; (c) the union must be representative only of the employees of the company (De Beers) but this does not prevent any affiliation to a Federation of Trade Unions; (d) eligible employees shall be free to join or not to join the union and both parties agree not to discriminate against any employee on account of his membership or non-membership; (e) the union agrees that it shall not actively support, concern itself or become affiliated to any political organisation (this applies to De Beers agreement); (f) recognition is granted on the basis of the union's constitution as registered by the Registrar of Trade Unions; and (g) any amendment to the union's constitution enabling the union to take any action contrary to or incompatible with the provisions of the agreement entitles the company to regard the agreement as having been terminated from the date of the amendment (Bamangwato Concessions agreement).

There is no recognition clause in the agreement dated 13 June 1974 between the Ghana Textile Corporation and the Industrial and Commercial Workers' Union of Ghana TUC or in any of the six collective agreements between the Association of Local Government Employers and the Kenya Local Government Workers' Union. The local government workers' agreements themselves are the product of the Joint Negotiating Councils set up in accordance with Sessional Paper No. 12 of 1967 issued by the Kenya Government. The Sessional Paper classified local government councils under three groups. Group 1 consists of the City Council of Nairobi and the Municipal Council of Mombasa. Group 2 comprises other municipal authorities, and Group 3 is made up of the county councils. The Local Government Workers' Union has the distinction of being the only union in Kenya recognised to represent every category of local government employees from the Town Clerk to the lowest labourer.

There are a few other interesting provisions in the agreements under discussion which merit further examination. The first concerns union security. In the Nigerian bank workers' agreement the check-off arrangement stipulates that member banks will 'deduct normal dues from the wages of union members and pay these directly to the union's banking account, provided each member authorises the deduction in writing subject to this item being covered in a separate agreement'. In other words although there are already two agreements (recognition and collective) and check-off has been agreed in principle, a third agreement must be concluded before it could be implemented. The agreement also provides that the union will elect its representatives to serve on negotiating bodies, and the names of all union officials, national and local, including elected representatives must be notified to the Association. All officials and representatives must be provided with proper credentials.

In the Ghana commercial workers' agreement provision is made that 'upon written instruction from the employee, the employer undertakes to deduct union dues monthly from the employee's salary and pay such amount to the union'. The agency shop clause is of particular interest not only because it is a welcome innovation but because of the argument used to justify it which could be emulated by other unions. It says: 'Employees shall have the right to voluntarily join or refrain from joining the union. Employees who choose not to join the union and who are covered by the terms of this contract, shall be required to pay, as a condition for enjoying the provisions of this agreement, a monthly service fee to the union for the purposes of aiding the union in connection with its legal obligation and responsibilities as the agent of the employees in the bargaining unit. The aforesaid fee shall be payable on or before the first day of each month, and such sums shall in no case exceed the membership dues paid by those who voluntarily choose to join the union.'

There is no provision in either the Nigerian bank workers' agreement or in the Ghana commercial workers' agreement obliging the employer to submit to the union a list of employees from whose wages and salaries deductions are made or the amount deducted. Such a provision exists, however, in the agreement between the State Shipping Corporation and the Ghana Union of Seamen. The Liberian mine workers' agreement provides that 'any worker covered by this agreement may arrange to have his or her union dues (US$1·00 per month) deducted from salary or wages by sending an individually written authorisation or relevant forms to be provided by the union. Only dues-paying members shall be represented by the union. No discrimination, intimidation or coercion shall be used to compel a worker to agree to check-off.'

In Annexure C to De Beers agreement a provision is made that the union shall appoint shop stewards in each department. Where departments work shift a shop steward must be appointed for each shift. Names of shop stewards must be submitted in writing to the manager and management must also notify the union and the individuals concerned of formal recognition. There are three qualifications for being a shop steward. The first is that the person must be elected or appointed in accordance with the provisions of the union's constitution; second, he must not be a learner or an apprentice; and third, he must have been employed by the company for a continuous period of one year prior to his nomination. Recognition of a shop steward does not confer any privilege or preferential treatment in relation to his position as an employee of the company. Shop stewards shall not instigate, incite, command aid, advise, encourage or procure any employee to take part in or continue an illegal strike. The company can, at any time, withdraw the recognition of a shop steward if, in the management's opinion, he is working contrary to the interests of the mine or the men he represents or contrary to the provisions of the agreement.

In the Bamangwato Concessions agreement, the company can raise objection to the appointment of any person as a shop steward. The appointment of a shop steward terminates if he is transferred to another department unless the company agrees that it should continue in respect of the department to which he has been transferred. A shop steward deals with all matters referred to him in the manner laid down in the agreement. On appointment, a shop steward is required to sign a declaration to the effect that he agrees to carry out his duties in strict conformity with the provisions of the agreement between the union and the company.

Another interesting clause in these agreements is the one covering grievance procedure. The Ghana commercial workers' agreement has four steps, but no time limit for management to make a decision or the aggrieved worker to file an appeal. The same thing applies to the seamen's agreement. There are five steps in the Liberian mine workers' agreement, and time limit at each step of the grievance procedure. At the fourth step either party may appeal to the Plant Grievance Committee which is composed of six employers and six workers' representatives. But according to the Rules of the Grievance Committee not more than five members should attend any one particular grievance meeting. If a case remains unsettled at the Plant Grievance Committee either party may appeal to the Ministry of Labour, Youth and Sports and forward to them a copy of the Committee's findings. The Bamangwato Concessions agreement has four steps in the grievance procedure, and there are time limits of two days in the first and second steps, but no time limit in the third though a meeting between the parties could be held within seven days. Within three days and not later than one week a case not disposed of at the third step must be referred to the union's head office. De Beers agreement has three steps with time limits of between two and three days. In all the agreements but three there are elaborate provisions relating to the procedure for handling group grievances.

On redundancy, all the agreements provide that adequate notice should be given to the union and the persons to be affected. 'Adequate notice' varies, however, from fifteen days in the Liberian agreement to one month in the others. All the agreements but one contain the principle of 'last in, first out', but there are different approaches to its application and payment of severance benefit. The Ghana commercial workers' agreement provides that in the event of redundancy, management will take into account length of service, efficiency, diligence, loyalty and health of the persons concerned before making a decision. Severance pay is one month's salary for each year of service. In the Liberian agreement it is provided that the principle will apply where skill, ability, past conduct and physical fitness are equal. Severance pay will be calculated on a sliding scale varying from one to three week's pay for each year of service. There is also a provision for recall in case of new employment opportunities, provided the ability of the person concerned is equal to that of a new employee. The Nigerian agreement provides that the principle will apply except in cases where merit and ability of a junior are greater than those of a senior employee. *Ex gratia* compensation varying from one month's salary for each year of service to a maximum of twelve months will be paid. There is also a provision for re-employment if vacancies occur within eighteen months.

Most of the agreements contain wages and salary scales, but only one gives a clear indication of the degree of improvement arising out of the bargaining process. This is the agreement between Gestetner Duplicators Limited and the Printing and Kindred Trades Workers' Union of Kenya in which it is stated that workers earning 600s. or less per month will receive 15 per cent wage increase with effect from 1 April 1976; those earning above that amount will receive 10 per cent. From April 1977 those earning 600s. or less will receive 13 per cent while those earning more than that amount will be paid 8 per cent. The agreement was concluded in 1976, and is valid for two years.

Elections

Union election is a crucial matter. The union will, or will not, be able to carry out its functions depending on the type of men and women the members choose to lead or represent them and the commitment and dedication of these people to the union. Being a group activity, trade unionism is basically a democratic organisation. It implies that those who lead or represent workers at all levels must not only derive their authority to function from those they represent, but must be seen to derive that authority freely and fairly. The law generally requires union elections; the union's constitution provides them accordingly; and members want them because they provide an excellent opportunity for them to demonstrate their confidence, or lack of it, in the men and women who come forward to assume leadership and representative functions in the trade union movement.

The problems with union elections in Africa arise not so much from the legal provisions nor the provisions of union constitutions but the method of conducting them. There are, of course, a few cases where the provisions of union constitutions have created difficulties, but these are exceptions rather than the rule. Union constitutions generally state when and where elections will be held, who is entitled to attend, the method of nomination and the voting procedure. Most union elections are held at annual, biennial or triennial conferences or annual general meetings in the case of branches. Usually the constitutions will provide that, in the case of election to national or district positions, nominations should be sent to the district or national headquarters of the union within a specified period. This means that before then branches will hold meetings, and discuss and decide who to sponsor or support, and delegates will have an indication as to whom their members want and will vote accordingly at the conference. Many unions and their branches follow this procedure. A good deal do not because the branches hardly meet before conferences. Some union constitutions provide that the principal officers of branches (chairman, secretary and treasurer or any two of them) shall represent the branch at conferences. Although the provision does not necessarily imply that members should not be consulted, some branch officials fail to convene meetings because their attendance is already assured by the provisions of the constitution, and they tend to vote at conferences, not in according to the wishes of their members, but purely on their own discretion. This partly explains the large-scale bribery which features in certain union elections.

In a previous work on the Nigerian trade union movement (*The Trade Union Movement in Nigeria*, London, 1969), I outlined some of the tactics which some union leaders in that country employ to sustain themselves in office when they have lost the confidence of their members. The Nigerian example is indicative of what happens in many other countries. Since the publication of that book there has been little improvement in the methods by which some union leaders derive their authority to function. Indeed, in certain respects the situation has worsened. If there are irregularities in the conduct of individual union elections, there are many more in the conduct of the elections of the national centres. The problem has been complicated by three developments. Election rigging is common place in Africa, and some union leaders think that they could use the same methods which certain politicians use to keep themselves in power. Since the emergence of one-party states and military regimes claiming to be anxious to secure trade union co-operation in the economic and social development of their countries, the leadership of many national centres has changed hands not through the votes of union members and their representatives but through the decisions and manipulations of the ruling parties or military juntas. In 1961 AATUF introduced 'election by acclamation' as a means of defeating those who would not subscribe to the decisions and tactics of the organisers of the Casablanca conference. Although most national centres in the continent at the time decried it as unconstitutional and undemocratic it has become the order of the day in many countries. To add insult to injury it has become the method of electing officers of OATUU.

Behind the acclamation façade lies strong allegations of irregularities. Two instances may be quoted. During the ULCN congress in 1971 a former President of the organisation, Alhaji H. P. Adebola, was chosen as a returning officer during the election of officers. When he came to the rostrum, he called for nominations and added, 'I, as a delegate of the Nigerian Railway and Ports Transport Workers' Union, would like to nominate the person I think should be the President of this organisation'.[15] He nominated Aljahi Yunusa Kaltungo, a former District Secretary of the Nigerian Nurses' Association, who succeeded him at the 1969 congress. That year, Kaltungo was facing a strong challenge from the Deputy President, J. O. James. Replying to an objection raised by those who thought it was irregular for a returning officer to nominate a candidate, Adebola said that he was exercising his right as a delegate. The nomination was greeted with shouts of 'unopposed, unopposed, unopposed!' Admidst that shouting, however, another voice was nominating J. O. James, but the nomination was not countenanced, so Kaltungo was declared elected unopposed. Kaltungo in turn nominated J. O. Adegbesan, President of Adebola's union, who, in turn, was also declared elected.

In April 1972 the Kenya Motor Engineering and Allied Workers' Union and many other unions affiliated to COTU filed objections to the elections held that month in Kajido which returned what was popularly known as the Karebe-Chegge group as COTU officers. The objectors claimed that the meeting which elected them was improperly constituted in that it had no quorum and that unqualified persons were allowed to participate and vote. The quorum argument arose out of an ambiguity in COTU's constitution, and highlights some of the problems which arise when an over-zealous government takes upon itself to perform an essentially trade union responsibility. Since the creation of COTU the Kenya Government has always drafted its constitution. According to COTU officials the Government has always done this because it believes that constitutions drafted by trade unionists fall short of expectation. But the ones drafted by Government officials do not seem to be better. Under Rule 4 (*g*) of COTU's constitution, 'the quorum of the Governing Council shall be two-thirds of the members entitled to attend and vote.' Under the constitution the president, general secretary and treasurer of the affiliated unions are, by virtue of their office, members of the Governing Council of ninety-two. The objecting unions argued that since the total number of members was ninety-two, two-thirds of that number was sixty-one. The total number of unions and delegates present at the Kajido meeting was forty-seven made up of (a) ten unions represented by three officers; (b) four unions represented by two officers; (c) five unions represented by one officer; and (d) four *ex officio* members. The objectors then asked two interesting questions.

First, if membership of the Governing Council was based on three principal officers from each affiliated union, could the attendance of one or two officers be said to be representative of the union? Second, if the quorum was based on the number of unions, it could only be constituted by eighteen unions each fully represented by its three principal officers. The objectors recalled a precedent created in 1970 when James Karebe walked out of a meeting of the Governing Council in Mombasa and later filed a petition against the election of F. E. Omido as Treasurer General of COTU on the ground that a quorum which he himself stated as being sixty-one was not constituted. They pointed out that Karebe's objection was accepted by the Registrar of Trade Unions and Omido's election was nullified, and stressed that it would be double standard if the Registrar did otherwise in 1972.

Under the Trades Unions Act any person convicted of fraud is prohibited from holding an office in a union. That was why, the objectors argued, three officials of the Civil Servants' Union, the Printing and Kindred Trades Workers' Union and the National Union of Teachers were banned from holding any union position. The objectors alleged that a key official of the Kenya Union of Journalists was allowed to participate and vote in the Kajido meeting even though he was prohibited by law from holding a trade union office. Another person, an Assistant Minister of Housing, who had ceased to be an 'official' or 'member' of a trade union was also allowed to attend and vote. The objectors argued that the Assistant Minister ceased to be a member or an official of a trade union in Kenya the day he was appointed to his post.

Labour Ministry officials who attended the Kajido meeting reported that 'the definition as regards the quorum of members entitled to attend and vote as contained in Rule 4 (g) is not clear to the supervisor of the elections. Therefore the meeting, if it so decides to go ahead with the election, must clearly understand that this question has still to be looked into by the Registrar of Trade Unions as to whether a quorum was realised.' The meeting accepted the warning and proceeded with the election. The quorum question and other points raised by the objectors were later referred to the Trade Unions Tribunal which ruled, among other things, that a fresh election was to be held within eight weeks and that the COTU constitution was to be reviewed. The election ordered by the Tribunal was held in June 1972. According to the Ministry of Labour Annual Report for that year, 'the group that had boycotted the Kajido meeting won all the seats. Objections were again raised by the losing group and the matters were referred to the Trade Unions Tribunal which nullified the election of the First Vice-President, Second Vice-President, Deputy General Secretary and one Trustee because of irregularities.' The Tribunal strongly recommended that COTU's constitution be amended to ensure that representation on COTU Governing Council reflected the numerical strength of the affiliated unions.

Defence of Human and Trade Union Rights

As a trade unionist, the question that worries me most is why trade unions which fought side by side with political parties to dislodge colonialists and in some cases filled the vacuum when political parties were banned, as in Kenya, are not now accepted by African Governments. As I write this, about ten leading trade unionists are in jails or detention in various African countries. Some are under investigation: splits are being encouraged to weaken trade union leadership, even though there is an OAU resolution calling for national unity of trade unions. Worse still, some unions are facing threats of dissolution. There are trade unionists living in exile because they have displeased their home governments. (J. D. Akumu, *Africa Magazine*, May 1975)

In these moving words the Secretary General of the Organisation of African Trade Union Unity describes the systematic erosion of human and trade union rights which has been going on since most African states attained independence. Cognate to these sad developments is a question which many observers have been asking namely, what role has the OATUU been playing in defence of human and trade union rights in Africa? African workers and those sympathetic to their cause believe that by virtue of its history, its connections and influence with African governments, the greatest and most urgent service which the OATUU could, and should, render is in this important field of defence of human and trade union rights. OATUU pledges in its Charter to 'forcefully recover, consolidate and defend trade union freedom'. The inclusion of the word 'recover' is an admission of the loss of trade union freedoms, which raises the question: 'How does the organisation live up to its pledges?' To put it mildly its performances are a great disappointment to most African workers. This is not altogether surprising judging from its history and the circumstances of its existence. But it highlights the hypocrisy, the pretence and downright deception to which African workers have been subjected for a long time by the propaganda that their salvation does not lie in organic links with international trade union organisations that have established reputation in defence of human and trade union rights but in a compulsory membership of a body created, financed and maintained by African governments for political and public relations purposes.

Any hope that the OATUU would live up to one of its principal objectives was extinguished by its reaction to the arrest and detention of leaders of the Confederation of Ethiopian Labour Unions in 1974 by the military authorities of that country. Fisseha Tsion Tekie, CELU's General Secretary, was the chairman of the founding congress of the OATUU in 1973, and Beyene Solomon, CELU's President, was a Vice-President of the organisation. Not only did the OATUU fail to do anything until the ICFTU had sent two unsuccessful missions to get the men released, but its Secretary General was quoted as having criticised ICFTU initiative, describing it as 'foreign interference in the internal affairs of an independent African state'. Solomon and his colleagues were eventually released in 1976 following constant pressure from the ICFTU and ILO. A few months after the arrest and detention of the Ethiopian labour leaders, demonstrating workers in Cotonou were shot by the Kerekou regime in the Republic of Benin. Again, OATUU is reported to have done nothing apparently because it was a domestic affair of an independent African country. Similar silence and apparent unconcern was also reported to have been shown by the organisation when the national Executive Councils of the trade union centres of Cameroun and the Central African Empire were dissolved by their governments and some of their leaders were jailed without trial.

Government spokesmen have often tried to justify the increasing curtailment of human and trade union rights with arguments of 'economic development' and 'national security'. It was apparently in answer to these arguments or excuses that one trade unionist made the point that 'workers and their families are part and parcel of the society in which they live and work. Whatever is done in the interest of workers is a service to their country: whatever is done against them is a disservice to their country.' Before and since the creation of the OATUU the only organisations which have been in the vanguard of the defence of human and trade union rights are the national centres in those countries where there are semblances of free and democratic unionism, the ICFTU and its African Regional Organisation, the International Trade Secretariats, WFTU and WCL. A few national centres and individual unions have filed complaints with the ILO when human and trade union rights have been infringed in their countries; others request international trade union organisations to which they are affiliated to take the necessary action on their behalf. As far as the ICFTU and the ITS associated with it are concerned, the method of approach varies from formal complaints to representations to governments, the OAU, personal visits and interviews with Ministers and Heads of States. The ICFTU and the ITS have been in the forefront of the struggles against the inhuman policy of apartheid and white minority regimes in Southern Africa. In recent years the OATUU has co-operated with the international trade union movement in anti-apartheid campaigns. The ICFTU has designated 1978 as a year of protest against apartheid in South Africa.

Non-bargaining Activities

Politicians, military leaders, economists and trade union leaders themselves have often urged African trade unions to expand their activities into fields beyond the traditional functions of collective bargaining and grievance handling. It has been argued that by so doing the unions make a positive contribution to the social and economic development of their countries. A wide range of activities has been suggested including the organisation of rural workers, creation of trade union sponsored co-operatives, housing, health and welfare schemes. Trade union reaction in the various countries has varied from positive response to total indifference. Co-operatives seem to be one activity in which the unions are mostly interested, and two aid agencies (the African–American Labour Centre (AALC) and the Friedrich Ebert Stiftung (FES)) have made remarkable contributions in helping African trade unions to acquire the necessary skills and experience. Of late, the ICFTU, the Africa Co-operative Savings and Credit Association (ACOSCA) and the International Co-operative Alliance have also made some contributions.

In Ghana, after the overthrow of the Nkrumah regime, the AALC and the FES helped the Ghana TUC and its affiliates to set up a mobile health scheme, thriving consumer co-operatives and credit unions and also a housing scheme. The credit unions became the saviours of the workers and full-time union officials during the difficult days of trade union confrontation with the Busia regime in 1971. In Kenya, AALC financed two high level national seminars on the role of trade unions in social and economic development which made detailed recommendations on how to promote co-operative activity among workers. Later it concluded a technical assistance agreement with COTU. Under the agreement which was valid for five years the AALC undertook to pay the salary and social charges of a co-operative officer to be attached to COTU and to provide technical assistance and advice in the promotion of co-operatives. Trade union sponsored co-operatives are increasing in Kenya. Two shining examples are the thrift and credit societies organised by Shell employees and the employees of the Nairobi City Council. In 1976 the Shell employees' society had a little more than 700 members with a share capital of 1·7 million shillings. The Nairobi City Council employees society known as Nacicco was founded in December 1975, and in November 1976, had a membership of 4,000 with a share capital of more than 1·4 million shillings. It is probably the fastest growing savings and credit society in Kenya. Civil servants and local government employees also have savings and credit societies, but the administration of the civil servants societies seems to leave much to be desired. UKCS Central Council which met in 1977 'noted with distress that the leadership of the Credit Societies had rendered the concept upon which these societies were founded dishonourable' and appealed to the Government to step in and improve the situation.[16]

In Tanzania and Zambia there are Workers' Development Corporations which are engaged in a wide range of economic activities. The Zambia Corporation was started with an initial capital of K100,000 from the Government and operates a shop and a printing press. In addition the Zambia Mine Workers' Union has one of the biggest and financially one of the wealthiest trade-union-sponsored credit unions in Africa. One small union which seems to have developed its co-operative activity almost unaided from outside sources is the African Timber and Plywood Workers' Union of Nigeria. In 1968 it sponsored its President, Gregory B. Tonukari, for training at the Co-operative College in Ibadan. On his return Tonukari organised the union's multi-purpose co-operative involving consumers, and thrift and credit functions. From a humble beginning of 220 members and assets of 9,901 Naira in 1969/70 its membership rose to 1,800 in 1973/4 with assets of 21,451 Naira.

In the early seventies the AALC awarded a scholarship to Samuel N. Padmore, a Liberian trade unionist, to undergo a diploma course at the Co-operative College in Ibadan. On his return he organised a consumers' co-operative shop in Monrovia which made some progress and inspired the decision to try the experiment in other parts of the country. Unfortunately this proposal was abandoned as the schism which eventually led to a split in the CIO developed. The Monrovia shop itself was closed, and Padmore joined the rival United Workers' Congress. In Sierra

Leone, a consumers' shop was started by the Sierra Leone Labour Congress in 1975 with financial and technical support of the Volunteer Development Corporation of Washington, the AALC, and Histadrut. In the first year of its operation it made a gross profit of Le 2,003·72 and in 1977 a gross profit of Le 7,000 was envisaged.[17]

In the French-speaking areas, trade-union-sponsored co-operatives seem to be well established in Madagascar and Tunisia. In Madagascar the unions started co-operative activities in the early 'sixties with the FMM in the vanguard. Financial and technical support was provided by ICFTU affiliates in Luxemburg and Israel. In Tunisia, UGTT also started various forms of co-operative activities in the early 'sixties. These included consumers, transport, fishing, clothing and insurance. Most of these co-operatives collapsed, but the consumers and fishing continued and have been in existence ever since. Besides the co-operatives, UGTT also owns a printing press and a 300-bed hotel which have been successful economic ventures. In Zaire the Caisse de Solidarité Ouvrière et Paysanne (CASOP) which is one of the seventeen national federations affiliated to UNTZa owns dispensaries and mobile clinics which cater for the health of workers and farmers. It also pays birth and death grants. CASOP is made up of workers and farmers.

9. FACTORS AFFECTING AND INFLUENCING UNION ACTIVITIES

The Legal Framework

The law regulating trade unions and trade disputes has undergone fundamental changes since the attainment of independence. Although Ghana set the pattern with its Industrial Relations Act, 1958, the most comprehensive, and in many respects the most advanced piece of labour legislation existing in English-speaking Africa is the Zambian Industrial Relations Act, 1971. It is sixty-four pages long and divided into eleven sections covering, among other things, the registration of trade unions, the establishment of the Zambia Congress of Trade Unions, control of trade union funds, employers' associations, the establishment of the Zambia Federation of Employers, works councils, joint councils and collective agreements, settlement of collective disputes and the establishment of an industrial relations court. Sierra Leone is another country having an Industrial Relations Act, but its provisions are not as comprehensive as the Zambian Act. Botswana, Kenya, Nigeria, Tanzania and Uganda have different laws regulating trade unions and trade disputes.

In examining the legal framework, we shall first consider some of the important provisions of the law relating to the organisation and administration of trade unions; later we deal with the law relating to trade disputes. Some of the Trade Union Acts provide for a mandatory recognition of registered trade unions. In this respect they differ significantly from the Trade Unions Ordinances and the rules of industrial relations practice which prevailed during the colonial rule. The arguments for the change have already been examined in the previous chapter. Under Section 16 (e) of the Botswana Trade Unions Act, 1969, a union which has 25 per cent of the employees of any employer as its members must be recognised by that employer. The Trade Unions Decree of 1973 makes two elaborate provisions under which recognition shall be accorded to trade unions in Nigeria. Section 22 deals with recognition where there is no rival trade union. Under that section a 'trade union shall be entitled to recognition by the employer in accordance with the terms of a recognition agreement voluntarily entered into by the employer and the union or, in default of such agreement, in accordance with a compulsory recognition order made by the Commissioner'. The Commissioner for Labour issues a compulsory recognition order taking into account all the facts and circumstances appearing to him to be relevant. Section 23 provides for recognition where there is a rival union. In this case recognition must be accorded to the union which has 60 per cent or more of the employees as members, and a recognition agreement must be signed.

Under Section 111 of the Zambian Act, employers and trade unions are required to conclude a recognition agreement within three months of the coming into effect of the Act. The recognition agreement must provide (Section 112) that the union has been recognised as 'the sole representative and exclusive bargaining agent for the employees'. It must also provide methods, remedies and rules relating to procedures for the settlement of disputes between employers and employees. Two copies of the agreement and any alterations thereon must be delivered to the Registrar of Trade Unions who forwards them to the Industrial Relations Court for approval and registration.

The laws of the various countries list between eleven and fifteen subjects which must be included in the constitution of every trade union. The Nigerian Decree provides that no illiterate shall become president, secretary or treasurer of a trade union; a person shall not be a member of a union unless he is, or has been, normally engaged in the trade or industry which the union represents; the committee of management shall consist of persons all of whom are members of the trade union, provided that if a person who is not a member of the union is appointed president or secretary he may be a member by virtue of his office; no member of a union shall take part in a strike unless the majority of the members have, in a secret ballot, voted in favour of the strike. The Zambian law provides for the disqualification of persons for election to any position dealing with the funds of a union who have been convicted of an offence involving dishonesty or members who are insolvent or who are undischarged bankrupts. The Botswana and Uganda Acts require provision to be made for the right of members to have a reasonable opportunity to vote. Both Acts provide that no person shall be a voting member of a registered union unless he is a member and his monthly subscription is not more than thirteen weeks in arrears.

In Botsawana, Kenya and Uganda not only must individual

unions be registered, their branches must also be registered. In Botswana and Uganda a branch union must be registered within twenty-eight days of its formation. The application for registration must show the name of the parent union, the name of the branch, its postal address, the place of meeting for carrying on the business of the branch, and the titles, names, ages, addresses and occupation of the officers of the branch.

The laws of five countries (Ghana, Kenya, Sierra Leone, Tanzania and Zambia) provide for the collection of union dues by check-off. The operation of check-off in Ghana has already been explained. In Kenya, the Minister of Labour is empowered to make an order in respect of check-off and order the proceeds to be paid by crossed cheque within fourteen days to the union concerned and COTU. Deducations can only be made from the wages of employees who are members of the union, and employees are free to contract out of check-off. The Sierra Leone law make a brief provision on the subject. It says (Section 9) that 'upon the request of a trade union to whom a collective bargaining certificate has been issued, the employer or employers concerned shall introduce the check-off system of collecting trade union dues'.

Until the publication of the report of the Presidential Commission on the NUTA, union dues in Tanzania were based on a sliding scale varying from 2s. to 10s. and were collected by check-off. The Commission recommended that check-off should be continued, but dues should be based on a flat rate of 2s. because 'all members stand the same chance of union protection and enjoy benefits of a similar nature'. In Zambia, check-off operates in two ways—by agreement and by a Ministerial Order. Under Section 19 of the Industrial Relations Act, 1971, an employer may deduct union dues from the wages of a worker if he is a member of a union and has signed an authorisation to that effect. He can withdraw the authorisation at any time. Under Section 20 the Minister can order an employer to deduct union dues from the wages of his employees whether or not they are members, provided they fall within the jurisdiction of the union and are sufficiently representive of the employees concerned. In this connection 'sufficiently representative' means that the union represents more than 60 per cent of the total number of persons employed who are eligible to join the union. The proceeds of the check-off must be remitted within fourteen days partly to the union concerned and partly to the ZCTU. Remittance must be made by crossed cheque marked 'not negotiable' and 'account payee' and accompanied by a list showing the amount deducted and the names of the employees from whose wages the deductions were made. A copy of the list must be sent to the

Labour Commissioner and the appropriate branch of the union concerned.

All the laws under review make elaborate provision relating to matters on which union funds may be applied. The financial provisions cover such things as accounting, auditing, rendition of annual financial returns, etc. In some laws the Registrar of Trade Unions is empowered to call for accounts at any time, to institute legal proceedings on behalf of a registered union in certain circumstances or institute proceedings against the responsible officers for failing to submit their fiancial returns. In extreme cases he is empowered to deregister the defaulting union. All the laws but one are silent, however, on the question of application of union funds for political activities. The Nigerian Decree provides (Section 15 (*i*)) that 'unless the rules of a trade union otherwise provide, in so far as the funds of a trade union represent the payments which the members are required to make under the rules, those funds shall not be applied (whether directly or indirectly, or through any other union, association or body or in any other indirect manner) to the furtherance of any political objectives'. The Decree defines political objectives as the making of contributions towards the funds of any political party, the payment of expenses incurred (directly or indirectly) by candidates for election to any political office in Nigeria, the holding of any meeting or the distribution of any literature or documents in support of any such candidate, the maintenance of any person holding a political office, the registration of electors, the holdings of any political meeting, or the distribution of political literature or documents of any kind.

The Botswana, Kenya and Zambia laws prohibit the affiliation of trade unions to any organisation outside their countries except with a written approval of the Minister of Labour. Under Section 62 of the Botswana Trade Unions Act no union can accept funds originating from outside the country without the written consent of the Minister of Labour. Funds include all donations, loans and other assistance of pecuniary value. The Zambian Act forbids any representative body or member thereof to accept assistance in the form of cash, gifts, loans, donations, property, travel vouchers or tickets from any government other than the Government of Zambia or from any agency or person acting on behalf of such other government or from any other body, agency or organisation situated outside Zambia without the prior written approval of the Minister of Labour.

The law relating to trade disputes varies in scope and content in the various countries. The Ghana and Sierra Leone Industrial Relations Acts provides for the certification of unions for collective bargaining purposes. A certified union is authorised to bargain on wages, terms of employment, hours of work and fringe benefits. In Ghana application for the certification of a union is made by the TUC on behalf of the union concerned or by the union itself if the TUC fails. The Minister of Labour cannot issue certificate in respect of unions representing civil servants, municipal and local government employees and teachers. The Sierra Leone Act establishes a National Joint Negotiating Body to determine and fix minimum rates of pay and paid holidays and maximum hours of work for employees below the supervisory level. In addition it establishes fourteen trade-group negotiating councils made up of equal representatives of employers and unions whose functions are to negotiate on wages, terms and conditions of service and conclude agreements relating to them. In the Ghana law agreements reached after collective bargaining can be extended to a class of employees who are engaged in the same kind of work or who work in the same area. Part V of the Act covers unfair labour practices which include discrimination against union members and officials, interference by employers in union affairs, refusal by employers to admit union officials, carrying on union activities in an employer's premises during working hours without his consent. The Act establishes an Unfair Labour Practices Tribunal which inquires into and determines cases brought before it and makes an order where necessary forbidding the continuance or repetition of the unfair labour practice. An appeal against the Tribunal's order can be made to the High Court within twenty-one days.

In Sierra Leone there is an Industrial Court for the settlement of industrial disputes. An award made by the court is binding on the parties, but an aggrieved party may appeal on a point of law only. The Sierra Leone Act classifies five public utilities—water, electricity, ports, posts and telecommunications and health services—as 'essential services' and provides that the Minister of Labour may from time to time classify any new trade group as an essential service. No strikes may take place in essential services, but they are permissible in other trade groups in certain circumstances provided twenty-one days notice is given.

The law governing trade disputes in Nigeria is contained in two decrees promulgated by the Federal Military Government in 1976 which repealed all previous laws on the subject. The two decrees are the Trade Disputes Decree No. 7 of 1976 and the Trade Disputes (Essential Services) Decree No. 23 of 1976. The principal Decree makes elaborate provisions for the reporting and settlement of trade disputes and forbids strikes and lock-outs until the procedures laid down have been exhausted. Section 2 provides that where there is any collective agreement for the settlement of a trade dispute three copies of the agreement must be deposited by the parties with the Commissioner for Labour. Where there is such an agreement the parties to the dispute must first attempt to settle it by that means. If the attempt fails or no such agreed means of settlement exists then the parties should within seven days meet under the presidency of a conciliator mutually agreed upon and appointed by or on behalf of the parties with a view to settling the dispute. If the dispute is not settled within fourteen days of the appointment of a conciliator then the dispute shall within fourteen days be reported by either party to the Commissioner. Within ten days of the receipt of the report the Commissioner refers the dispute to the Industrial Arbitration Panel, established by the Decree, the chairman of which is empowered to appoint an arbitration tribunal to settle it.

Section 9 requires the tribunal to make an award within forty-two days of its constitution or such other longer period as the Commissioner may allow. Within twenty-one days of the publication of the award any of the parties to the dispute may raise an objection. If no objection is raised within that time, the award is confirmed and published in the Gazette and becomes binding on the parties. If an objection is raised, the dispute is referred to the National Industrial Court also established by the Decree whose decision is final and binding. The Court has exclusive jurisdiction over questions of interpretation of an award made by it or an arbitration tribunal, the contents of collective agreements or the terms of settlement of any trade dispute by a conciliator.

Disputes involving workers in 'essential services' are referred directly to the National Industrial Court. Essential services include any service established, provided or maintained by the Federal or State governments, local government councils, town councils or any municipal or statutory authority or by private enterprise for, or in connection with, the supply of electricity, water, fuel of any kind, sound broadcasting, postal, telegraphic, cable wireless or telephonic communications; for maintenance of ports, harbours, docks or aerodromes, or for, or in connection with, transportation of persons, goods or livestock by rail, sea, river or air; for, or in connection with, the burial of the dead, hospitals, the treatment of the sick, the prevention of diseases, sanitation, road cleaning, the disposal of night soil and rubbish, for dealing with the outbreaks of fire, service in any capacity in the Central Bank of Nigeria, the Nigerian Security Printing and Minting Company and any licenced bank. A strike may not take place in essential services unless at least fifteen days notice is given. Contravention is punishable by a fine of 100 Naira or imprisonment for six months.

The Trade Disputes (Essential Services) Decree empowers the Head of the Federal Military Government to proscribe a trade union if he is satisfied that its members are engaged in acts calculated to disrupt the economy or obstruct the smooth running of any essential service or failed to comply with the procedure laid down in the Trade Disputes Decree for the reporting and settlement of disputes. Where a union has been proscribed no other union consisting of the same members can be registered until at least six months has elapsed. An official of a proscribed union can be detained if the Inspector General of Police or the Chief of Staff, Supreme Headquarters, is satisfied that his acts are prejudicial to industrial peace or are calculated to obstruct or disrupt the running of any essential service.

The Kenya Trade Disputes Act of 1965 establishes an Industrial Court, apparently the oldest of its kind in black Africa, whose functions are to inquire into disputes referred to it by the Minister of Labour and make an award. The Court is made up of the President appointed by the Chief Justice and two other members appointed by the Minister of Labour, one representing employers and the other representing employees. Where the members of the court are unable to agree on their award, the matter is decided by the President acting with full powers as an impartial umpire. The Act obliges the parties to a dispute to adhere to agreements where they exist for the settlement of disputes and to respect awards made by the Industrial Court. The Minister has power to declare any strikes or lockouts illegal if he satisfied that the procedure laid down for the reporting and settlement of disputes has not been followed. The Act classifies fourteen services as essential and these include almost all the services covered by the Nigerian Essential Services Decree.

In 1967, Tanzania created a Permanent Labour Tribunal whose functions are to hear and determine any trade dispute referred to it, register negotiated and voluntary agreements, inquire into any matter referred to it and report to the Minister of Labour, advise the Labour Commissioner on any matter referred to it and exercise such functions and powers as are conferred on it by the Act or any written law. Section 6 of the Act provides that where a dispute is settled by conciliation the Labour Commissioner must submit the text of the negotiated settlement to the Minister of Labour with a report setting out the rate of wages payable prior to the agreement, the date of the last revision of wages, the increase in labour costs in the event of the agreement being enforced, the expected increase in labour productivity in the trade or industry affected by the agreement, whether any redundancy in such a trade or industry is likely to occur, the effect of the agreement on the price of the product concerned, and whether the agreement, if enforced, is likely to affect any plan for expansion in the trade or industry concerned. On receipt of the agreement and report the Minister refers them to the Permanent Labour Tribunal together with any comments he may wish to make. The Tribunal examines the documents with a view to determining whether they meet the ten criteria stipulated in Section 22 for making an award. If it is satisfied, the agreement is then registered as an award. If it is not satisfied, it may make modifications before registering it or refuse registration altogether. The same procedure is adopted in the case of registration of voluntary agreements. If a dispute is not settled by conciliation it is reported to the Minister who refers it to the Tribunal within twenty-one days. The Tribunal receives and hears evidence from the parties concerned, and may seek advice on the Government's economic and financial policies as well as consider the provisions of Section 22 (e) before making an award. Every award and decision of the Tribunal is binding on the parties concerned and cannot be questioned in any court of law save on the grounds of jurisdiction. The Act does not apply to civil servants and local government employees.

The Zambia Industrial Relations Act, 1971, stipulates in Section 87 that every collective agreement must provide two statutory clauses, namely the duration of the agreement and the method and procedure of amending, terminating or replacing it. Copies of collective agreements must be sent to the Industrial Relations Court. The Court may direct its Registrar to register the agreement or refer it back to the parties concerned with its reasons for not registering it and give direction as to its re-submission. A collective agreement cannot be implemented until it has been registered. The Court has a similar jurisdiction like its counterpart in Nigeria and the Permanent Labour Tribunal in Tanzania. Under Section 55 of the Act, works councils must be established in every undertaking employing twenty-five eligible employees. 'Eligible employees' means those not serving probation or employed on temporary basis or employees in managerial positions. In 1976 the number of eligible employees was raised from twenty-five to 100. Every works council must consist of not less than three nor more than fifteen members of whom two-thirds must be elected by the eligible employees and one-third appointed by the management of the undertaking. The principal objectives of works councils are to promote and maintain effective participation of workers in the affairs of the undertaking for which such councils are established and to ensure the mutual co-operation of workers, management of the undertaking and the trade union in the interests of industrial peace, improved working conditions, greater efficiency and productivity. Every council must be consulted in all schemes and programmes relating to the health and welfare of the eligible employees of the undertaking. Every council must be informed of the decisions of the board of directors, the proprietors or management of any undertaking in relation to investment policy, financial control, distribution of profits, economic planning, job evaluation, wage policy and the appointment of senior management executives in the undertaking. Section 72 (*i*) provides that 'after the establishment of a council for an undertaking, a decision by the management in the field of personnel management and industrial relations shall be of no effect unless it is approved by the council established in such undertaking, which approval shall not be unreasonably withheld'. This applies particularly to recruitment of employees and assessment of their salaries, transfer of employees from one undertaking to another owned by the same employer, disciplinary rules applicable to the employees in an undertaking, redundancy, bonuses and incentives and mode of their payment, and safety of the employees.

International Relations and Aids
Before 1959 trade unions in Africa enjoyed almost an unfettered freedom in their international relations. Whether a union or a national trade union centre should or should not affiliate to an industrial or global trade union organisation depended on the wishes of its members. It was generally recognised by the unions, employers and governments themselves that international affiliation is a basic trade union right enshrined in Convention 87 of the ILO. It was also generally agreed that membership of an international trade union organisation is beneficial for the healthy development of African trade unions. Membership, it was felt, provided a useful forum for young and inexperienced trade unions to associate with their older, well established and experienced counterparts in the industrialised countries, exchange views and ideas and generally try to find a common solution to some of the problems facing the working people of the world. International affiliation carried obligations, rights and privileges. The main obligations were, and still are, willingness to respect and abide by the constitution of the organisation to which a union or national centre is affiliated, payment of affiliation fee on applying for affiliation and payment of dues periodically as provided for in the constitution of the organisation. The rights and privileges consist of participation in meetings and congresses of the organisation, moral and sometimes

financial aid to the affiliated organisation to help it achieve some of its objectives, e.g. to organise the unorganised, or simply to purchase furniture and office equipment for the union's secretariat. In cases of unions from countries under colonial rule or white minority domination, grants are given to further not only trade union objectives but also to aid the struggles for independence.

The bigger and well established national unions and national centres in the industrialised world felt they had a moral obligation to help build sound and viable trade unions in Africa and other parts of the developing world. This obligation derives from the concept of international solidarity of the working class and the Manifesto on Economic and Social Demands adopted by the founding congress of ICFTU in 1949. The Manifesto declares that 'labour is not a commodity ... the fundamental right of workers—that which underlies all other rights—is to economic security and social justice. We therefore pledge ourselves to the supreme task of advancing the interests of workers throughout the world and of enhancing the dignity of labour'.

In 1959 most of the national trade union centres in Africa were affiliated to one or the other of the three global internationals—ICFTU, WFTU and IFCTU now known as the World Confederation of Labour. Most national centres were affiliated to ICFTU, and most individual unions were also affiliated to the international trade secretariats associated with it. As a result of that relationship ICFTU and the ITS sent various forms of aids to help develop free and democratic trade unions in Africa. Aids to African trade unions were originally not meant for affiliates alone: they were intended for trade unions and national centres which believed in the principles of free and democratic unionism. Although receipient organisations were not obliged to affiliate, aids nevertheless constituted a formidable moral inducement, particularly as it became increasingly clear that the ICFTU and the ITS had their primary obligations to their affiliates. Indeed, it is generally believed by many African leaders that the desire to receive aids and nothing more was the principal motivation for seeking international affiliation. Although many trade union leaders have denied it the impression is still there. It was a powerful ammunition in the hands of AATUF leaders and has been an ammunition for OATUU leaders in their anti-affiliation crusade.

Originally there were five main forms of aids—invitations to conferences and meetings with all expenses paid by the host organisation, financing trade union education programmes, grants for organising campaigns or the purchase of office furniture and equipment, material donations (cars, scooters, bicycles, books to set up small trade union libraries) and assigning an experienced trade unionist from an industrialised country to a given area to render technical and advisory services to the unions in that area and generally to administer grants made to the unions from the ICFTU International Solidarity Fund. But in trying to help African trade unions zeal sometimes outran judgment, and in recent years has raised doubts in the minds of critical observers as to the real intentions of the aid programmes. The error of judgment was committed in four of the five forms of aids—invitations to conferences and meetings, financial grants, accepting full responsibility to finance education programme and choice of personnel—each of which has created problems the end of which is nowhere in sight. Some of the current difficulties facing the trade union movement in Africa including the apparent low esteem in which the international trade union movement is held in certain African countries are a direct consequence of that error of judgment.

The opportunity to travel, most times to Europe and North America, at other people's expense, soon created an army of itinerant trade union leaders who spent more time travelling and very little actually building their organisations and servicing their membership. Travels to Europe and North America were usually undertaken by the top leadership of the unions and national centres. When the leaders travelled they generally requested aids from their hosts. To support their requests they told incredible stories, some true, some false, of the tremendous difficulties created by governments and employers which make it a herculean task for the workers to organise. European and North American trade unionists were and still are generally impressed by such stories, remembering their own experiences in the early days of building their organisations. In the spirit of international solidarity they appealed to their members to help and they did. In time what began as a kind gesture to help African trade unions to tide over a difficult period became the mainstay of the trade union movement in the continent. By 1965 the ICFTU found itself saddled with the responsibility of paying subsidies for the maintenance of national centres which had little or no support from their affiliates. Most of these national centres did not pay dues, not even the token contribution of 10 per cent of the normal dues rate which the ICFTU Executive Board had permitted them to pay because of their financial situation. Yet they received aids. To ensure that they paid dues the ICFTU adopted the practice of deducting their dues from grants made from the International Solidarity Fund. In other words, workers in industrialised countries not only helped African trade unions financially but also paid their dues to ICFTU.

Three main problems arose out of this development. It is now common knowledge in many countries that much of the aids received through appeals made by union leaders during their overseas trips was not used for the purposes they were meant: they frittered away into the private pockets of the leaders. Realising that some leaders had been benefiting from their trips the idea of going abroad became a crucial matter to trade union leaders in several countries. It has been reported that in certain countries where there were more than one national centre union leaders changed their union's affiliation according to opportunities offered to them to travel abroad. Secondly, seeing that the national centres were often in receipt of funds to operate, their affiliates saw no need to pay dues. No national centre would dare to apply that provision of its constitution relating to default in dues payment. In some countries, Kenya and Nigeria for example, the unions expected their national centres to finance their operations rather than the other way round. Owing to the rivalry between the opposing national centres in both countries (in the case of Kenya before the creation of COTU) the national centres adopted the ridiculous method of winning affiliates through the bribery of officials in the unions concerned.

Those who conceived the idea of giving subsidies to national centres grossly under-estimated the harmful effects they would have on the trade union movement in those countries. The problems which these subsidies created are a constant reminder of the differences which arose between the British and American trade union leaders at the ICFTU Executive Board meeting in 1959 over methods and strategy in building trade unions in Africa. The British wanted attention to be concentrated on the development of national unions, believing that when such unions were properly established they would see the need to create national trade union centres and support them. Here they were probably guided by their own experience in establishing the Trades Union Congress, probably the oldest and one of the strongest national centres in the world today. The Americans, on the other hand, wanted to see strong national centres established, believing that these centres would undertake the responsibility of organising the unorganised, strengthening weak unions and generally becoming the representative and spokesman of organised labour in community and national affairs in the various countries. The American belief was probably based on their own experience in creating the former Congress of Industrial Organisations and was intended to strengthen their anti-colonial stand which endeared them to the trade union leaders from countries then under colonial rule. The American case, though ridiculed by some critics as having been motivated by the desire to recruit agents for their anti-communist crusade, could have worked had the trade union leaders lived up to expectation. There were and still are arguments for both cases, but as experience has shown the British case was sounder.

The willingness of the international trade union movement to accept full responsibility for financing trade union education programmes accounts for the small number of educational activities organised and financed by the unions and national centres in the various countries. The situation has been worsened since the emergence of several organisations all claiming to be engaged in workers' education in Africa. Probably the single factor which has done more damage to the image and reputation of the international trade union movement as represented by the ICFTU and ITS is the choice of some of the people assigned to work with the unions in certain countries. As individuals they were excellent in many respects and knew their jobs. But thanks to WFTU and AATUF propaganda and their impact on certain African Governments, they were suspected of serving other interests, and believed to be engaged in subversive activities in Africa. It is against this background that subsequent developments should be considered.

In 1959 the whole idea of unfettered freedom of association was called to question by the Preparatory Committee of the All-African Trade Union Federation. Its meeting in Accra was called to sabotage the ICFTU African Regional Conference scheduled to take place in Lagos in November 1959. Writing on the strategy adopted, Colin Legum reports that 'knowing of the venue and the timing of the second ICFTU conference in Lagos, they [the Ghana TUC] announced their resignation from the ICFTU and a decision to inaugurate the AATUF in Accra to coincide with the Lagos meeting. The decision to launch AATUF was taken without consulting the Committee of the All-African Peoples' Organisation (or even its chairman, Mr. Mboya) which originally decided to sponsor the new body.'[1] At first, the campaign of the national centres from the old Casablanca Group for the revocation of the right of international affiliation was not taken seriously by the majority of African states nor was it supported by them. But after the creation of the OAU, and particularly following the resolution adopted by its Council of Ministers in September 1967, in Kinshasa, which drew 'the attention of the member states to the necessity for the African representatives of the ILO (governments, employers and workers) to present a united front with a view to defending African interests at the ILO conference', the campaign was given a unanimous backing.

Although aids created problems, they nevertheless made positive contributions towards the development of African trade unions. One form of aid which has been highly appreciated by the unions, employers and governments, including unions and governments hostile to the ICFTU, is its education programme. The earlier contributions of the ICFTU and the ITS have been outlined in the previous chapter. In recent years the ICFTU has been concentrating on creating a better awareness of the basic functions of trade unions through its monitors' training programmes, organising the unorganised through theory and practice training programmes for union organisers and encouraging the unions and national centres to play a meaningful role in the social and economic development of their countries through its seminars on development and employment policies in Africa. The new approach to trade union education is the outcome of a series of regional and international events which the Confederation organised in 1972 in an effort to evaluate its educational activities with particular reference to needs, who should be served, relevance of existing education programmes, with particular regard to the problems facing the trade union movement generally and in a given area, the demands of the Second Development Decade, teaching methods and techniques.

Government Policies and Tactics

At independence government policy towards the unions was generally liberal. Policy tended to change as some of the weaknesses which led to the collapse of most of Africa's First Republics began to emerge thus creating frustration and resentment among workers and their organisations. Claims for improvement in wages and working conditions were generally frowned at, not because they were unjustified but because of their likely consequences on the public service, as the governments—and local authorities and institutions created by them—were the largest employers in practically every African country. Attempts by the ruling parties to transform the unions from the status of being a fearless spokesman and champion of workers' rights to mere rubber stamps of party or government decisions marked the first incidents of the parting of ways between the estwhile comrades in arms during the struggles for independence. The governments and ruling political parties reacted in a number of ways. In some countries harsh laws which severely curtailed trade union freedoms were passed. In others the governments and ruling political parties tried to woo the unions by referring to them as the industrial wings of the parties and as such were obliged to support the Government, implement its policies and increase productivity. Ghana, Ivory Coast, Tanzania, Tunisia and Zambia are cases in point. Union leaders were brought into the Executive of the ruling parties and sometimes given ministerial appointments in an effort to demonstrate that workers were participating in the decision making process in the country.

Kenya went a step further. The Government concluded an Industrial Relations Charter with the employers and the unions aimed at preserving industrial peace and creating employment. It served its purpose for a while, and in due course the Uganda Government, employers and trade unions concluded a similar charter. Tanzania wanted to follow a different path to achieve the same objective by incorporating the national trade union centre as a division of the Ministry of Labour. When the unions rejected the plan, the TFL was dissolved and NUTA was created in its place. The experiments in industrial peace were disrupted in Kenya and Uganda by the activities of dissident groups in the trade union movement of both countries and by influential elements in the ruling political parties who wanted to change the style and character of the trade union movement. To restore peace in Kenya the existing national centres were dissolved and a new one created. In Uganda where the ruling élite felt that their ambition to change the attitude of the unions to the ruling party was being frustrated by the alleged 'foreign influence' in the unions, the Trade Unions Ordinance, 1952, was repealed and a new Trade Unions Act was passed in 1965 which prohibited non-Ugandans from holding office in the unions. As a result of the Act all Kenyans and Tanzanians who held union positions were removed from office. Three years later, a dissident group with the active support and encouragement of a section of the Government tried to occupy the offices of the Uganda Labour Congress. When they failed because of police intervention, the Government reacted by closing the offices of the Congress throughout the country and the ICFTU African Labour College. The College had been under threat of closure or government take over since 1963. In order to save it the ICFTU Executive Board appointed a high level delegation led by the Confederation's President, Arne Geijer, which visited Uganda in May 1964. The delegation was shabbily treated by the then Minister of Labour, George Magezi. Seven months later, he told the Uganda Parliament 'I am going to leave the College to die its natural death and it is going to come very soon.'[2]

In Malawi, following the decision of the ruling Congress Party to accept trade unions into affiliation, all union leaders known or suspected of not being loyal to the party were removed from their posts. Repression of political opponents which followed the cabinet crisis of 1965 forced certain trade unionists into exile. In Nigeria where there had been perennial splits in the trade union movement until 1975, the attitude of successive governments to the unions was more or less ambivalent. Government had not been able to accord sole recognition to any national centre as long as there was a split, but in 1962, after the Ibadan merger conference, that policy was changed. The United Labour Congress of Nigeria enjoyed sole recognition until the military administration of Major General Aguiyi-Ironsi changed the policy and granted recognition to other national centres including the Labour Unity Front which was up until then not a national centre. In 1968, the Nigerian Government promulgated Decree No. 21 which forbade strikes and lockouts. Although it was said to be an emergency measure necessitated by the civil war, that Decree was not repealed until 1976, six years after the end of the war. If the war situation was actually the reason for the Decree, it would be understandable. But government spokesmen who continued to defend it even after the war often created the impression that the real reason was the number of man-days lost during that year through strike actions. In other words, the world was left with the impression that the right to strike was withdrawn because it had been abused. Table III shows the man-days lost through strike actions from 1962 to 1968 in thirteen African countries. From it we learn that compared with other relatively big African countries Nigeria had a low strike record, and in the year 1968 it had the lowest strike record during the seven-year period.

In December 1975 the Nigerian Commissioner for Labour, Brigadier H. E. O. Adefope, announced a new labour policy which, he said, aimed at giving a new sense of direction and a new image to the Nigerian trade union movement. This meant the prohibition of the activities of international trade union organisations with the exception of the ILO and the OATUU, the restructuring of the trade unions on national industrial basis, introduction of compulsory check-off with built-in safeguards to ensure the judicious application of the proceeds to legitimate trade union aims and objectives including in particular the provision of welfare schemes for union members and their dependents, provision of trade union education through the establishment of a national institute for labour studies and the take over, with immediate effect, of all foreign-sponsored labour institutions established and operated in the country. Later a tribunal of inquiry into the activities of trade unions was appointed. Government refused to accord recognition to

Table III. MAN-DAYS LOST THROUGH STRIKES IN 13 AFRICAN COUNTRIES 1962–68

Country	1962	1963	1964	1965	1966	1967	1968
Cameroun	4,896	3,084	235	7,509	591	538	10,206
Gabon	4,028	1,705	12,388	2,942	690	47	—
Ghana	2,800	2,850	1,073	23,389	25,712	6,758	100,017
Kenya	745,749	235,349	167,767	345,855	127,635	109,128	47,979
Madagascar	27,456	20,181	2,588	36	455	—	—
Malawi	6,502	7,069	24,647	20,248	3,211	4,862	4,863
Mauritius	13	3,719	11,253	3,862	3,514	1,050	15,845
Morocco	278,426	351,700	337,400	207,785	91,486	134,459	162,883
Nigeria	57,237	53,797	90,875	276,175	76,704	92,373	18,444
Sudan	—	985	31,759	223,170	194,570	58,016	58,010
Tanzania	417,474	77,195	5,855	1,825	8,825	7,224	5,757
Uganda	96,986	94,292	39,737	55,937	12,917	12,864	—
Zambia	561,534	409,559	123,317	22,493	579,280	46,088	65,898

Source: ILO Year Book of Labour Statistics 1972.

the newly formed Nigerian Labour Congress which, it claimed, was not democratically set up. In 1976, the former four national centres—ULCN, NTUC, NWC and LUF—were dissolved by Decree, and M. A. Abiodun, a former senior official of the Federal Ministry of Labour, was appointed Trade Union Administrator, and was charged with the responsibility of restructuring the unions and helping create a new national centre. In 1977, it was announced that a total of sixty-one trade unions and nine employers' associations would be set up. The sixty-one unions were to be made up of forty-three national industrial unions and eighteen senior staff associations. A new national centre was to be set up in 1978 after election of officers of the national unions had been completed.

For organising what was said to be an 'illegal strike' the Gambia Workers' Union was deregistered in January 1977. But the real reason for the measure appears to be its militancy in pursuing a pay claim which had led to the appointment of a commission of inquiry. The commission recommended substantial increases in the wages of workers, but the Government refused to accept the recommendation and the union called a strike two days after a new law had been rushed through Parliament making it obligatory for twenty-one days notice to be given before workers could go on strike.

A wave of industrial actions which shook Douala in January 1976, forced the Cameroun Government to grant wage increases varying from 5 to 18 per cent. The strikes were organised in defiance of the 'Government union', the Union Nationale des Travailleurs du Cameroun (UNTC), and led to the removal of UNTC President Moise Satounghe Defith. The wage increases were not extended to dock workers and this led to a one-week strike which paralysed the Douala docks. Hundreds of strikers were black-listed from employment in the docks and new hands were employed from the mass of the unemployed. In the weeks which followed the strikes some of the strike leaders were arrested, detained and tortured, and some were later released. In the Central African Empire, a move to integrate the national centre, UGTC, with the ruling political party was successfully resisted by the unions. At its Congress in April 1977, the General Secretary spoke eloquently in favour of freedom of association and his organisation's adherence to ILO Conventions 87 and 98. Shortly after the congress he was placed under house arrest and the UGTC was allegedly dissolved. The ICFTU sent a cable to Emperor Bokassa seeking clarification. In his reply, the Emperor confirmed the house arrest and accused the ICFTU of being communist-oriented and of interfering in the Empire's internal affairs.

Under the arrangement governing union-party relations in Zaire, the General Secretary of the UNTZa is a member of the governing body of President Mobutu Sese Seko's ruling party, the MPR. One day in 1977 he was going to attend a meeting of that body when he was stopped at the gate and asked to return home; the gateman who stopped him claimed to have acted on instruction from higher authorities. Later Kikongi di Mwinsa was invited by President Mobutu and told that he had been relieved of his union and party positions. His offence: he had taken photograph of the President's villa in Geneva and distributed copies to certain persons. He was later arrested and jailed for fifteen days without trial. In Mozambique, following FRELIMO's third congress in 1977 which provided guidelines for the destruction of capitalism and the construction of a workers' and peasants' state based on 'scientific socialism', 'production councils' which have nothing to do with trade unions are being set up. Labour matters are no longer being dealt with by the Ministry of Labour but by the party.

Employers' Attitude
Mention has already been made of employers' attitude with particular reference to recognition of unions and the steps taken by certain countries to deal with the problem. Here I intend to focus attention on other aspects of employers' attitude which also affect union activities. There are still many employers in the various African countries who do not want their employees to form or join trade unions of their choice. They include certain multinational corporations, medium-sized foreign companies and indigenous employers. Opposition to unionism takes various forms. It includes outright rejection of any form of unionism and various devices by management to gain control of unions representing their employees. Where unions are organised on plant or enterprise basis hostile employers would prefer that pattern of organisation to industrial unions embracing their employees and other workers in the same industry. The reason often given to justify that attitude is that they would like 'to deal with people who know the economics of the industry'. Actually the reason is to enable the employer to control or dominate the affairs of the union, for 'industry' does not necessarily mean the particular industrial sector but the firm or enterprise. Where there is animosity between the workers from the various ethnic groups which make up the workforce, some employers play one group against the other and thus create problems in organising and strengthening workers' solidarity. A pathetic story was told in July 1975, in an application for a compulsory recognition order made by the Onitsha branch of the Nigerian Textile, Garment, Leather and General Workers' Union

to the Federal Commissioner of Labour, Brigadier Adefope. The story may be summarised as follows:

The Nigerian Textile, Garment, Leather and General Workers' Union (NTGLGWU) had been organising the employees of the General Cotton Mill Limited, Onitsha, a joint venture of the former East Central State Government and a Hong Kong firm. In 1974 a branch of the union was formed at Onitsha where the General Cotton Mill was located, and it had 1,600 members out of a workforce of 2,000. The branch union approached the company for recognition, and the management made two promises to that effect. The first was on 5 March 1974, before the Labour Officer, Onitsha, and the Resident, Onitsha Province, the principal administrative officer of the Province. The second was on 17 April 1974, before the union's National President, Alhaji A. D. O. Abutu, and the Obi (King) of Onitsha. None of these promises was fulfilled. Employers in Nigeria usually ask unions seeking recognition to tender proof of their membership among the workers they seek to represent as a condition for according recognition. It would appear that the same procedure was adopted in this case. What followed after tendering that proof is better narrated by the branch secretary. He says: 'Instead of according recognition, the management took our nominal roll which they effectively utilised to dismiss our members. ... By 31 December 1974, 400 members of our union had been dismissed.'[3]

In June 1974 a rival union, apparently sponsored by the management, was formed. It was called the 'General Cotton Mill Workers' Union'. Management urged the workers to join it and dissociate themselves from the NTGLGWU which they described as the 'Hausa/Yoruba irresponsible union'. 'All the agents of the management baby union were made sectional or departmental heads and detailed to report any member of the NTGLGWU which order had been effectively carried out.'[4] Throughout 1974 the General Cotton Mill management failed to recognise the NTGLGWU. Twice that year (August and December) the Labour Officer, Onitsha and the Principal Labour Officer, Enugu, asked the workers to prepare for a plebiscite, the aim being to determine which of the unions claiming to represent them had a majority support. For reasons which were never made known to the workers the plebiscite was not held. The NTGLGWU later described the plebiscite suggestion as a deceit and added that the Principal Labour Officer's attitude did not command the respect of the workers. On 31 January 1975 the NTGLGWU Onitsha branch organised a strike in furtherance of its claim for recognition. Management reacted by declaring the entire workforce as having been dismissed. Eventually 1,500 were re-engaged on the specific condition that they joined the General Cotton Mill Workers' Union. A few months after the strike the Principal Labour Officer who had played a role in the dispute retired from the public service and took up appointment with the General Cotton Mill Limited as a Personnel Officer. In July 1976 the company concluded a recognition agreement with the NTGLGWU, Onitsha branch.

It is still a problem for union organisers to gain access to the premises of certain employers. Farms and plantations of certain foreign companies and parastatal development corporations are cases in point. Farms and plantations are usually located in remote areas, and the workers live in company housing estates close by. Although members of the public could visit them and their families without previous authorisation, that facility is not always open to union organisers if they are known as such. In certain countries, and even in certain areas of the same country, organisers must first obtain permission from the company before entry otherwise they could be prosecuted for trespass because the housing estates are deemed to be private property. To obtain permission organisers must disclose the object of their mission, and this places them under the surveillance of hostile employers. Spies report on contacts, meetings held and decisions taken. In due course management announces reorganisation programmes and declares some of the key men redundant or finds other excuses to terminate their employment. In East and Central Africa it used to be a fashion for agricultural and plantation workers' unions to conclude access agreements before undertaking any meaningful organisation programmes. That practice has almost been completely abandoned with the growth of comprehensive collective agreements covering this and other provisions.

Check-off is not operated by every union in Africa. It takes a long time to negotiate check-off in certain countries and almost as much time to pass the administrative bottleneck to put the agreement into operation. In the meantime, the union must collect dues from its members. The normal practice is for shop stewards or specially designated collectors to collect during pay day, and their task is made easy by management agreeing that collectors be supplied with tables and chairs and be allowed to sit near the paymaster. Such a facility is still a dream for certain unions in certain countries.

In most countries employers have yet to shed themselves of some of the tactics they used to employ in industrial disputes during the colonial period. One is refusal to bargain at all with trade unions or, if pressed to do so, bargaining in bad faith. The other is the habit of using the police to break strikes. It is not uncommon to hear union leaders complaining that some employers would negotiate and reach agreements with them but these agreements would not be implemented for one reason or the other. The growth of industrial courts or similar bodies charged with the responsibility of adjudicating industrial disputes, interpreting collective agreements and making legally binding awards owes its origin to the desire of governments to find a solution to this perplexing problem.

Police involvement in industrial disputes often arises in this way. If a dispute is declared, or the union gives notice of a strike action, the employer contacts the local police and asks them to send a detachment to protect his property and keep the peace because, according to him, a breach of the peace is apprehended. The police dutifully comply. When they arrive, and the strikers are outside the workplace they order them to disperse, including the pickets. Sometimes they do not stop there, but try to help the employer to make way for strike breakers or 'scabs' (in American terminology) to get in. It is this action which often leads to clashes between strikers and the police. It has been reported that following mounting criticism of their role, the police in certain countries have modified their methods of operation in industrial disputes. Instead of pleasing the employer by doing whatever he asks, they invite the appropriate union officials to their office for what they describe as a 'chat'. The chat may go on for some days and ultimately the strike may be called off without achieving its objective, particularly in a situation where the union cannot pay strike benefit. The Nigeria Police has been reported as having used this method several times.[5]

Quality of Union Leadership

To a certain extent, the state of a union is a reflection of the quality of its leadership. A leader must lead. But to be able to lead properly he must derive his authority from the members and he must be guided by what they want or desire. Leadership imposes an obligation to think and originate ideas, to discuss these ideas with other colleagues and members of the union, a willingness to receive and consider suggestions from them, tender advice when necessary, and generally to guide the union in making decisions. A good union leader knows that the union is not his private affair, and avoids running it like his private vineyard. Although he may have his own ambitions he tries to subordinate them to the interest of the union. How do union leaders in Africa meet these basic qualifications of leadership?

In considering this question it must be borne in mind that there are two main categories of union leaders in Africa—the elected and the appointed. The elected are usually employees of companies, factories, the public services, public utilities and local government bodies. They hold such offices as President, Vice-President, General Secretary (if the position is honorary), Treasurer, Auditor or Trustee. The appointed are full-time salaried officials of the secretariat headed by the General Secretary. In some unions the General Secretary is elected by a delegates conference for a specified period, but before the end of that period his position is made permanent, and he is therefore not liable for election at a succeeding conference. In others he is appointed by the Executive and he holds office at their pleasure. The General Secretary may be appointed by means of an advertisement in the local press, and sometimes he may not have had any previous trade union experience. In most unions the full-time salaried officials and other staff members are not members of the union or of any trade union. There appears to be no arrangement similar to that of Europe and North America whereby when a leader is elected to a full-time position he is granted leave of absence by his employers during his tenure of office and he has the right to return to his job when he is voted out. Thus you have an army of people who claim to be trade union leaders but who actually do not belong to the trade union family. Some of the problems of the trade union movement in Africa owe their origin to this state of affairs.

There is no doubt whatsoever that certain African trade union leaders compare favourably in competence, dedication and militancy with their counterparts in other parts of the world. It is equally true that there are many others who do not deserve to be in the trade union movement at all. In every country you find these types of union leaders, but the latter tends to predominate hence the instability in the movement. What may be described as the legion of mercenaries in the movement exists for a number of reasons. Workers tend to vote or appoint some of their leaders because such leaders come from the same ethnic origin, or belong to the same political party or religion with them rather than base their choice on proven ability to discharge the responsibilities of the office and dedication to the union. Many union leaders see the trade union movement as a springboard for higher ambitions. These higher ambitions may be to secure a political office or acquire wealth at all costs. It is not uncommon to hear that some full-time salaried officials of trade unions are on the pay roll of the employers whose workers they represent. 'Gin and tonic' is a popular nickname in Nairobi. It refers to a union official and his connections and deals with employers. In Lagos one union leader is said to be in regular receipt of cheques and other presents from employers. The Adebiyi

Tribunal report tells incredible stories about the low quality of some Nigerian trade union leaders. One union leader, Alhaji Babs Animashaun, was not only the proprietor of a large transport company but he had unexplained lodgment of 255,457.54 Naira (£N127,728 6s. 5d.). This case is particularly interesting because what helped him to start the transport business was a loan of 300,000 Naira (£N150,000) granted to him by the United Bank for Africa whose employees were members of the National Union of Nigerian Bank Employees (NUNBE) of which he was the General Secretary. Before getting the loan Animashaun had overdrawn his personal account by 59,000 Naira. Between December 1971 and February 1972 the bank had nine industrial disputes with NUNBE over pay claims, improvement of the conditions of service, non-granting of loans to staff and termination of the appointment of a senior management staff. The Tribunal found 'that the grant of these loans totalling 359,000 Naira to Alhaji Animashaun was a favour to him which naturally, would attract a *quid pro quo*. A good trade unionist should not put himself in a position where his private interests would conflict with his duty to his employers, i.e. the bank employees in this case. The bank is no less culpabable in the matter'.[6] Animashaun's union was proscribed before the appointment of the Adebiyi Tribunal.

The quality of union leadership may also be examined in the light of its effect on full-time salaried union officials and staff and the loss to employers and governments in many African countries of able union officials. It is an irony that African trade unions are possibly the worst employers in the continent, in contrast to trade unions in other parts of the world, which not only offer attractive terms but sometimes exceed those offered by industry as part of their commitment to use their own example to justify some of their demands. Israel is a case in point. Trade unions in Africa often fight for what they generally call 'better conditions of service', meaning higher wages, and improvements in fringe benefits and other terms of employment. How many unions extend these conditions to their full-time officials and staff? Experience varies from country to country and from union to union in a single country. It is not uncommon to hear full-time union officials and staff complain that their salaries, which are well below comparable pay in positions in industry and the public service, are not paid on time or may not be paid at all for some months; that those entitled to overtime may not be paid or the payment may be delayed for an unreasonably long time; that leave and leave allowance are poor compared with conditions in industry and the public service; and that it is usually difficult to get reimbursement for medical expenses. How many unions and national trade union centres ever think that their full-time salaried officials and staff may one day reach retiring age and that in the absence of a national pension scheme provision ought to be made for their retirement benefit? The men and women who work full-time for trade unions in Africa are like any other workers—they have families and obligations and are entitled to some of the good things of life; they also have their ambitions. If the union does not create the objctive conditions for them to remain they will leave—which is largely the reason for the loss of able trade unionists.

Who should be blamed for this state of affairs—leaders or members, or a combination of both? Are African workers, who are generally sensitive to exploitation, particularly interested in exploiting those they employ to represent and service them? In the absence of conclusive evidence, the ordinary union members must be given the benefit of the doubt. It is the responsibility of the leaders to formulate good personnel policies and proposals for their implementation. Much of this responsibility lies with the General Secretary, who is usually the head of the secretariat. In some of the big national unions and national centres some of these things are being done, but in the great majority the General Secretaries do not take their responsibilities seriously, and therefore fail.

Effects
How do the factors we have just examined affect the union on the shop floor? In particular, how does the ordinary member see his union and the trade union movement in general? Here again experience varies from country to country and from one union to the other in the same country. It all depends on the average member's understanding of what the union is all about, what successes or failures the union has to its credit or debit in relation to its primary responsibility of protecting and improving the lot of its members, the relationship existing between the unions and the ruling political parties or military regimes, the degree of free thinking existing in the country and the freedom to give expression to it without the fear or prospect that by so doing one would disappear or be victimised in one form or the other, the influence which the union's head office has on the shop floor and the influence of members' views in the decision making process of the union. In those countries where there have been no ties between the unions and political parties or where such ties have been tenuous, there seems to be a better understanding and appreciation of what unions are and how they help the workers and their families. Members are quick to point out that their wages and salaries and

working conditions have been improved through the union's efforts. They generally acknowledge that the effectiveness of the union depends largely on their support and the fact that it is an independent bargaining agent of the workers. They would like the unions to maintain their independence.

In those countries where there are close ties between the unions and ruling parties or military juntas, members' understanding of what the union is depends on the definition given by the parties or juntas. Thus if the parties or juntas think that the unions are not free instruments for safeguarding the social and economic interests of the workers but merely tools for the implementation of party and government policies, members tend to accept that concept, particularly if the magic words 'economic development' are given as a justification. This desire to convert the unions from what William H. Friedland calls a 'consumptionist' to a 'productionist'[7] role is mainly responsible for the spate of 'reorganisation' of trade unions in many countries claiming to be of socialist or egalitarian orientation. It explains why in certain countries union leaders are imposed rather than elected by the workers they are expected to represent, or why elections are conducted in such a manner that only the 'good boys' or 'good girls' of the parties or governments are elected. Union officials and representatives on the shop floor operate not in keeping with the wishes of their members but in accordance with the decision of the parties or juntas. In some countries, Zanzibar for example, the union has ceased to exist on the shop floor and throughout the island, and its functions have been taken over by 'party cells'. During the International Conference on Adult Education and Development which was held in Dar-es-Salaam in 1976, the participants (of which I was one) went on an excursion to Zanzibar. In this rare visit to the island a guide conducting visitors round a sugar factory built by the Chinese made no efforts to disguise the situation: 'We have no unions here; workers' problems are being taken care of by the party and party cells in the factory and other workplaces.'

Nothing does greater damage to the union's image in the eyes of the ordinary member as insincerity, dishonesty and abuse of office by union officials and functionaries be they at the shop floor, the branch, district or national level. When such weaknesses are known members' confidence in the union declines, support weakens, and sometimes members quit in disgust. Organisers generally report that it is easier to recruit workers who have never been union members before than regaining the membership of those who left the union because they were cheated by certain union officials.

The array of laws aimed at forestalling labour disputes and

preventing strikes has not achieved its purpose in many countries. The Nigerian experience is a good example. During the period 1968–75 when most of these laws were promulgated more than 2,500 disputes were declared of which more than 50 per cent led to strikes. The 1976 Decrees which repealed all previous laws governing trade disputes and enacted more stringent measures including the proscription of trade unions and the detention of trade union leaders in certain circumstances were defied in nineteen strikes which took place in 1976 at Ikeja industrial estate, about 15 kilometres from Lagos, and which led to the loss of 29,433 man-days. In the same year, one dock workers' union contravened the provisions of the Decree regulating disputes in 'essential services' by failing to give the statutory fifteen days' notice before ordering the workers out. The union argued that the men were 'working to rule'.

As a result of the campaign which has been going on since 1960 namely, that international affiliation by African trade unions is an evil thing, the average union member seldom realises that he has common problems with his counterparts in other parts of the world, and that international solidarity of the working class is the best solution to the systematic erosion of trade union rights in many areas of the world and the problems created by multinational corporations. For good or for ill, Africa is the only continent in the world where you have a so-called continental trade union organisation created and maintained largely by governments. The wider implications of the campaign against international affiliation are discussed in Chapter 10.

10. PROSPECTS AND PROBLEMS

What are the prospects of the trade union movement in Africa? In considering the question one must think of the social, political and economic conditions of the continent, the existence of the OAU and the OATUU, the concept of Pan-Africanism, the performances of the unions themselves, the activities of international trade union organisations, the ILO and aid agencies operating there. Trade union development cannot proceed in isolation of these factors. A columnist of the *New African Development* summed up the social conditions of Africa in a short article captioned 'Time for Bitter Home Truths'. Writing in the November 1977 issue he said, among other things, that 'it is not just that nothing seems to work from the telephone to the airlines: not that public officers see themselves as masters rather than servants of the people; that bank clerks think that their duty is to take money from customers and insult them when they want to make withdrawals (except, of course if you are an Alhaji or an Alhaja); that everybody if trying to cheat every body else; that corruption has become an accepted way of life; or that the whole place has become an open lavatory where men and women, boys and girls, strip at will and do their thing without a care for hygiene and decency. No; what gets me more is that people you expect to know better won't stand you complaining and asking that things be done properly. They quickly dismiss you as a black European who has been brainwashed to see nothing good in his own people. Worse, they cannot accept that there is any thing wrong with us ... it is always the fault of the white man, the legacy of colonialism and imperialism ... when the electricity and telephone fail, it is not because we have incompetent engineers, but because the whiteman sold us obsolete equipment or because the whitemen in our employ are sabotaging our efforts ... Well, I don't know. But I cannot see the future for the black race if we continue to think and act like that. Call it a chip on the shoulder, inferiority complex or what you like. What I say is if after two decades of self-rule we still blame colonialism for our ills then we can never grow up.'

Observers of the political scene sometimes refer to Africa as the 'turbulent continent', an expression depicting the great changes that have been taking place since 1963. For it was that year that Africa and the world witnessed two changes of government—one peaceful, the other violent—which have since become common place. President Sylvanus Olympio of Togo died of an assassin's bullet, and Abbe Fulbert Youlou of Congo was forced out of office by protest demonstrations in which the trade unions played a leading role. The Zanzibar revolution and the army mutinies in Kenya and Tanganyika in 1964 were further evidence of signs of things to come. Ben Bella of Algeria, Kasavubu of the Congo (now Zaire) and David Dacko of Central African Republic (now Empire) were overthrown in 1965. In 1966 the most significant military coups took place in West Africa. Maurice Yameogo of Upper Volta gave way on 3 January to Lt. Col. Sangoule Lamizana. Twelve days later, a rump cabinet in Nigeria called upon Major General Aguiyi-Ironsi to take over the administration of the country, Balewa's broad-based Government having been overthrown by a dissident group in the army. Barely one month after the great event in Nigeria, a combined operation of the army and the police force removed the Nkrumah regime in Ghana. Since 1966, hardly has a year passed without one African government being overthrown. Writing in *New African Development*, May 1977, Umunna reported that of the twenty-nine heads of states and governments who formed the Organisation of African Unity and signed its Charter on 23 May 1963 only seven were still in office; four heads of state died natural deaths while in office; two were killed by their soldiers and sixteen were overthrown by military coups.

What went wrong? Why did people who traditionally show great respect and loyalty to authority suddenly become restive and went to the extreme measure of adopting unconstitutional methods to change their governments. These questions are a constant reminder of some of the weaknesses of Africa's first republics. At independence practically all African governments inherited the norms of government and administration bequeathed by the former colonial powers of Britain, France and Belgium. (Spain and Portugal relinquished their own colonial authority only recently.) These norms, with varying details, had certain common features, among them were guarantees for security of life and property, free and fair elections based on the principle of one man one vote, an impartial and independent judiciary, adherence to the rule of law, freedom of association, of speech, of political and religious belief. During the elections which preceded the attainment of independence, the ruling political parties made certain promises to the electorates in exchange for the mandate to govern. After independence the people naturally expected the fulfilment of these promises or some of them. Rising expectations not only came in conflict with various constraints which were not necessarily the making of the politicians, but also with the personal interests of the ruling élites. Allegations of corruption, nepotism and abuse of office were rife. To protect themselves and silence criticism the ruling élites took harsh measures against their opponents and in the name of 'national security'.

Besides the trade unions which were generally considered as 'agitators' the press was one of the earliest objects of attack. Laws and regulations restricting press freedom were promulgated in many countries. It was generally argued that the press were too critical of governments and did not give a fair and accurate coverage of their activities. Some governments alleged that the most powerful and influential sections of the press did this because they were foreign-owned. This allegation decided the action of several governments to set up their own newspapers or compulsorily acquire most of the foreign owned and well established newspapers in their countries. With the possible exception of a handful, there is hardly an independent African country where independent newspapers and magazines worthy of their name exist. Press freedom is intimately related to the ownership of the press concerned.

In the art of government certain principles and certain institutions have been developed almost to the point of sacredness. The concept of representative government derives from the fact that since all the citizens of the country cannot be assembled together in one place because of the sheer size of number and limitation of space, the people should participate in the government of their country through the periodical election of representatives in the legislature. The method generally adopted for this election is secret ballot by eligible voters, and the election must be fair and free. The concept of an impartial and independent judiciary derives from the assumption that where two parties are quarrelling, a neutral third party should step in and settle the quarrel after hearing evidence from both sides. It also implies that those who make the law should not interpret or execute it: interpretation and execution should be left to law enforcement agencies like the police and the courts. Cognate to the concept of an impartial and independent judiciary is the rule generally referred to as The Rule of Law, which stipulates that no person should be punished except for a definite breach of the law and proof of that breach should be established in a court of law. The African Conference on the Rule of Law (Lagos, Nigeria, January 1961) attended by 194 judges, practising lawyers and teachers of law from twenty-three African countries as well as nine countries in other continents emphasised the importance of the rule when it declared that:

The Rule of Law is a dynamic concept which should be employed to safeguard and advance the will of the people and the political rights of the individual and to establish social, economic, educational and cultural conditions under which the individual may achieve his dignity and realise his legitimate aspirations in all countries whether dependent and independent ... that in order to maintain adequately the Rule of Law all Governments should adhere to the principle of democratic representation in their legislatures; and that fundamental human rights, especially the right to personal liberty should be written and entrenched in the constitutions of all countries and that such personal liberty should not in peace time be restricted without trial in a court of law.[1]

The Law of Lagos (as the Declaration was later known) eventually came to be more honoured in the breach than the observance as Africa's first republics collapsed in quick succession and military regimes and one-party states substituted multi-party governments. Even before that development, Nigeria, the host country, created the precedent in the breach when the ruling élite, obsessed by the desire to destroy the Opposition declared a state of emergency in the former Western Region. It was during the debate on a bill to that effect that Chief Anthony Enahoro, then an Opposition frontliner in the House of Representatives, made his famous prophesy when he said that Nigerian Parliamentarians were 'setting in motion a chain of events the end of which no one can tell.' From the state of emergency Nigeria steadily went down the precipice of disintegration culminating in thirty months of savage civil war. States of emergency followed in many other countries with the ruling élites assuming incredible powers of arrest and detention of political opponents and any person who would not agree with them or support their policies. In such conditions most of the people arrested and detained are not charged or tried in any court of law, yet they are kept in jail for months or years and, in some cases, tortured, maimed or killed. Writing in *New African Development*, August 1977, Ali Mazrui pointed out that 'since 1963 a lot of blood has flowed under Africa's continental bridge. It is now less a case of protecting African presidents from the violence of their adversaries than of protecting African people from the violence of their presidents.'

Free and fair elections hardly exist now in Africa except in those few countries where the right to govern is still based on the verdict of the ballot box rather than the barrel of the gun. But even in those places the results of elections have often been disputed. The general elections in Sierra Leone in May 1977 were a farce. Journalists covering the elections reported that 'even before a single ballot had been cast the ruling party had claimed half the contested seats through unopposed candidates ... the elections were traditionally conducted in the style of minor civil wars ... and in the pitched battles which the two sides fought in the streets the APC stalwarts often had an edge thanks, in part, to little help from overzealous law officers.'[2]

Some people have tried to suggest that political instability in most African countries owes its origin to the adoption of what they call 'Westminster-style democracy', and argue that that style of democracy cannot work in Africa because 'Africans are a different kind of people'. The very nature of politics implies the existence of different viewpoints and methods of achieving certain political objectives whether the game of politics is played in Africa or in other parts of the world. The problem with African politics is not whether there should be different view points and methods, but how safe can those who hold them be in exercising that fundamental human right. Secondly, will the ruling élite in any country tolerate views and methods aimed at convincing the electorate to vote for an alternative government at another general election without labelling such views or methods as subversion or treason? To suggest that the existence of more than one political party in a given country is the cause of political instability is merely begging the question. It ignores a basic weakness in most African political leaders—deep-rooted intolerance of opposition. Those who maintain a public posture of welcoming opposition at best merely tolerate them: there is no heart to accommodate opposition and allow them freedom of action and expression that would enable them become an alternative government. Some African political leaders, particularly those who led their countries to independence, still believe in something akin to the theory of Divine Right of Kings.

The argument against Westminster style democracy does not impress. It assumes that because a part of humanity inhabits a geographical area called Africa, therefore, a system of government evolved in a different continent over the years and which has in many respects proved effective and efficient, should not be applied to that section of humanity called 'Africans'. The attempt to dilute the concept and practice of democracy with the appellation of 'Westminster' is the old tactic of the rabble rouser who lacks argument and tries to substitute argument with prejudice. It is like saying that a hospital in Britain, France or the United States serves a different purpose from one in Accra, Kisumu or Kitwe. But perhaps the most ridiculous argument advanced to justify the so-called Westminster style democracy is the one based on tradition. It is said that in traditional Africa, there was no party system and Africans were not divided into opposing camps. Africans should therefore return to their traditional ways of doing things. The party system of government as is known today might not have existed in traditional Africa, but its ingredients of consultation and discussion were deeply rooted in almost every African society. The apostles of tradition ignore the fact that there are now very few things which can be said to be traditionally African either in origin or development. Our governmental structure, education, banking and insurance, modern business methods and trade unionism are but a few of the institutions and services now existing in the various African countries which could hardly be said to be traditionally African in origin and development. Africa has benefited tremendously from the wealth of human knowledge and has made her own contributions. The idea, therefore, that certain norms are suitable for certain sections of humanity and unsuitable to others because 'Africans are a different kind of people' must be dumped into the rubbish heap.

Africa is a potentially rich but actually a poor continent because her economy has not been developed. Mineral resources abound in several African countries, but their exploitation in the interest of the people has been limited by several constraints. Since independence, practically every government has been doing whatever it could to achieve economic growth and improve the living standard of the people. Some governments believe in a mixed economy, and allow both private and state capital to be involved in the development of the economy. Others believe in socialism as an economic and political philosophy, but its application differs from country to country. No government appears to have adopted capitalism as an economic philosophy. Two contributions to economic and political thought may be examined. The Kenya Government claims to believe in what it calls 'African Socialism' and declares its development efforts to be based on that concept. 'African socialism' is defined as an 'African political and economic system that is positively African not being imported from any country or being a blueprint of any foreign ideology but capable of incorporating useful and compatible techniques from whatever source. The principal conditions the system must satisfy are (i) it must draw from the best of African traditions; (ii) it must be adaptable to new and rapidly changing circumstances; and (iii) it must not rest for its success on a satellite relationship with any other country or group of countries'.[3]

Tanzania also believes in socialism but adds a rider to its accomplishment—self-reliance. Clause 9 of TANU's creed on which the Arusha Declaration was based states that 'it is the responsibility of the state to intervene actively in the economic life of the nation so as to ensure the well-being of all citizens and so as to prevent the exploitation of one man by another, and so as to prevent the accumulation of wealth to an extent which is inconsistent with the existence of a classless society.'[4] Socialism, the pamphlet adds, implies four principal tenets—independence, absence of exploitation, the major means of production must be under the control of peasants and workers, and democracy, with strict adherence to its principles. Independence means self-reliance. Independence cannot be real if the country depends on gifts and loans from another country for its development. The Arusha Declaration of January 1967, stipulates that every TANU and Government leader must be either a peasant or a worker and should in no way be associated with the practices of capitalism or feudalism; no TANU or Government leader should hold shares in any company or directorship in any privately owned enterprise; no TANU or Government leader should receive more than one salary or own houses which he rents to others. For the purpose of the Declaration the term 'leader' means members of TANU National Executive Committee, Ministers of State, Members of Parliament, senior officials of organisations affiliated to TANU, senior officials of parastatal organisations, and all those elected or appointed under any clause of the TANU constitution, councillors, civil servants in high and middle cadres and includes a man and his wife, a woman or a woman and her husband. Prior to the publication of the Arusha Declaration, President Julius Nyerere had announced, in a nation-wide radio broadcast, the nationalisation of eight food processing plants, and eight purchasing and distribution companies which, he said, would constitute the nucleus of a State Trading Corporation and would be responsible for external and wholesale trade. In addition the state was to take controlling shares in seven giant companies engaged in the manufacture of beer, tobacco, shoes and cement. Whether the Government's policies and measures were right or wrong may be measured from the results. In a review of them sometime in 1976 President Nyerere admitted that while remarkable progress had been made in certain areas, e.g. the banks and some of the big commercial undertaking, notable failures had also been recorded in others, e.g. the *ujamma* village scheme which was not well received in certain areas, and in the organisation of co-operatives by government officials rather than by the traditional method based on the Rochdale principles.

In most African countries the notion of 'nation state' is synonymous with the man at the helm of affairs. Disagreement with him and his policies or disagreement with the policies of his government is often interpreted as subversion or treason. Pan-Africanism and the existence of the OAU and the OATUU have added new dimensions to the political and trade union situations. Article III of the OAU Charter is both the strength and weakness of the organisation. In so far as it bans interference in the internal affairs of its member states it provides a basis for unity. But when non-interference becomes a shield or a licence in certain African states for the wanton destruction of lives and property and the OAU keeps silent or appears helpless or when the authors of non-interference who themselves are members of international organisations arrogate to themselves the right to dictate the international relations of trade unions they provoke resentment and criticism. In so far as it reaffirms the policy of non-alignment to all blocs the OAU is merely restating what its members have adopted as the corner-stone of their foreign policy. But non-alignment means one thing to certain African leaders and quite a different thing to others. The late Pandit Jawaharlal Nehru, India's first Prime Minister, who coined the phrase and introduced 'non-alignment' to political discussions gave an indication in 1961 of what he had in mind. Addressing the first summit conference of the Non-Aligned States in Belgrade he said:

We call ourselves non-aligned countries. The word 'non-aligned' may be differently interpreted, but basically it was coined and used with the meaning of being non-aligned with the power blocs of the world. 'Non-aligned' has a negative meaning. But if we give it a positive connotation it means nations which object to lining up for war purposes to military blocs, to military alliances and the like. We keep away from such an approach and we want to throw our weight in favour of peace. In effect, therefore, when there is a crisis involving the possibility of war, the very fact that we are non-aligned should stir us to feel that, more than ever, it is up to us to do whatever we can to prevent such a calamity coming down upon us.[5]

Colin Legum reports that a preliminary meeting held in Cairo to prepare the way for the Belgrade conference defined officially for the first time what non-alignment means. He says, 'To be non-aligned a country must (i) pursue an independent policy based on peaceful co-existence; (ii) not participate in multilateral military alliances (e.g. NATO, the Warsaw Pact, SEATO or CENTO); (iii) support liberation and independence movements; and (iv) not participate in bilateral military alliances with great powers, nor should it have foreign military base on its territory set up with their agreement.'[6]

If non-alignment means non-involvement in military alliances how did it become an issue in the trade union movement in Africa? Are African trade unions or the international trade union movement military blocs or alliances? To understand this development it is necessary to bear in mind the opposition to colonial rule and the effect which state-sponsored propaganda had and is likely to have in people's minds. Nkrumah's Ghana, the AATUF, the Casablanca powers and the WFTU bear full responsibility for it as well as the pathetic inability of certain trade union leaders to distinguish the wheat from the chaff. The international trade union movement as represented by the ICFTU and the ITS associated with it is made up of trade union organisations from the non-communist world. Merely because some of these trade union organisations come from the former colonial powers of Britain, France and Belgium, the impression was created that they were tools of their governments and would be used by them to perpetuate what was generally known as 'neo-colonialism' in Africa. For that reason African workers were to have nothing to do with the ICFTU and ITS. What probably could have been dismissed out of hand was given some measure of credibility by a strange document circulated during the ILO First African Conference in Lagos in 1960 captioned 'The Great Conspiracy Against Africa'. The document, said to have been issued by the All-African Trade Union Federation (AATUF) which was yet to be formed, was alleged to be an annex to a British Government White Paper on policies in Africa. It said that 'recent developments there have greatly increased the importance of the unions as alternative instrument of western influence and especially as a brake on unchecked political and national movement. Since it is difficult to accuse trade unions of serving colonial ends, with their aid it should be possible to establish harmonious relations with the new social and political institutions in Africa now being created and with the administration of industrial and agricultural interests, which we hope to maintain after any political changes. Trade unions will be needed to check irresponsible nationalisation and to maintain control of the key sectors of the economy in the newly created African states. The principal aim should be the development in Africa of a genuine trade union movement as we know it in Britain and on the continent. This must be done with our help and under our influence from the start'.[7] Although the document was denounced as a forgery it nevertheless did the desired damage, namely to create hostility against the ICFTU and ITS in Africa. OAU and OATUU continued the propaganda when they came into existence. Non-alignment was equated with non-affiliation to international trade union organisations, particularly affiliation to the ICFTU.

In view of the noise often made against international affiliation the time has arrived for a brief discussion of the matter. International affiliation is one of the basic trade union rights enshrined in Convention 87 of the ILO. Article 5 of that Convention reads: 'Workers' and employers' organisations shall have the right to establish and join federations and confederations and any such organisation, federation or confederation shall have the right to affiliate with international organisations of workers and employers.' Up till July 1977 Convention 87 had been ratified by only twenty-four African states. It is true that under the rules governing legal obligations deriving from conventions, legal obligation arises only when a country has ratified a convention. It is equally true that member states of the ILO which have not ratified any particular convention have a moral obligation to do so having undertaken, on joining the organisation, to respect international labour standards established by its Conventions and Recommendations. The Africans themselves seem to recognise this fact when they adopted a resolution at the Fourth African Regional Conference of the ILO meeting in Nairobi in 1973 concerning the ratification and implementation of international labour standards. The resolution noted that 'while progress has been made in the ratification of international labour conventions by African states since they became Members of the International Labour Organisation ... the possibilities for the acceptance and implementation of ILO standards have in most countries not been fully or systematically explored'. It reiterated 'the special importance attached to the ratification and strict application of Conventions relating to the protection of certain fundamental human rights (freedom of association, elimination of discrimination in employment and occupation, abolition of forced labour and penal sanctions for breach of contracts of employment), which *the First African Regional Conferences (Lagos, 1960) declared to be a question of honour and prestige for all African States.*' The resolution then invited 'African States encountering difficulties in the implementation of ILO standards to have recourse to the procedure of direct contacts with the International Labour Organisation, and where appropriate, to have recourse also to technical co-operation as a means of overcoming these difficulties.'

The most surprising thing about the denial of the right of international affiliation is that it appears to be limited to trade unions. As far as is known no Government in Africa has prohibited its employers' organisations, youth movements, students or womens' organisations from international affiliation. The word 'international' is often misused in this context. Opponents of international affiliation create the impression that they are merely against organic links with organisations outside the African continent. But the meaning of 'international' is 'between different nations', and implies therefore that organic link with an organisation grouping the various national centres in Africa like the OATUU is also international.

The obligations and benefits of international affiliation have already been outlined in Chapter 9. Now I wish to examine its intrinsic value and its significance to the concept African Personality which Pan-Africanism tries to foster. As indicated earlier, international affiliation brings African trade unions in contact with their counterparts in the industrialised and Third World countries of Asia, the Caribbean, Latin America and the Pacific. It creates a forum for an exchange of views and experiences and finding solutions to some of the problems facing the working people of the world, and all parties benefit one way or the other from the exercise. Affiliation obliges African trade unions to pay dues which help to maintain the organisations to which they are affiliated. This is a universal trade union obligation and indeed the universal obligation of organisations which are affiliated to other organisations. Through participation in the activities of the organisations to which they are affiliated African trade unions make the voice of Africa heard in one of the most important councils of the world. African personality may be projected anywhere, but there is no doubt that the most important and effective forum to do so is international gatherings where non-Africans may wish to see Africans and hear African voice. African governments themselves have set an example by their membership of such international organisations like the Commonwealth, the UN and its Specialised Agencies like the ILO, WHO, FAO, UNESCO etc. If the Governments have done this, is any thing fundamentally wrong in allowing the trade unions to do the same? Should government spokesmen be the only medium of projecting the African Personality in international gatherings?

Some governments have tried to justify the denial of the right of international affiliation with the argument of the alleged corruption of union leaders which is said to be one of the effects of that relationship. No attempt is being made here to ignore some of the weaknesses of certain trade union leaders. Suffice it to say, however, that union leaders are not the only corrupt people in Africa or in any given African country. Corruption exists in government, the public service, commerce and industry, but no one has tried to suggest that because of it government or the public service should cease to exist, or that the wheels of commerce and industry should grind to a halt. Denial of the right of international affiliation is having an adverse moral effect on African trade unions. Besides the wild and wholly unsubstantiated allegation that international affiliation is against African interest no one has been able to adduce any tangible reason why there should be no affiliation. The attitude of certain union leaders to the question is baffling. Not infrequently one sees them as the greatest apologists of the policies of their governments. The law of certain countries provides that affiliation should not be undertaken without the approval of the Minister of Labour. Most leaders of unaffiliated national trade union centres interpret the provision as a blanket prohibition against international affiliation. Until there has been a test case, certain Governments will continue to argue that international affiliation is not prohibited as such, but that the unions have failed to comply with the provisions of the law relating to it. While many African union leaders consider organic link with international trade union organisations as an abominable thing they do not think it humiliating to approach these organisations and their affiliates in Europe and North America for funds and technical assistance. In other words, it is a bad thing to affiliate to international organisations, but it is a good thing to accept their money. Only people devoid of principle and pride will behave like this or encourage people to behave like that. Through such an ambivalence most African trade unions have formed the habit of wishing to benefit from trade union funds without any regard for their obligation to contribute to them. This is the well known attitude of the 'free rider' whom the trade unions condemn unequivocally. This 'free riding' attitude is not limited to global internationals like the ICFTU, WFTU and WCL but is also extended to ITS and OATUU. Only two of the eight remaining affiliates of the ICFTU in Africa pay dues.

Of the fifty-seven African trade unions affiliated to four International Trade Secretariats in 1974—FIET, IFPAAW, ITGLWF and MIF—only ten paid dues regularly to their respective ITS, five paid irregularly and the rest paid nothing. The MIF received dues regularly from 58 per cent of its African affiliates; the ITGLWF received regularly from 17 per cent and irregularly from 11 per cent while the IFPAAW received regularly from 22 per cent and irregularly from 30 per cent. Between April 1973 and June 1975, only seventeen of the OATUU's forty-eight affiliates paid dues. How regularly these payments were made is unknown. The highest amounts were paid by the UNTC (Cameroun), NUTA (Tanzania) and UNTZa (Zaire). Between July 1975 and February 1976 only six of its affiliates—the CNTG

(Guinea), ZCTU (Zambia), NOTU (Uganda), UMT (Mauritania), SWC (Somalia) and UMT (Mali)—paid dues. The audited accounts of the organisation during the period 13 April 1973 to 30 June 1975 shows an income of 316,499.99 Ghanaian cedis ($\mathcal{C}$) made up as follows: subventions from OAU $\mathcal{C}$193,280.31 (61 per cent); special contributions $\mathcal{C}$79,941.75 (25·2 per cent); Government grants $\mathcal{C}$19,986 (6·3 per cent); and affiliation dues $\mathcal{C}$23,281.93 (7·3 per cent). According to the unaudited account for the period 1 July 1975 to 29 February 1976 presented to the OATUU Second Congress in Libya in April 1976 the total income for the period was $\mathcal{C}$190,780.95 made up as follows: subventions from OAU and the Ghana Government $\mathcal{C}$114,716.57 (60·1 per cent) (OAU $\mathcal{C}$104,716.51, Ghana Government $\mathcal{C}$10,000.06); and dues $\mathcal{C}$14,272.95 (7·4 per cent). For the financial year July 1976 to June 1977 the OATUU Secretariat prepared a budget of US$1,539,662 of which, if receipts matched estimates (which seldom happens), the organisation hoped to realise only $904,000 (58·7 per cent) made up as follows: dues from forty-eight affiliated organisations at $3,000 each $144,000 (9·3 per cent); OAU subventions $130,000 (8·4 per cent); government donations $480,000 (31·1 per cent); pledges by affiliates $100,000 (6·4 per cent) and other sources (sale of badges, fund-raising activities etc.) $50,000 (3·2 per cent). As much as $635,662 (41·2 per cent) of the budget is categorised as 'deficits'. When presenting the budget to the Libyan Congress, Chief E. O. A. Odeyemi, Assistant Secretary General in charge of Finance and Administration, gave no indication of a concrete proposal of how the decifits were to be covered. He merely suggested to the Congress to appeal to the OAU and African Governments and 'any organisations that can help us without any strings attached' to increase their subventions and grants. Although the secretariat could not balance its 'Consolidation Budget' which increased the 1975 'Austerity Budget' by 88·6 per cent nevertheless it proposed a 15 per cent salary increase for all officers and recommended the setting up of regional offices in all the five regions of the continent.

The significance of these figures is that there has been no remarkable improvement in the attitude of African trade unions to dues payment to organisations to which they are affiliated despite the wide spread use of the check-off as a method of dues collection. As long as this attitude continues, as long as there are paymasters like the OAU, African Governments and 'any organisations that can help us without strings attached' the prospects of building a strong, effective and viable continental trade union organisation to defend and promote the economic and social interests of African workers will continue to be dim.

It is now time to take a look at aids and developments in trade union aid programmes since 1965. An objective consideration of aids raises certain philosophical and policy questions. What should be the primary aim of any trade union aid programme? On what principles should trade union aid programmes be based? Should public funds be used to finance certain trade union activities? Should 'strings' be attached to trade union aid programmes? If so, what type of strings? These are some of the questions we shall be considering in this brief discussion. Aids must be understood in their proper context. The dictionary meaning of the word 'aid' is help. Help is usually required or sought because a person or an organisation is unable, owing to certain constraints, to do what he or it should do or plans to do. The constraints may be the result of a lack of finance, equipment, or the necessary knowledge or skill. Aid is usually requested by the person or organisation in need, and not the other way round. The request for aid may be made by correspondence, or during a personal discussion between the donor and the receiver, or by a combination of both methods. It implies that before making the request, the person or organisation making it must have thought of what should be done, how it should be done, and the means of doing it. Technical advice by the donor or any other competent person may facilitate the process of making a decision. It also implies, with particular reference to the financial aspect, a willingness on the part of the person or organisation in need to make a contribution, no matter how small. Aid is a supplement to, not a substitute for, what a person or an organisation has or ought to have. Aid enables a person or an organisation to achieve certain objectives and should, therefore, be limited in scope and time. It should aim primarily at helping people to help themselves, and should not create an 'overdependence' on the donor, otherwise it defeats its objectives. Unfortunately this cannot be said of most of the current aid programmes.

Whether public funds should be used to finance certain trade union activities in the Third World has been a controversial question in the international trade union movement since 1959, particularly after the First World Economic Conference of Free Trade Unions organised by the ICFTU. That conference recommended, among other things, that industrialised countries should donate one per cent of their gross national product as aid to developing countries, an idea which the United Nations accepted a few months later. Each time the suggestion was made in the ICFTU that public funds be accepted to finance certain trade union activities in the developing countries it was rejected on the ground that doing so would compromise the cherished principle of free trade unionism. Two developments seem to have changed the attitude of leading trade unionists in Europe and North America. The first is the concept of life-long learning and the universal acceptance of the theory that education involving an overall development of man is state responsibility. It was felt that if public funds could be used to educate and train public servants and business tycoons part of the funds should also be used to educate and train workers. The second is the decision of the ICFTU First World Conference on Education in the Labour Movement which was held in Montreal in 1967. That conference welcomed a proposal that public funds should be accepted for workers' education, provided the acceptance did not compromise the militancy and independence of the unions, and provided also that the orientation, planning and direction of such programmes were left with the unions.

Concerning 'strings' the question is raised as to whether in fact there can ever be any 'aid without strings'. One observer put the matter in perspective when he remarked during a heated argument on the subject that 'the problem is not strings, but the thickness of the strings'. No person or organisation gives money or materials to another without knowing what the money or materials will be used for. That piece of information constitutes part of the 'strings' generally attached to trade union aids. Any person aiding another wants to know that the aid is used for the purpose it was given. In the international free trade union movement the main strings attached to aids to African trade unions are three in number and may be summarised as follows: (a) they should be used for the purpose(s) for which they were intended; (b) accounts supported by receipts and vouchers should be submitted to the donors or their administering agencies in keeping with audit requirements; (c) periodical reports showing progress made or difficulties encountered should also be sent to the donors or their administering agencies. Many trade union leaders want money and/or materials, but are not prepared to meet these requirements.

Since 1965 a new phenomenon has entered the aid programmes for African trade unions, and that is trade union programmes financed from public funds made available by certain governments in Europe and North America. During that year, the Americans, disenchanted by what they considered to be the inability of the ICFTU to make the best possible use of the money in its International Solidarity Fund to build strong trade unions in Africa, decided to withdraw their contributions to the ISF and set up the African–American Labour Centre whose main activities were said to be trade union education, vocational training and economic co-operation. A number of vocational training and a workers' education institutes were set in certain African countries with American citizens at the helm. Between 1965 and August 1967, the AALC spent a total of US$2,251,539[7] made up as follows: $1,769,539 (78·5 per cent) from the US Agency for International Development; $425,000 (18·8 per cent) from the AFL–CIO and individual unions and $57,000 (2·5 per cent) from private contributions. Its expenditure has increased tremendously ever since. The American initiative was followed in a modified form by Canada and a number of European countries, among them were Denmark, Holland, Norway and Sweden. Each of these countries set up agencies for international development. The West Germans operate through the Friedrich Ebert Stiftung and the British through the TUC. These agencies operate in a different way from the Americans. Canada and the other European Governments allocate a certain amount every year for development aid which is administered by their agencies. The administering authorities invite non-governmental organisations in their countries, interested in carrying out certain development projects in developing countries, to apply for part of the allocation. Among the non-governmental agencies which apply are the trade unions. The application is usually made by the national trade union centre(s), and it may be for the purpose of financing educational programmes, or other trade union sponsored projects of a developmental nature. Some of the national centres carry out their programmes on a bilateral basis, others choose to work with the ICFTU because it has the contacts and the experience. ICFTU submits projects to its affiliates in the countries having these international development agencies. These projects are generally based on requests received from its affiliates in Africa and other Third World countries including those received from non-affiliated organisations with which the organisation maintains friendly relations.

Aids sometimes create problems not only for the donors and recipients but also for the brokers. It was apparently to avoid such problems that the ICFTU Finance and General Purposes Committee issued certain guidelines in 1974 governing projects financed from external sources. These guidelines may be summarised as follows: (*a*) Such external financing is a supplement to, and not a substitute for, the use of ICFTU's own resources for development projects. (*b*) Project proposals must first of all be approved by the ICFTU governing bodies prior to taking them up with external agencies. (*c*) External financing applies to ad hoc projects limited in time in the field of development aid and does not touch on the structure and ongoing activity of the ICFTU and its regional organisations. (*d*) Programmes and applications for funds should be worked out by or in collaboration with ICFTU headquarters and submitted by headquarters. (*e*) ICFTU priorities and not donor priorities should be strictly adhered to. (*f*) Projects should be of such dimensions that they can be handled through existing ICFTU machinery.

The preponderance of aids has added a new dimension to trade union activities, particularly in the educational field, and created problems in its train. The greatest and most regrettable is the seeming 'prostitute mentality' noticeable in many trade unionists. It is not uncommon to hear them say, in connection with some of the unreasonable demands they make during the organisation of trade union courses, that 'if you cannot do it, we shall approach the Americans or the Germans and we shall get what we want. We are not affiliated to them, but they help us'.

If it is a good thing to accept public funds for certain trade union activities or trade union sponsored projects, is it also a good thing to accept the funds from another government instead of the government of one's own country? Two schools of thought have emerged in connection with this question. One favours accepting funds from any public source in so far as the conditions do not conflict with the decision of the Montreal Conference on the subject. Another favours accepting only from one's own government because the workers are direct contributors to the fund through their taxes, but it readily acknowledges that, besides the OATUU, the possibility of any trade union or national centre getting it is remote. In any case, it points out, such a grant would provide another opportunity for the Government to exercise further control over the unions.

Whether the funds are derived from workers' contributions or from public sources in the industrialised countries, benefiting from them without making a contribution or satisfying the basic conditions governing their grant is a sad commentary on African trade unions and their leaders. It means that African union leaders cannot do what their counterparts in other parts of the world have been able to do namely, build strong, viable and self-supporting trade unions. Secondly, it destroys the African's claim to equality with other races. Equality is not measured by mere verbal claim: willingness and ability to accept the responsibilities which others are willing and able to accept are some of the yardsticks.

What all this means is that the time has arrived for Africans and all those interested in African development and progress to take a new hard look at the trade union movement in Africa from the branch level to the pinnacle of the OATUU, its aims and objectives, its promise and performance, its successes and failures, and consider what it should do in the years ahead. Close scrutiny should be extended to every aspect of union activity, and should aim, among other things, at finding a solution to three basic problems which the ICFTU Working Party on Trade Union Education identified in 1975 as the 'perennial problems manacing trade unions in developing countries—fragmentation, defective structures and maladministration'.

Although such hard looking is basically the responsibility of African trade unions themselves, the international free trade union movement can make a useful contribution assuming, of course, that such a contribution would be welcome and would not be regarded by the ultra-sensitive elements in the trade unions and governments as an unnecessary interference in African trade union affairs. The first task requiring urgent attention in every country is organising. It is a strange paradox that, in spite of the great changes in the laws of many countries enabling the unions to organise almost 100 per cent of their potential, trade union membership in most countries is still less than 50 per cent of that potential. The old difficulty with dues collection has been considerably minimised by the adoption of check-off as a means of dues collection. What remains now is to ensure the introduction of the system in those unions which do not yet have it, and make arrangements, similar to the provisions of the Zambia Industrial Relations Act, 1971, relating to the remittance of dues to national unions and national centres. Many things have been asked of the trade union movement in Africa; some are within its competence, others without. But it is not often remembered that its capacity to meet these demands depends, in the final analysis, on whether there is an effective organisation already in existence.

Union administration is a problem in almost every country, and deserves equal attention. In the important areas of grievance handling and collective bargaining much more has to be done than hitherto to make the unions more meaningful to workers by attending to their complaints on time and without asking for inducements, and by bringing many more workers under the coverage of collective agreements. None of these things is beyond the capabilities of the present trade union leaders. But will they sit down in their offices and apply their brains and energy to basic trade union functions? Will union members in every country be prepared to act as checks and balances on their leaders? Will there be free and fair elections in African trade unions? On the basis of existing evidence the future is not bright. But although the prospects may be dim, the future is not entirely without hope. A new generation of trade unionists is emerging in many countries. They are the products of trade union education programmes which have been going over the years, and which have been intensified within the last decade. They may rise, as some of their forerunners did, to top level positions in their unions and national centres, particularly in those countries now under military rule. The return of civilian rule would offer opportunities for election and provide outlets for some of the politicians who dominate the leadership of many trade unions and national centres assuming, of course, they would be acceptable to the electorates. Assuming they would be, the unions would still be faced with the problem of deciding whether their full-time salaried officials could efficiently and effectively combine the responsibilities of their office with those of a parliamentarian. For although the voice of labour ought to be heard in parliament, the greater part of union work belongs outside parliament. Almost every trade union in the world faced with this problem has had to make a decision like this at certain stages of its development, and African trade unions cannot be an exception to the rule.

But the new generation of trade unionists could succeed in creating a new image for the unions and making them more meaningful to the workers if governments, political parties and military leaders would change some of their attitudes to trade unions and some of their misguided concepts about unions and their role in society. The independence of trade unions must be recognised, and strong trade unions must be accepted. Whether Africa needs strong trade unions is sometimes a controversial question. The phrase 'strong trade unions' carries fearful connotations in certain quarters in Africa, hence the systematic erosion of trade union rights and freedoms in most African countries. Some people only think of trade unions in the context of strikes and the inconveniences they create. Little or no thought is given to the cause of strikes. To some people unions are a liability rather than an asset; they are luxuries intended for the developed economies of the world and not the developing countries of Africa. Some think unions are good only in so far as they are instruments for implementing party or government decisions or working 'co-operatively' with employers.

Man in Africa is like man in other parts of the world. Similarly, workers in Africa are like workers every where. As already pointed out in Chapter 7, workers form and join trade unions because they have certain problems at their workplace which they think the union can help to solve; they have certain needs which they think the union can help to provide; they have certain dreams of a better life which they hope the union can help them to fulfil. Some people have tried to argue that in practically every African country the men and women in wage earning employment constitute an infinitesimal minority of the total population. That being the case, their needs and hopes must be subordinated to 'the greatest good of the greatest number'. To achieve that objective, they argue, wages should not be increased even when there is ample justification for an increase. Granted that workers constitute a minority of the total population in every African country, there is no doubting the fact that they are a qualitative minority. Without them government cannot function; without them commerce and industry would cease to operate. Moreover, the obligations inherent in the extended family system are clear proof that wages paid to African workers are often not only for them and their immediate families: they are common assets shared by their fathers and mothers, brothers and sisters and others of the extended family.

Historians and other scholars of the social sciences readily acknowledge that the great improvements in the standard of living of mankind could not have been attained without workers and their organisations. Africa could also pay a similar compliment to its workers and their organisations. That fact underscores the need for strong and effective trade unions in every African country. Such unions cannot exist if the law is heavily weighted against the workers and their organisations and in favour of the employers, be they private or public; they cannot develop if labour administrators are biased against unions and their leaders; they cannot exist if the unions are dominated by employers, politicians, military leaders, religious and ethnic organisations or secret societies; nor can they exist if the unions themselves are not democratic organisations responsive to the wishes of their members. Trade unions in Africa are entitled to the basic rights and freedoms enshrined in ILO Conventions 87 and 98. The extent to which these rights and freedoms are seen to be enjoyed by workers and their organisations in every African country is the yardstick of real progress. The truth must be acknowledged that what is done in the interest of workers and their organisations is a service to their countries: what is done against them is a disservice to their countries.

NOTES

CHAPTER 1. WEST AFRICA

1. Quoted by Ukandi G. Damachi in *The Role of Trade Unions in the Development Process with a Case Study of Ghana*, New York, 1974, p. 21.

2. Ibid., p. 22.

3. Ibid., p. 22.

4. Ibid., p. 22.

5. Ghana Industrial Relations Act, 1958.

6. GTUC Constitution adopted by the Steering Committee meeting held at Aburi, 2–3 September 1958, p. 2.

7. ICFTU letter dated 22 December 1958, addressed to John K. Tettegah, Secretary General of the Ghana Trades Union Congress.

8. Check-off is an arrangement between a union and an employer whereby the employer undertakes to deduct trade union dues from the wages of the members and pays the proceeds to the union.

9. Report to 39 ICFTU Executive Board Meeting, 1–3 February 1966 on the relaxation of the control of trade unions.

10. Report to 40 ICFTU Executive Board Meeting, 28–30 June 1966 on trade union developments in Ghana.

11. Ibid.

12. For a detailed account of communist overtures to take over control of the trade union movement in Nigeria see Wogu Ananaba, *The Trade Union Movement In Nigeria*, London, 1969, pp. 142–54.

13. Ibid., pp. 215–6.

14. Evidence given by Solomon Aladepo Alamu, Acting Registrar of Trade Unions, Nigeria, at the Activities of Trade Unions Tribunal of Inquiry, Lagos, Day 11 of 40 ICFTU Executive Board Meeting. Proceedings, p. 40.

15. List of registered trade unions issued by the Registrar of Trade Unions, Nigeria. The number of 'genuine trade unions' has been arrived at by identifying, mainly from their names, 248 organisations of employers and the self-employed which were included in the Registrar's list.

16. Report to 35 ICFTU Executive Board, 30 Nov.–3 Dec. 1964.

17. Report on the Gambia by M. E. Jallow.

18. Ibid.

19. *Labour and Development*, a monthly review of African socio-economic events of interest to trade unions, published by the Regional Economic Research and Documentation Centre, Lome, Togo, No. 9, p. 12.

20. *Labour and Development*, No. 14, p. 17.

21. Ibid.

22. Report by Irving Brown on the UGTAN Congress, Conakry, 16–19 January 1959, p. 7.

23. *African Trade Unions*, Ioan Davis, Penguin African Library, 1966, p, 156.

24. Ibid.

25. Ibid.

26. *African Trade Union News*, Regional Economic Research and Documentation Centre, Lomé, No. 12, p. 1.

27. *Labour and Development*, No. 11, p. 15.

28. *African Trade Union News*, No. 30, p. 1.

29. *African Trade Union News*, Nos. 15–16.

30. Report of an interview published in *Labour and Development*, February 1975, p. 17.

31. *African Trade Union News*, No. 31, p. 3.

CHAPTER 2.   EASTERN AFRICA

1. Proposals of the Tanzania Government on the Recommendations of the Presidential Commission of Inquiry into the National Union of Tanganyika Workers (NUTA), Dar-es-Salaam, 1957, p. 2.

2. Ibid.

3. Report to 35 ICFTU Executive Board, 30 November–3 December 1964.

4. Report to 35 ICFTU Executive Board, 30 November–3 December 1964.

5. Ibid.

6. Roger Scott, *The Development of Trade Unions in Uganda*, Nairobi, p. 22.

7. Ibid., p. 173.

8. Ibid., p. 146–7.

9. Report to 41 ICFTU Executive Board, 22–24 November 1966.

10. Report of the Commission of Inquiry into the Dispute Affecting the Executive Board of the Uganda Labour Congress, Entebbe, p. 29.

11. Ibid., p. 31.

12. Report, dated 31 October 1966, on the trade union situation in Ethiopia by Lennart Kindstrom, ICFTU representative in Ethiopia.

13. Ibid.

14. Report to 62 ICFTU Executive Board, 21–22 November 1974.

15. *Labour and Development*, No. 14, p. 15.

CHAPTER 3.   CENTRAL FRICA

1. Ministry of Labour Report 1963–7, Zomba, Malawi, p. 17.

2. Ibid., p. 20.

3. Report on the trade union situation in Malawi.

4. Knight Maripe, 'Discrimination in Rhodesia: Based On Merit or Race?' *Free Labour World*, February 1968, p. 8.

5. 'Role of Trade Unions in the Liberation Struggle in Zambia', lecture

by E. C. Chalabesa at ZCTU/ICFTU Seminar on Multinationals and Employment, Lusaka, 28 January 1976 (mimeo), p. 7.
6. Lecture on Zambian Trade Unions by Prof. Simmonds, at the ZCTU/ICFTU Seminar on Multinationals and Employment, Lusaka, 28 January 1976, mimeo, p. 3.
7. 'Brief History of the Zambian Labour Movement', issued by Department of Workers Education, ZCTU, mimeo, p. 9.
8. Ibid., p. 9.
9. Report to 35 ICFTU Executive Board, 30 November–3 December 1964.

CHAPTER 4. SOUTHERN AFRICA
1. Report on 1966 visit to Swaziland by W. G. Lawrence, ICFTU Representative in Rhodesia.
2. Report on 1970 visit to Swaziland by W. G. Lawrence, ICFTU Representative in Rhodesia.

CHAPTER 5. NORTH AFRICA
1. Secretariat report to 33 ICFTU Executive Board, 11–14 March 1963.
2. Appendix III to secretariat report to 33 ICFTU Executive Board. Appendix III is a report entitled 'Putsch against Freedom and Democracy in Algeria' by Giacomo Bernasconi, a member of the ICFTU delegation which visited Algeria during the first congress of the UGTA in January 1963.
3. OEF Newsletter of 10 July 1969 (OEF = Organisation of Employers' Federations and Employers in Developing Countries).
4. Ibid.
5. Secretariat report to 31 ICFTU Executive Board, 3–4 July 1962.
6. IFPCW Petrogramme, No. 71–39, 24 September 1971.
7. Secretariat report to 35 ICFTU Executive Board, 30 November–3 December 1964.
8. Ibid.
9. Georges Fischer, 'Trade Unions and Decolonisation', *Présence Africaine*, Vol. 6/7, No. 34/5, p. 139.
10. Ibid.
11. Ioan Davies, *African Trade Unions*, Harmondsworth, 1966, p. 165.
12. Ibid., p. 166.

CHAPTER 6. CASE STUDIES
1. Quoted in *The Export of Apartheid to Lesotho: A BCP Case Study* published by the Permanent Secretariat of the Afro-Asian People's Organisation, Cairo, 1971, p. 14.
2. Ibid.
3. BCP Appeal to the UN Commission on Human Rights, Geneva, 1975, Part 5, pp. 1–3.
4. Ibid., Part 6, p. 9.
5. Ibid.

6. Ibid., Part 3, pp. 1–23.

7. Extrtacts of the judgment in *Rex* v. *Mofelehetsi Moerane and thirty-one others.*

8. Report dated 11 April 1966, by W. Ananaba, on the trade union situation in Liberia.

9. Report dated 14 November 1966, by W. Ananaba, on 'The Mission to Nimba'.

10. ILO Official Bulletin, Supplement II, Vol. L, No. 3, of July 1967, p. 76.

11. Ibid.

12. Letter dated 5 April 1976, from James Bass, Executive Vice President of the CIO, to Miss Thelma Nelson, Assistant Minister of Labour, Youth and Sports.

CHAPTER 7.   CONTINENTAL TRADE UNION ORGANISATIONS

1. Report by Stefan Nedzynski, ICFTU Assistant General Secretary, on 'The First All-African Trade Union Conference, Casablanca, 25–31 May 1961.'

2. Secretariat report to 37 ICFTU Executive Board, Amsterdam, 5–6 July 1965.

3. Nedsynski's report.

4. Ibid.

5. B. A. Bentum, *Trade Unions In Chains*, Ghana Trades Union Congress, p. 27.

6. Ibid., p. 31.

CHAPTER 8.   AFRICAN TRADE UNIONS AT WORK

1. Eleazar C. Iwuji, 'Employment Promotion Problems in the Economic and Social Development of Ghana', paper prepared for International Institute for Labour Studies, Geneva, 1972, p. 22.

2. Ibid., p. 21.

3. *Trade Union Education in the '70s: Report of the Pan-African Seminar on Trade Union Education Policy*, Lagos, Nigeria, 7–11 February 1972, p. 37 (An ICFTU publication).

4. General Secretary's Report to ZCTU General Council, 5–6 December 1970.

5. *Labour and Development*, No. 26, February 1977, pp. 13–14.

6. Report of the Tribunal of Inquiry into the Activities of Trade Unions, Federal Ministry of Information, Lagos, pp. 18, 32, 55 and 63.

7. Proceedings of the Tribunal of Inquiry into the Activities of Trade Unions, Nigeria, Day 14, p. 10.

8. Report by W. Ananaba on Trade Union Courses held in Victoria, Mahé, Seychelles, 12–23 August 1974.

9. Report of the Tribunal of Inquiry into the Activities of Trade Unions, Federal Ministry of Information, Lagos, 1977, p. 25.

10. Ibid., pp. 33–49.

11. Ibid., p. 58.

12. Discussion between John Gould, AALC East Africa Representative, and W. Ananaba in Nairobi in July 1976.

13. Proceedings of the Tribunal of Inquiry into the Activities of Trade Unions, Nigeria, Day 37, p. 94.

14. *UKCS News*, August 1977.

15. Proceedings of the Tribunal of Inquiry into the Activities of Trade Unions, Nigeria, Day 41, p. 56.

16. *UKCS News*, August 1977.

17. *Labour and Development*, No. 32/33, August/September, 1977.

CHAPTER 9. FACTORS AFFECTING AND INFLUENCING UNION ACTIVITIES

1. Colin Legum, *Pan Africanism*, London, 1962, p. 83–4.

2. *Uganda Argus*, 11 December 1964.

3. Letter dated 10 July 1975, from Peter Otta, Onitsha Branch Secretary of the Nigerian Textile, Garment, Leather and General Workers Union, to Brigadier H. Adefope, Federal Commissioner for Labour, Nigeria.

4. Ibid.

5. For a full account of police activities during industrial disputes, see 'Strikes and the Institutionalisation of Labour Protest: The Case of Nigeria', paper presented by A. Adeogun, Faculty of Law, University of Lagos, Nigeria, to the 'Seminar on Third World Strikes', 12–16 September 1977, Institute of Social Studies, The Hague.

6. Report of the Tribunal of Inquiry into the Activities of Trade Unions, 1977, Federal Ministry of Information, Lagos, p. 86.

7. William A. Beling (ed.), *The Role of Labour in African Nation Building*, New York, 1968, p. 20.

CHAPTER 10. PROSPECTS AND PROBLEMS

1. Quoted by Colin Legum in *Pan-Africanism*, London, 1962, p. 202.

2. 'Election Victory with a Question Mark', *Africa Magazine*, June 1977, p. 28.

3. *'African Socialism and its Application to Planning in Kenya'*, Republic of Kenya, Nairobi, 1965, pp. 2–3.

4. 'The Arusha Declaration and TANU's Policy on Self-Reliance', TANU, Dar-es-Salaam, 1967, p. 1.

5. Quoted by *Indian National Herald*, 15 August 1976.

6. *Pan-Africanism*, *A*, op. cit., p. 60.

7. Wogu Ananaba, *The Trade Union Movement in Nigeria*, London, 1969, p. 189.

8. AALC Geneva, 1967, Proceedings of a meeting with Workers' Delegates attending the 51 Session of the ILO Conference, p. 51.

GUIDE TO ABBREVIATIONS AND TERMINOLOGY

Organisations

AALC: African-American Labour Centre. An organisation created by the American trade union federation, AFL–CIO, in 1965 to provide trade union education, vocational training and other forms of technical aids to trade unions and workers in Africa. Identical bodies exist in Asia and Latin America.

AATUF: All-African Trade Union Federation. Founded in Casablanca in 1961 at the instance of the national trade union centres of Algeria, Egypt, Ghana, Guinea, Mali and Morocco. Its basic policy was that a national trade union centre could not obtain or retain membership of the organisation if affiliated to international trade union organisations like the ICFTU, WCL and WFTU. It argued that membership of international trade union organisations was contrary to the policy of non-alignment adopted by most African states as the corner-stone of their foreign policy.

AFRO: African Regional Organisation of the International Confederation of Free Trade Unions. Created in 1960 in response to the wishes of ICFTU affiliates in Africa.

ATUC: African Trade Union Confederation. A rival continental organisation set up in Dakar in January 1962 by national centres believing in the principles of free and democratic trade unionism and which would not subscribe to the view that international affiliation was contrary to the policy of non-alignment.

ACOSCA: Africa Co-operative Savings and Credit Association. Created in 1968 to assist in the organisation and promotion of co-operative savings and credit societies, otherwise known as credit unions, in all African countries and adjacent islands. Its headquarters are in Nairobi, and it is affiliated to the World Council of Credit Unions based in Madison, Wisconsin, USA.

FES: Friedrich-Ebert-Stiftung, otherwise known as the Friedrich Ebert Foundation. A foundation created in Germany in the 1920s to award scholarships to gifted students, German and foreign, whose parents could not finance their studies, to provide civic and adult education and promote

232

international understanding and co-operation. It is named after the First President of the German (Weimar) Republic, who himself rose from the working class and was proud of it.

FIET: Fédération Internationale des Employés et des Techniciens, otherwise called the International Federation of Commercial, Clerical and Technical Employees, is one of the ITS associated with the ICFTU. It has its headquarters in Geneva and in 1976 represented 5,937,075 workers. African affiliates were twenty-one from fourteen countries representing 61,373 workers. Founded in Copenhagen in 1910, it aims, among other things, at co-operating in establishing a new social order based on the unity of all peoples in freedom and equality and the common utilisation of the world's resources, and to promote international solidarity by bringing together the free trade unions of commercial, clerical and technical employees in commerce and industry regardless of nationality, race or creed.

ICFTU: International Confederation of Free Trade Unions. An international trade union organisation founded in London in 1949. It is mainly an organisation of national trade union centres, and has its headquarters in Brussels, Belgium. In June 1978 it had 122 affiliates from 88 countries representing a membership of 58,766,775. The concept of free and democratic trade unionism which it stands for and promotes implies, among other things, that the union or the national trade union centre (*a*) is created by its members or in their interest; (*b*) is in constant receipt of subscriptions from the members; (*c*) the leaders derive their authority to function from the members through periodical free and fair elections; (*d*) is responsive to the needs and aspirations of the members; and (*e*) is not dominated by extraneous influences like governments, political parties, military leaders, religious or ethnic organisations, employers or secret societies.

IFPAAW: International Federation of Plantation, Agricultural and Allied Workers. One of the international trade secretariats (see ITS below). In 1977, the IFPAAW had nine affiliates from Africa representing 137,666 workers.

ILO: International Labour Organisation. Created in 1919 to ensure universal and lasting peace based on social justice. It tries to achieve the objective of social justice by constant research to labour problems and publication of its findings, setting international labour standards through its Conventions and Recommendations, the application of which it oversees and offering technical assistance to governments, employers and trade unions as requested. A Specialised Agency of the UN, it is the only organisation of its kind with a tripartite structure made up of governments and employers and workers' organisations.

IMF: International Metalworkers' Federation. One of the oldest and probably the biggest of the ITS, founded in Amsterdam in 1904, with its headquarters in Geneva. In 1975 it had a total membership of 13,000,000.

ITF: International Transport Workers Federation, founded in London in 1896, aims at embracing transport workers' unions of all countries, irrespective of race, creed, colour or nationality. With its headquarters in London, it is about 5,000,000 strong and in 1977 had 42 affiliates from ten African countries.

ITGLWF: International Textile, Garment and Leather Workers Federation. Founded in 1970 as a result of the amalgamation of the former international organisations of clothing, shoe and textile workers, and is about 5,000,000 strong, it has its headquarters in Brussels. In 1975 it had eighteen affiliates from nine African countries representing a total membership of 171,065.

ITS: International Trade Secretariats. International trade union organisations grouping individual unions in identical trades or industries, e.g. plantation and agriculture, mines, postal, telegraph and telecommunication services, public service, teachers, etc. The ITS are sometimes referred to *industrial internationals* while organisations of national trade union centres like the ICFTU, WCL and WFTU are referred to as *global internationals.* The ITS are autonomous international organisations which believe in and promote the principles of free and democratic unionism; fourteen of them are associated with the ICFTU. They have a General Conference which meets annually. Four of their representatives are members of the ICFTU Executive Board.

MIF: Miners' International Federation. An ITS of mineworkers, founded in Belgium in 1890. In 1977 its total membership was 1,269,825, of which 48,200 were from nine affiliates from nine African countries.

OATUU: Organisation of African Trade Union Unity. Created in 1973 at Addis Ababa under the auspices of the Organisation of African Unity (OAU), it replaced the AATUF and ATUC, and is largely financed by OAU and certain African governments. On the question of international affiliation it has taken off where AATUF stopped, namely that national centres should sever links with international trade union organisations. Its Secretary General was reported as having appealed to African labour ministers in 1978 to put pressure on their national centres to comply.

PSI: Public Services International. A new name adopted in 1958 by the International Federation of Unions of Employees in Public and Civil Services, itself a merger in 1935 of the International Federation of Employees in Public Services (founded 1907) and the International Federation of Civil Services (founded 1925). The PSI is about 4,000,000 strong and has its headquarters in London. In 1975 it had twenty-nine affiliates from eleven African countries.

PTTI: Postal, Telegraph and Telephone International. Its name indicates its jurisdiction. Founded in Milan in 1920, the PTTI had a membership of 3,246,417 in 1975. In 1977 it had twenty-three affiliates from fifteen African countries. Its headquarters are in Geneva.

WCL: World Confederation of Labour (a new name adopted in 1968 by the International Federation of Christian Trade Unions). WCL represents about 3,000,000 workers, and is believed to be the smallest of the 'global internationals'.

WFTU: World Federation of Trade Unions. Founded in 1945 by the national centres of the various countries which allied to fight and defeat Nazi Germany in the Second World War. The major national centres in what came to be known as the Western World and the national centres of some of the countries in Europe, Asia and North America withdrew from the WFTU in 1949 following disagreement over trade union attitudes to the Marshall Plan, which the Russians condemned as American imperialism and wanted the unions, through the WFTU, to reject. Trade unions from war-torn Europe joined their governments in welcoming it, arguing that it would help rebuild their shattered economies, create jobs and increase trade union membership potential. The split in the WFTU led to the founding of the ICFTU.

Explanation of terms

Agency shop clause (sometimes known as dues shop). A provision in a collective agreement stating that non-union members will pay a stipulated amount monthly, quarterly or annually to the union representing the workers in a given trade or industry. The concept of agency shop is based on the argument that the union is recognised as an exclusive bargaining agent in the trade or industry; that wages, hours of work and other terms of employment therein are determined through collective bargaining between the union and the employer; and that concessions won are usually applied to all the workers in the bargaining unit and not just to union members only. That being the case, any worker who benefits, and for one reason or the other does not wish to join the union, ought to pay a fee for the benefits enjoyed which are direct consequences of union action. Agency clause is a North American innovation, and was evolved as a solution to the problem of the 'free rider'—the worker who likes to benefit from the union but has no interest in supporting it financially.

Check-off. An arrangement between a union and an employer whereby the employer undertakes to deduct trade union dues from the wages of the members and pays the proceeds to the union.

Collective bargaining. Negotiations between employer(s) and trade union(s) regarding wages, hours of work, fringe benefits and other terms of employment due to workers in exchange for their labour. If both sides reach agreement it is reduced to writing in the form of a binding contract called collective agreement and signed by the representatives of both sides. In many countries the law or practice requires the agreement to be ratified by the members before it is signed.

Grievance procedure. Procedure established either unilaterally by the employer or jointly by the employer and a trade union outlining the process of handling and disposal of workers' individual or group complaints or grievances. If the procedure is established by the employer it is generally embodied in the company's rules or staff regulations. If jointly established, it is embodied in the collective agreement between the parties.

JIC: Joint Industrial Council. A machinery (based on the British model of industrial relations) for collective bargaining between employers and trade unions. JICs have written constitutions with elaborate provisions covering composition of the council, the officers and rules governing the conduct of meetings.

Non-bargaining activities. Activities not related to collective bargaining carried out by trade unions to improve the social and economic interests of their members and their families, e.g. co-operatives (consumer and thrift and credit), family planning, clinics, recreational facilities, etc. Non-bargaining activities are an extension of the old concept of benefit schemes which was the foundation-stone of trade unions.

Shop steward. A union representative on the shop floor, who recruits new members, collects dues where there is no check-off arrangement, takes up workers' complaints or grievances and generally is the liaison officer between the union and members on the shop floor. Shop stewards may be elected by the workers they represent or may be appointed by the union. In big factories or establishments they are elected or appointed to represent the various departments or sections. If the workforce is large in the section or department, they are elected or appointed to represent between twenty and fifty workers.

Organising. The job of creating union strength, discipline and self-confidence among groups of disunited and weak workers. One writer has defined organising as "a social system that has an unequivocal collective identity, an exact roster of members, a programme of activity, and procedures for replacing members". (Theodore Caplow, *Principles of Organisation*).

Trade union. A continuing, permanent and democractic organisation created by the workers to protect themselves at their work; to improve the conditions of their work through collective bargaining; to seek to better the conditions of their lives; and to provide a means of expression for the workers' views on the problems of society.

Trade union rights. Rights established by law or collective agreement or both guaranteeing, among other things, the legal existence of trade unions; the right of individual workers, individual unions and national trade union centres to form and join trade unions or trade union federations and confederations of their choice without interference from administering authorities; the right of workers to bargain collectively with their employers and to participate in discussions on company policies which affect their lives; and the right of workers to withdraw their labour (go on strike) in furtherance of their claims.

Union security. A provision in a collective agreement guaranteeing protection for union representatives, including shop stewards, from victimisation because of their union activities. Protection against victimisation may take the form of the official or representative not being transferred during the tenure of his or her office.

INDEX

Abboud, Gen., 83
Abdoulaye, D., 23
Abid, T., 88
Abidjan, 27
Abiodun, M. A., 197
Abutu, A. D. O., 199
Achampong, Col. I., 13
Achour, H., 79, 85-7
ACOSCA, 177
Adebiyi Tribunal, 157, 158
Adebo, Chief S. O., 16
Adebola, H. P., 173
Adefope, H. E. O., 195, 199
Adegbesan, J. O., 173
Addis Ababa, 43, 45, 122, 123, 136, 137
African–American Labour Centre (AALC), 46, 48, 57, 114, 144–5, 147, 148, 154, 159, 177, 178, 222
African National Congress, (ANC) Zambia, 57, 58
African Regional Organisations (AFRO), 11, 120, 122, 123, 124, 135
African Representative Councils (Zambia), 58
African Socialism, 212
African Trade Unions, 4
African Trade Union Confederation (ATUC), 7, 15, 120, 132, 133, 134, 136, 137
Agege Commission, 20
Agency shop, 168
Aguiyi-Ironsi, Major Gen., 195, 208
Ahidjo, Pres., 29
Ahmed, A. M., 84

Aikpe, Capt. M., 29
Ajayi, Dr. F. A., 97
Akumu, D., 38, 88, 136, 139, 140, 175
All-African People's Conference (1958), 11, 45, 54, 192
All-African Trade Union Federation, 7, 12, 27, 41, 76, 82, 89, 120–5, 127, 129, 130–7, 172, 192
Algeria, 59, 74
All-Nigeria Peoples' Conference, 14
All-Nigeria Trade Union Federation, 14
Amalgamated Transport and General Workers' Union (Uganda), 41
American Federation of Labour-Congress of Industrial Organisations (AFL–CIO), 56, 78, 222
Americo–Liberians, 101, 102
Amoa-Awaah, K., 12
Ampah, J. K., 129
Angola, 63, 125
Animashaun, B., 203
APRONA, 49
Arab Socialist Union, 77
Armed Forces Co-ordinating Committee, 46
Arusha Declaration, 213
Assimilation policy, 5
Association des Fonctionnaires et Agents de la Colonie (Zaire), 61
Association Indigène de la Colonie (Zaire), 61

Baganda, 40
Bah, A., 20, 21

Bamako, 129
Bamgbala Commission, 159–60
Bamhawer, Dr. O., 93
Banda, Dr. H. K., 51
Banyanga, A., 41
Bare, Gen. M. S., 50
Bass, J., 102, 103, 104, 107, 108, 111, 114
Bassey, S. U., 14, 157
Basutoland Congress Party, 89, 93, 94, 97, 98, 99; — Federation of Labour, 89, 93, 97, 98, 99, 100, 101, 138
Basutoland National Party, 89, 93, 94
Bantu Labour Relations (Amendment) Bill, 72
Bechuanaland Federation of Labour, 64; — Front Party, 64; — Trades Union Congress, 64; — Workers' Union, 64
Becu, O., 7, 75
Beleke, V., 62
Belgium: colonies, 6; and territories, 5; unions, 6
Bellagha, B., 133
Belkhodja, T., 87
Ben, R., 103
Ben Bella, A., 75, 76, 208
Benani, 79
Benin, 28
Bentum, B. A., 12, 130
Bérenger, P., 68, 69
Berry, S., 104
Binaisa, G., 44
Binaisa Commission, 44
Bintu, R., 62
Bo-Boliko, A., 62
Bokassa, Emperor, 197
Booka, T., 62
Borha, L., 125, 128, 132, 133
Botswana, 64, 90, 144, 145
Botswana Federation of Trade Unions, 65
Bourguiba, Pres., 84, 85
Brandie, J. S., 3
Brown, I., 56
Brussels, 33, 76, 123

Buganda, 41
Bunyoro, 41
Burombo, B., 54
Burundi, 49, 61

Cameroon (West), 29; — Republic, 29
Casablanca (Group of African States), 45, 82, 121, 125, 127, 131, 132, 133, 172
Central African Empire, 30, 145
Central African Federation, 51
Central Organisation of Trade Unions (Kenya) (COTU), 40, 143, 145, 178, 182, 191
Central Sindical Angolana, 63, 64
Cessay, M. A., 20
Chad, 30
Chakulya, W., 148
Check-off, 10, 67, 81, 141, 142, 149, 150, 151, 154, 182, 200
Chikura, T., 56
Chimusoro, D. T. G., 56
Chipembere, H., 51, 52
Chiume, K., 51
Cisse, A., 26
Colbert, E., 109, 111, 112
Colonial Development and Welfare Act, 1940 (U.K.), 2
Colonial Office, 2
Colonies, Secretary of State for, 1
Compagnie de Phosphate de Gasfa, 86
Conakry, 27
Confédération Africaine des Travailleurs Croyants (CATC), 23, 26, 31, 32, 59, 60, 61, 132
Confédération des Syndicats Chrétiens de Belgique (CSCB), 61
Confédération des Syndicats Chrétiens du Congo et Rwanda–Urundi (CSCC), 61
Confédération Française des Travailleurs Chrétiens (CFTC), 21
Confédération Générale du Travail (CGT), 21, 23, 26
Confédération Générale du Travail-Force Ouvrière (CGT–FO), 21

Confédération Générale des Travailleurs Africains (CGTA), 23

Confédération Générale des Travailleurs Camerounais (CGTC), 29

Confédération Nationale des Travailleurs de Guinée (CNTG), 27, 28, 60

Confédération Nationale des Travailleurs du Sénégal (CNTS), 31

Confédération Nationale des Travailleurs du Togo (CNTT), 31

Confederation of Arab Trade Unions, 76, 81

Confederation of Ethiopian Labour Unions (CELU), 46, 47, 137, 176

Confédération Syndicale Congolaise, 60

Confédération Syndicale Voltaïque, 31, 151

Confederazione Somala du Lavoratori, 50

Congress of Industrial Organisations (CIO) (Liberia), 102, 103, 110, 113–18, 137, 139, 179

Convention People's Party, 3, 9, 10, 129

Cost of living allowance, 2

Dacko, D., 207

Dahomey (Rep. of Benin), 27, 29

Dangiwa, A. M., 16

Davies, I., 4, 5, 27, 85

Debat, M., 60

De Gaulle, Gen. 25

Dhili, A., 79

Djilani, 79

Dlamini, Col. M., 67

Dlamini, Prince M., 66

Dombal, G., 30

Douala, 197

Dube, J. J., 56

Duncan, B., 114

Duval, G., 68

East Germany, 28

Egypt, 59, 77, 127, 128

Egyptian Federation of Labour, 77

Emergency Powers Act, 1966 (Liberia), 106, 110

Enahoro, Chief A., 210

Entrup, Dr. J. L., 93

Essential services, 4, 20, 185, 186

Ethiopia, 45, 141

Ezzedine, B., 79, 137

Fédération des Syndicats des Travailleurs Madagascar (FISEMA), 73

Fédération des Travailleurs du Burundi, 49

Fédération Générale du Travail de Belgique, 61

Fédération Générale du Travail de Belgique–Congo Belge, Rwanda–Urundi (FGTB–CBRU), 61

Fédération Générale des Travailleurs Kongolais (FGTK), 61

Federation of Civil Service Trade Unions, 68

Federation of Rhodesia and Nyasaland, 58

Federation of Uganda Trade Unions (FUTU), 42, 44, 131

Fédération Syndicale du Cameroun (FSC), 29, 30

Fédération Syndicale Gabonaise (FESYGA), 61, 145

Firestone Co., 101, 105, 106, 113

Fivondronambenny Mpiasa Malagache (FMM), 73

FLING, 32, 33

Ford, C., 2

France, 5, 9, 26; National Assembly, 22

Francistown African Employees Union (FAEU), 73

French community referendum, 26

Friedland, W. F., 206

Friedrich Ebert Stiftung (FES), 34, 145, 147, 148, 177

Gabon, 60, 144, 150

Gadaffi, Col., 81

Gambia, The, 17, 32, 138, 142, 154;

— Labour Union (GLU), 17; —Utilities Corporation, 21
Gbatu, 115
Gebre, G., 47
General strike, 3, 46, 69
General Workers' Federation (GWF) (Mauritius), 68, 69
General Workers' Union of Guinea-Bissau (UGTGB), 32, 33
Georgestone, H. N., 17
Germany, Federal Republic of, 9
Ghana, 9, 38, 127, 128, 144; — Government, 11, 12
Ghorbal, A., 87
Gnawi, A. N., 84
Goodrich, 101, 111
Gorralah, N. O., 30
Grant, M., 17
Gray, A., 102, 103, 104, 116, 117, 118
Grievance procedure, 170
Gris, C., 27
Gueye, A., 26
Gueye, B., 133, 135
Guinea, 9, 22, 25–8, 127, 128
Guinea–Bissau, 32
Gwetu, M. M., 56

Habeas Corpus, 93, 108
Habyalimana, Major Gen. J., 49
Hached, F., 84
Hajbi, H., 82
Hargesia, 54
Harmon, E., 117, 118
Hassan II, King, 82
Hill, P., 104
Holden, R., 63
Hood, W., 66
Hooper, N., 92
Horton, A. R., 103, 109
Houphouet–Boigny, Pres., 25, 26

Ijeh, E. U., 163
Independent Forward Bloc (IFB), (Mauritius), 68, 69
Independent United Labour Congress (IULC), 15
Industrial Arbitration Panel, 185

Industrial Conciliation Act, 1959, 52, 53
Industrial Relations Act, 1958 (Ghana), 10, 141, 142, 180; — 1974 (Mauritius), 69; — 1971 (Zambia), 146, 180, 182, 187, 224; — (Amendment) Act, 1971 (Ghana), 13
Inland Revenue Staff Federation (Rhodesia), 55
International affiliation, 11, 14, 108, 126, 137, 188, 216, 217, 218
International Confederation of Free Trade Unions (ICFTU): 6, 7, 10, 14–16, 21, 24, 30–3, 38–9, 46–7, 49, 55, 59, 60, 63, 66, 68, 73, 75–9, 80, 82, 87, 101, 107, 108, 110, 121–9, 132, 136, 145–8, 154, 159, 159, 164, 176–97, 215, 216, 220, 221–4; African Labour College, 39, 43, 130, 147, 194; Executive Board, 10, 39, 72; — International Solidarity Fund, 55
International Federation of Christian Trade Unions (IFCTU), 6, 132, 189
International Federation of Plantation, Agricultural and Allied Workers (IFPAAW), 108, 109, 110, 111
International Labour Organisation (ILO), 6, 9, 15, 31, 43, 45, 68, 75, 79, 85, 89, 97, 100, 108, 112–13, 132, 147–8, 176–7, 192, 197, 207, 215–17, 227
ILO Fact Finding and Conciliation Commission, 79, 97
ILO Governing Body, 80, 96
International Metalworkers' Federation (IMF), 7, 218
International Textile, Garment and Leather Workers' Federation (ITGLWF), 7, 218
International Trade Secretariats (ITS), 146, 147, 176, 189, 192, 193, 215
International Trade Union Conference Against Apartheid, 71

Intersyndicat des Travailleurs de la Fonction Publique, 26
Istaqlal Party, 82
Ivory Coast, 22, 26, 27, 144, 145, 150

Jacob, L. B., 104
Jacobs, J., 92, 93
Jallow, M. E., 12, 21, 122, 123
Jamela, R., 54, 56, 57
James, J. O., 173
Jawara, Sir D., 18
Joint Action Committee (JAC) (Nigeria); 16
Joint Industrial Council (JIC) (Gambia), 19, 165
Jomah, J. O., 102, 103
Jonathan, Chief L., 90–4
Jones, E., 80

Kalangari, J. K., 45
Kaltungo, Y., 173
Kamaliza, M., 34, 35
Kamara, E. T., 17
Kampala, 39, 130
Kanyago, P., 7
Karebe, J., 174
Karebe-Chegge Group, 173
Kasavubu, 208
Kasalo, H., 42
Katilungu, L., 54, 57–8
Kawah, A., 107, 114
Kenya, 2–4, 38, 40, 144, 151
Kenya African National Union (KANU), 39
Kenya African Workers' Congress (KAWC), 39–40
Kenya Federation of Labour (KFL), 4, 38, 40, 126
Kenya Federation of Progressive Trade Unions (KFPTU), 38, 39, 40, 131
Kerekou, Pres., 28, 29, 176
Kersten, O., 87
Khama, Sir S., 64
Khumalo, M. G., 56
Kibuka, E., 42–4
Kindstrom, L., 102

Kirkaldy, H. S., 97
Konrad Adenauer Foundation, 92
Ksar, H., 86

Labour Party: (British), 4; (Mauritius), 68–70
Labour Practices Review Board, 105, 106
Labour Relations and Public Employment Administration Order, 1962, 45
Labour Unity Front, 15, 197
LAMCO, 106, 107, 109, 115–18
Lamine-Gueye Law, 5
Lamizana, Lt. Col. S., 32, 208
Law and Order Maintenance Act, 55
Law of Lagos, the, 209
Lawrence, W. G., 55
Legon, 12
Legum, C., 214
Lepole, T., 99
Lebotho la Khotso, 93
Lesotho, 7, 90, 138
Lesotho Congress of Trade Unions (LCTU), 89
Lesotho Council of Workers (LCW), 89, 97, 100, 101
Lesotho General Workers' Union, 96
Le Soleil, 29
Liberia, 7, 138, 142, 154
Libya, 78, 81
Libya General Workers' Union (LGWU), 78, 80, 81
Libyan Labour Code, 79
Libyan National Federation of Trade Unions, 81
Ligue Générale du Travailleurs de l'Angola (LGTA), 63
Luande, H., 44
Luvualo, M., 63

Maachou, 79
Mak' Anyengo, O., 38
Madagascar, 73, 138
Magezi, G., 42, 131
Makhosini, Prince, 67

Malainine, C., 30
Malawi Congress Party, 51, 54
Malawi Trade Unions Congress
     (MTUC), 51
Mali, 127, 150
Malik, F., 135
Maluleke, J., 54
Mancham, J., 47, 49
Maodzwa, 57
Mapetla, Mr. Justice, 95
Marematlou Party, 89
Maripe, K., 53
Marklouf, 85
Marxist Groups, 14
Marxist–Leninist ideology, 28, 29,
     31
Masuku, W. V., 56
Mau Mau, 40
Mauritania, 30, 150
Mauritius Confederation of Labour
     (MCL), 68
Mauritius Federation of Trade
     Unions (MFTU), 68
Mauritius Labour Congress (MLC),
     67, 69, 145, 154
Mawema, M., 54
Mazrui, A., 209
Mboya, T., 39, 126, 127, 128, 132
Mhungu, A. J., 56
Micombero, Col., 49
Milton Obote Foundation, 43
Mindolo Ecumenical Foundation,
     146–7
Miners' International Federation
     (MIF), 108, 111
Mmusi, G., 64, 65
Mohamed V., 82
Moise, S. D., 136, 197
Monckton Commission, 58
Monger, P., 107
Morocco, 5, 138
Moslem Committee for Action
     (MCA) (Mauritius), 68
Motshidisi, K. K., 64, 65
Mouvement Militant Mauricien
     (MMM), 68–70
Mouvement Populaire de la Révolu-
     tion (MPR) (Zaire), 62

Movrommatis, A., 97
Moyo, J. S., 54
Mozambique, 73
MPLA, 63, 64
Mugabe, R., 56
Murray, R., 107
Muzorewa, Bishop A. 56
Mwinsa, K. di, 62, 198
Mwnogozo, 37

National African Federation of
     Unions (NAFU), 54, 55
National African Trades Union
     Congress (NATUC), 56, 57
National Bureau of Investigation
     (Liberia), 103, 104
National Confederation of Angolan
     Trade Unions (CNTA), 63, 64
National Council of Trade Unions
     (Nigeria) (NCTUN), 14
National Development Levy (Gha-
     na), 12
National Farmers and General
     Workers' Union (NFGWU), 17
National Front for the Liberation
     of Angola (FLNA), 63
National Industrial Court (Niger-
     ia), 185
National Liberation Council (Nig-
     eria), 12
National Liberation Front (Algeria)
     (FLN), 74, 76
National Organisation of Trade
     Unions (Uganda) (NOTU), 4,
     143
National Revolutionary Movement
     (Congo), 60
National Trade Union Education
     Committee (Botswana) (NTUEC),
     65
National Union of Tanganyika
     Workers (NUTA), 34, 37
National Union of Tanganyika
     Workers (Establishment) Act,
     1964, 34–6
Ndong, E., 60
Nefishi, 140
Nehru, J., 214

Neo-Destour Party, 84
Neto, Dr. A., 64
Ngo, B. Y., 26, 27
Ngom, S. E. D., 140
Ngwanya, T., 67
Ngwanye National Liberatory Congress (NNLC), 66, 67
Ngwerume, B., 56
Niger, 27
Nigeria, 2, 14–16, 143, 144
Nigeria Labour Congress (NLC), 15, 154
Nigerian Trade Union Congress (NTUC), 14, 15, 154, 158, 159, 197
Nigerian Workers' Council (NWC), 15, 154, 160, 197
Nimba, 106, 107, 111
Nkomo, J., 54, 56
Nkrumah, K., 3, 4, 10, 129, 208, 212; — Government, 11, 12
Nkumbula, H., 58
Northern Federation of Labour (Somalia) (NFL), 50
Northern Rhodesia Mineworkers' Union (NRMU), 57
Northern Rhodesia Trades Union Congress (NRTUC), 58
Nouira, H., 85
Nyasaland African Congress (NAC), 51
Nyerere, Pres. J., 35, 213
Nyyueque, A. E. O., 139

Obote, Milton, 130
Odero–Jowi, J., 39
Odeyemi, Chief E. O. A., 140, 219
Oduleye, J. A., 15
Olympio, Pres. S., 208
Omido, F. E., 174
Organisation of African Trade Union Unity (OATUU), 15, 81, 88, 118, 124, 131, 134–5, 137, 139, 140, 147, 164, 175–6, 189, 195, 207, 214–5, 223–4
Organisation of African Unity (OAU), 48, 133, 137, 140, 207, 214–5

Organisation Voltaïque des Syndicats Libres (OVSL), 31, 151
Ottenyo, W., 38, 39
Overseas Territories Labour Code (France), 5, 22

Padmore, S. N., 176, 177
PAIGC, 32, 33
Palmer, G. E. E., 17
Pan-Africanism, 6, 11, 39, 54, 120, 214, 217
Pan-African trade union organisation, 11
Pan-African Workers' Congress (PAWC), 89
Papenfus, S. J., 91
Parti Démocratique de la Côte d'Ivoire (PDCI), 26
Parti Mauricien Social Démocratique (PMSD), 68, 69
Parti Sénégalais Démocratique (PSD), 26
Passfield, Lord, 1, 2, 3
Patrick, J., 3
Permanent Labour Tribunal (Tanzania), 186, 187
Pires, Major P., 32
Poaching, 16
Pongault, G., 60
Portugal, 32
Pratt, J. T., 144, 116–8
Programme for Progress (Ghana), 12
Progress Party Government (Ghana), 12, 13
Public Services International, 55
Pyke, Sir Philip, 67

Radio Moscow, 80
Railway African Workers' Union (RAWU), 52–3, 55–6
Rake, A., 35, 37
Ramoabi, T., 93
Ramoreboli, 95
Randrianatoro, C., 73
Raphael, A., 71
Rassemblement Démocratique Africain (RDA), 21

Rassemblement du Peuple Togolaise (RPT), 31
Redundancy, 170
Reformed Trades Union Congress (RTUC), 58
Regional Economic Research and Documentation Centre (RERDC), 164
Registrar of Trade Unions, 53, 151
Reich, J., 41, 42
René, F. A., 47, 49
Revolutionary Council, 43
Rhodesia, North and South, 52, 55, 143
Roach, F., 93
Robel, 137
Roberts, J., 109, 111, 112
Ross, W., 117
Rubber Tappers' Association, 108–9, 113
Rule of Law, 208
Rwanda, 49, 61
Rwanda–Urundi, 5, 61

Saillant, L., 84
Sawyerr, L., 101–2, 104
Scott, R., 40, 42
Security (union), 168
Seddik, M. B., 79, 82, 125, 126, 131
Seku, Gen. M. S., 61, 198
Selah, B., 84, 85
Selassie, Emperor Haile, 45
Senegal, 22, 23
Senegalese Deputy, 5
Senghor, Pres. L., 25, 31
Seton, V., 102, 104
Seychelles Democratic Party (SDP), 47, 48, 49, 141
Seychelles People's United Party (SPUP), 47, 48, 49, 141
Seychelles Workers' Education Committee, 48, 49
Seydou, D., 126
Sherif, E. A., 118
Shita, S., 78, 79, 80
Sierra Leone, 2, 3, 154
Sierra Leone Council of Labour (SLCL), 16, 17, 138, 144

Sierra Leone Federation of Trade Unions (SLFTU), 17
Sierra Leone Labour Congress (SLLC), 17, 138, 139, 146, 154
Sihwa, Mrs. L., 56
Silungwe, H., 147
Sissoko, F., 131
Sithole, Rev. N., 54
Sithole, P. F., 55
Soares, Dr. M., 32
Sohbuza II, King, 67
Solomon, B., 47, 176
Somalia, 50
Somali Youth League, 50
Soumah, D., 132, 133
South Africa, 70–3, 90
South African Confederation of Labour (SACL), 70
Southern Rhodesia Trades Union Congress (SRTUC), 54, 55
Springer, Mrs. M., 56
Statut de la Fonction Publique (France) 1959, 26
Sudan Federation of Workers' Trade Unions (SFWTU), 84, 138
Sunmonu, H., 16
Swaziland, 65, 90
Swaziland National Movement (Imbokodvo), 66
Sweden: LO and TCO, 72
Sy, M., 22, 24
Sylla, L., 136
Syndicat Chrétien du Burundi (SCB), 49
Syndicat des Agents de l'Administration du Burundi (SAAB), 49
Syndicat des Travailleurs et Paysans Malagaches (STPM), 73
Syndicat Libre des Travailleurs du Burundi (SLTB), 49

Tandau, A., 37, 140
Tanganyika African National Union (TANU), 34, 35, 37, 42
Tanganyika Federation of Labour (TEL), 34, 35, 194
Tanzania, 34, 38, 59, 66, 143

Tekie, F. T., 47, 176
Telli, D., 135
Tettegah, J. K., 9, 10, 24, 126–31
Tlili, A., 79, 128, 132, 133
Togo, 31, 150
Tolbert, A. B., 118
Tolbert, Pres., 118–19
Tonukari, G. B., 178
Touré, Pres. S., 9, 22–3, 25, 27
Toweh, J., 114–5
Trade Disputes Act (Kenya), 1965, 186
Trade Disputes Decree No. 7 (Nigeria), 1976, 184
Trade Disputes (Essential Services) Decree No. 23 (Nigeria), 1976, 184
Trade Union Council of South Africa (TUCSA), 70–1
Trade Unions Act (Botswana), 1969, 65
Trades Union Congress: (British) (TUC), 3, 66, 68, 72; (Ghana) (GTUC), 9–13, 24, 126, 129, 142, 145; (Malawi) (MTUC) 51; (Nigeria) (TUCN), 14; (Sierra Leone), 16
Trade Unions Ordinances, 2, 141, 158, 180; (Ghana) 1941, 10
Transkei, 90
Transport and Allied Workers' Union (Malawi), 51
Traore, Z., 32
Tsirinana, Pres., 73
Tsvaringa, E., 56, 57
Tubman, Pres., 101–3, 109, 114, 119
Tubman, S., 101
Tueh, W. B., 109
Tugbeh, W. B., 103
Tumelo, Miss B. C., 65
Tunisian Association of Industry, Trade and Crafts, 86

Uganda, 3, 40–1, 44, 143
Uganda Federation of Labour (UFL), 41, 125

Uganda Labour Congress (ULC), 43, 44
Uganda People's Congress (UPC): Youth Wing, 42
Uganda Public Employees' Union (UPEU), 41, 44
Uganda Trades Union Congress (UTUC), 41, 44
Ujamma village, 213
Unfair Labour Practices Tribunal (Ghana), 184
Union Camerounaise des Travailleurs Croyants (UCTC), 29
Union Démocratique Mauricienne (UDM), 69
Union des Forces Ouvrières Voltaïques (UFOV), 31
Union des Syndicats Autonomes du Cameroun (USAC), 29
Union des Syndicats Croyants du Cameroun (USCC), 30
Union des Syndicats Libres du Cameroun (USLC), 29
Union des Travailleurs du Burundi (UTB), 49
Union Générale des Travailleurs d'Afrique Noire (UGTAN), 9, 21–3, 25–7, 125
UGTAN (Autonome et Unitaire), 26
Union Générale des Travailleurs Algériens (UGTA), 74–6, 79, 125
Union Générale des Travailleurs Camerounais (UGTC), 29
Union Générale des Travailleurs de la Côte d'Ivoire (UGTCI), 27
Union Générale des Travailleurs du Dahomey (UGTD), 27
Union Générale des Travailleurs Sénégalais (UGTS), 26
Union Générale des Travailleurs Tunisiens (UGTT), 79, 84, 85, 86, 88
Union Marocaine du Travail (UMT), 79, 82
Union Nacional dos Trabalhadores Angolana (UNTA), 63, 64

Union Nationale Camerounaise (UNC), 30
Union Nationale des Travailleurs Centrafricains (UNTC)
Union Nationale des Travailleurs de Dahomey (UNSTD), 28, 29
Union Nationale des Travailleurs du Cameroun (UNTC), 30
Union Nationale des Travailleurs du Tchad (UNTRAT), 30
Union Nationale des Travailleurs du Togo (UNTT), 31
Union Nationale des Travailleurs du Zaïre (UNTZa), 62
Union Progressiste Sénégalaise (UPS), 26, 30
Union Syndicale des Travailleurs Voltaïques (USTV), 31, 32
United Africa Company Workers Union, 10
United African National Congress (UANC), 56
United Arab Republic see Egypt
United Committee of Central Labour Organisations (UCCLO) (Nigeria), 16
United Labour Congress of Nigeria, 15, 146, 154, 163, 195
United Mine Workers' Union (Sierra Leone), 17
United National Independence Party (UNIP) (Zambia), 58
United Nations, 16, 32
United Nations Human Rights Commission, 93
United Workers' Congress (Liberia), 117, 178
Universal Declaration of Human Rights, 98

Vandervaken, J., 88
Vewesse, C. P. N., 109
Viannini arrears, 107, 109
Viljoen, M., 71
Vote valuation, 53

Wablo, T., 114
Walker, F., 117, 118
Waller Commission (Gambia), 19, 20
West African Community States, 26
West Cameroon Trades Union Congress (WCTUC), 30
Williams, P., 103
Wilson, D., 109
Wolo, F., 103
World Assembly of Youth (WAY), 75
World Confederation of Labour (WCL), 6, 11, 68, 73, 125, 147–8, 154, 189, 218
World Confederation of Organisations in the Teaching Profession (WCOTP), 29
World Federation of Trade Unions (WFTU), 11, 14, 16, 23, 32, 59, 68, 73, 75, 77, 83, 125, 129, 131, 146, 147–8, 154, 189, 215, 218

Yace, P., 26
Yameogo, Pres., 32
Yancy, F. W., 103–4
Youlou, Pres. F., 59, 208

Zaire, 61–2, 144, 146, 150, 179
Zambia, 51–2, 54, 57, 143–6, 154, 197
Zambia Congress of Trade Unions (ZCTU), 59, 143, 147, 148, 154, 180, 182, 219
Zimbabwe African Congress of Trade Unions (ZACTU), 54
Zimbabwe African National Union (ZANU), 54, 56
Zimbabwe African Peoples' Union (ZAPU), 54, 56
Zimbabwe Federation of Labour (ZFL), 57
Zwane, Dr. A. P., 66